CW00349433

**THE NAKED KING, THE SHADOW
& THE DRAGON**

THE NAKED KING,
THE SHADOW
& THE DRAGON

Yevgheny Shvarts

*Translated from the Russian and with an introduction by
Elisaveta Fen*

MARION BOYARS · LONDON

A MARION BOYARS BOOK
distributed by
Calder & Boyars Ltd
18 Brewer Street London W1R 4AS

First published in Great Britain in 1976
by Marion Boyars Publishers Ltd
18 Brewer Street London W1R 4AS

© This translation Marion Boyars Ltd 1975

All performing rights in these plays are strictly reserved and
applications for performances should be made to

The Secretary
The League of Dramatists
84 Drayton Gardens London SW10 9SD

No performance of the plays may be given unless a licence
has been obtained prior to rehearsal.

ALL RIGHTS RESERVED

ISBN 0 7145 2538 3 Cased Edition
ISBN 0 7145 2539 1 Paperback Edition

Any paperback edition of this book whether published
simultaneously with, or subsequent to, the cased edition
is sold subject to the condition that it shall not, by way
of trade, be lent, resold, hired out, or otherwise disposed
of, without the publishers' consent, in any form of binding
or cover other than that in which it is published.

All rights reserved. No part of this publication may be
reproduced, stored in a retrieval system, or transmitted,
in any form or by any means, electronic, mechanical,
photocopying, recording or otherwise, without the prior
permission of the copyright owner.

Typesetting by Gilbert Composing Services, Leighton Buzzard
Printed by Unwin Brothers Limited
The Gresham Press, Old Woking, Surrey.
A member of the Staples Printing Group.

CONTENTS

INTRODUCTION

Yevgheny Shvarts was born on the 21st of October 1896 in the country near Petersburg, and died on the 15th of January 1958. In the posthumous Soviet edition of his plays and film scenarios in 1960, he is described as one of 'the leading Soviet dramatists'. His plays, however, were not published in a separate edition until that year and, until recently, have had only a few performances.

Shvarts's interest in the theatre dates back to the early twenties when he was a member of a 'Theatre Workshop' at Rostov-on-Don. His literary career began in 1925 when he gave up acting and became a contributor to, and later, one of the editors of a children's magazine in Leningrad. He wrote several plays for children, but his reputation as a dramatist is based on three remarkable satirical plays for adults, although these, too, like his plays for children, contain a strong vein of fantasy.

It is perhaps not surprising that the ideas and feelings which underlie these three important plays, *The Naked King, The Shadow* and *The Dragon,* had to be disguised by clothing them in the garb of fairy-tales — for they were written during the decade of 1934-44), the years dominated in Russia by the 'cult of personality' and the ruthless persecution of all dissenters from the official ideology of Stalinism.

Most of the themes Shvarts used to convey the covert meaning of his plays were borrowed from the well-known tales of Hans Andersen. No less than three Andersen stories underlie the plot of *The Naked King* — 'The Princess and the Swineherd', 'The Princess on a Pea' and 'The Emperor's New Clothes'. Written in 1934, it is, of the three plays, the most light-hearted. It might appear on the surface no more than an amusing 'take-off' of the more comic peculiarities of the Nazi régime in its early years — its emphasis on ethnic purity (the scene between the King, the Princess's fiancé, and the Court Scientist in Act Two) and the quasi-military discipline inculcated in the Hitler youth (the scene with the marching ladies-in-waiting in the same act).

Yet there are shafts of satire obliquely aimed at individuals and situations nearer home. In 1934, the Hitler regime had not yet produced its full crop of political murders, whereas Stalinist terror was getting well into its stride: dissenters were 'liquidated', millions of *'kulaks'* were being transported to the desert regions of Kazakhstan. Both 'kings' in *The Naked King* (the Princess's father and her fiancé) are ready with the threat of immediate execution whenever someone displeases them. The Princess's fiancé in a black mood commands the presence of his jester, who succeeds in making him laugh only when he tells him a sadistic 'anecdote', consisting of a series of accidents happening to several people. It was known that one of Stalin's favourite amusements was listening to 'jokes' told by the chiefs of his political police about their victims' behaviour before their execution. In the final scene of the play, when the people turn against the king and his overthrow is imminent, one of his ministers takes flight, screaming: 'I'm for the people! My mother is a locksmith, my father's a laundress! Down with the monarchy!' The proof of 'proletarian' origin was certainly not demanded by the bureaucrats of the Nazi Germany, but by the officialdom of Stalin's régime. Clearly, the latter smelt the rat, for after having been performed once in Leningrad in 1935, the play was immediately taken off and not staged again until 1960 at the Leningrad Comedy Theatre, and in Moscow at the *'Sovreménnik'* Theatre during the 1960-61 season, where it was a 'wild success'. The present writer saw it billed at one of the theatres in Moscow in the autumn of 1965.

The Shadow, written in 1940, reflects a much more sinister and sombre state of affairs. It is based on Andersen's story of a man becoming separated from his shadow. The main protagonist of the play, a young 'Savant', called Christian-Theodore, is visiting a country which encourages tourists. The daughter of the innkeeper at whose inn he is staying, a young girl called Annunziata, tells him that her country is far from ordinary and that 'all that is said to happen in fairy-tales and is a mere invention as far as other countries are concerned, does really happen in our country every day'. She gives as an example the existence of an Ogre, who is an employee at the city bank. When the Savant replies that this is most interesting and that they should put it into their tourist brochures, she glances over her shoulder and whispers: 'Not everyone likes fairy-tales. We're very afraid that if people find this out, they'd stop coming to our country. This will be very unprofitable. Please, don't give us away.' The Savant protests that he thinks the contrary. 'I think', he says, 'that more people would come to your country if they hear that fairy-tales have become reality here.' Credulous visitors, such as Bernard Shaw, the Webbs and hordes of others, who went to the Soviet Union in the thirties, and saw their private fairy-tale realized in that country, inevitably come to mind. They apparently had no idea that an 'ogre' might be concealed behind the mask of every bureaucrat who welcomed them.

Shvarts conveys extremely well the sinister undertow which ran beneath the ordinary flow of everyday life in Russia during the years of Stalin's reign — for reign it was, more absolute and arbitrary than that of any medieval tsar. The Savant opens the window of his room and hears the street vendors' cries: 'Water, water! Who wants icy-cold water?' 'Water melons, ripe water melons!' Then suddenly: 'Knives for murderers! Who needs a murderer's knife?' 'Flowers, flowers! Roses, lilies, carnations!' And again: 'Poison for sale! Fresh poison!'

The atmosphere of mutual suspicion and a paranoid fear of betrayal is amusingly portrayed in the scene between two government ministers, who have a confidential meeting in the middle of a vast garden lawn to escape eavesdropping. Even then they prefer to converse in truncated language, in half-words. Nor do the business habits of the capitalist world escape Shvarts's ridicule: the two ministers do their best to safeguard their ill-begotten riches by transferring them to 'safer' countries. One even sends his artificial set of gold teeth abroad, so that he is prevented from enjoying his food. Yet the final twist to their discourse is surely an arrow aimed at the Soviet reality: determined to destroy the young Savant, the ministers decide they must find a close friend of his 'because only a close friend would know him well and so know how to go about delivering him into our hands.' This treacherous friend happens to be the Savant's own shadow.

The Savant is duly 'framed' and handed over to his enemies, who do not want him to gain the throne by marrying the Princess who reciprocates his love. The reactions of his friends to the Savant's downfall are familiar to all who had followed Stalinist 'purges' and trials. With the exception of the devoted Annunziata, none dare defend him and all are ready to confirm his non-existent guilt.

The Savant's Shadow, Theodore-Christian, who usurps

9

his place beside the Princess and persuades her that she loves him, orders the execution of Christian-Theodore. However, when the Savant's head is chopped off, the Shadow's head also drops off, and the Princess finds a headless fiancé at her side.

Despite a Soviet critic's warning against 'de-coding the primitive images of fairy-tales', because this 'impoverishes and narrows the philosophical thought of the fairy-tale and turns it into primitive and ambiguous allegory', it is impossible to ignore the allegory of *The Shadow.* One wonders, if by the execution of the Savant and the Shadow's loss of his own head as a result, Shvarts wanted to convey that by destroying so many gifted and intelligent men, the Soviet dictator was in danger of metaphorically losing his own 'head', that is, depriving himself of the means of administering his country. The symbolism of the characters' names hardly needs to be stressed: Christian-Theodore, personifying all that is gentle, wise and noble in human nature; Annunziata, the bringer of 'good news' of truthfulness and devotion, and other startling names with their historic sinister associations. Christian-Theodore and Annunziata are the only good persons in the country of time-servers, power-seekers, denunciators and executioners, with the exception of the rather inefficient 'doctor'. And the two decide to leave the country 'where fairy-tales come true', because the Savant refuses the Princess's offer of love and throne. He rejects power, even if it gave him the opportunity to do good; power is too corrupting. In this way, Shvarts seems to imply, Soviet Russia loses some of its best people by emigration or by their withdrawal into deeper privacy.

The Shadow was published in Moscow in 1940 in the magazine *'Literatúrny Sovreménnik'* (Literary Contemporary). In the spring of the same year it came out under a separate cover published by the Lenin State Theatre in an acting edition. It was staged that autumn but almost immediately taken off. It was not staged again until the 1960-61 season when it was produced by N.F.Akimov at the 'Comedy Theatre' in Leningrad and was a great success. It is still in the repertory of that theatre on its tours of the provinces. The stage sets designed for the play were exhibited at the Royal Festival Hall in London during the visit there of the Kirov Ballet Company in the mid sixties.

10

The Dragon, written by Shvarts in 1944, is one of the
most eloquent and powerful portrayals of the degrading
and destructive effects of totalitarianism on the minds of
the enslaved and exploited population. The Soviet
critics may well point out the many similarities between
the character and behaviour of the 'Dragon' and Adolf
Hitler, yet the Dragon has just as many attributes which
liken him to Stalin. It is, however, the people who accept
the tyrant's domination that arouse the dramatist's
deepest scorn and pity. While trying to dissuade the
Knight-Errant, Lancelot, from battling with him on
behalf of the people, the Dragon tells him that his subjects
are not worth fighting for: 'My people are a dreadful
lot. You won't find such people anywhere else. It's my
work: I've made them like that.' 'But they're still human
beings,' protests Lancelot. 'Only in appearance,' replies
the Dragon. 'If you could look inside their souls, you'd
shudder, you'd turn to flight. You would not risk death
for the sake of such cripples. You see, I've crippled them
myself and I've made a pretty good job of it. Human
souls, you know, are made of very durable stuff. If you
chop up a man's body, he'll die, but if you tear a man's
soul to pieces, it just becomes more yielding, more
pliable. I assure you that you won't find anywhere such
souls as I have here, in my city. Here, I have souls
without arms or legs, deaf-and-dumb souls, souls like
chained dogs, slavish souls, damned souls. Here there
are souls pierced with holes, mercenary souls, souls that
are burnt right through, dead souls. A pity that souls are
invisible, that you can't see them with your own eyes
and be persuaded.'

His warning is proved correct because the people for
whose sake Lancelot battles with the Dragon and kills
him, all but losing his own life in this encounter, make
no good use of their liberation but immediately accept
the tyranny of another despot, the Dragon's former
yes-man, the Mayor of the town. However, in contrast
to Christian-Theodore of *The Shadow*, Lancelot does not
abandon the struggle; he recovers from his wounds and
returns to overthrow the tyrant. With the help of Elsa,
the girl he loves, he decides to assume power over
the city and its population. 'We have a long and dreary
task in front of us,' he tells Elsa. 'We shall have to kill
the dragon in every one of them. But we shall succeed,
and we shall all be happy in the end!'

The Dragon had only one performance in the Leningrad

'Comedy Theatre' in 1944, and was then withdrawn. It was revived in 1962, but again, in spite of favourable notices, was taken off and has not reappeared in the Soviet repertory since.

One wonders to what extent Yevgheny Shvarts himself believed in the ultimate victory of courage and love over cowardice and hatred. It is the theme that is woven like a golden thread into all his work. He was himself a deeply honourable, compassionate and gentle person, who lived through the horrors of the siege of Leningrad in 1941-42 without succumbing to any of its terrible temptations. His contemporaries in Soviet Russia remember him with great affection and respect. His plays have been produced at different times in Poland, Rumania, Czechoslovakia, East and West Germany, Israel and America. In this country they had no more luck than in Shvarts's own. *The Naked King* in this translation was accepted by the Royal Shakespeare Company (Aldwych Theatre) in 1969 and an acting edition was prepared, but the change of management resulted in its being dropped without explanation. The same play was also accepted by the BBC. Radio Drama Department, but was not broadcast. *The Dragon* (in Max Hayward's translation) was staged at the Royal Court in 1969, but had only a short run.

Elisaveta Fen

THE NAKED KING

CHARACTERS

Henrik
Christian
Princess
Ladies-in-Waiting
The King-Father
Minister of Tender Feelings
Chamberlain
Governess
Prime Minister
The King
Nose. Kettle. Gendarmes. Mayor. Conductor. Boot
Polishers. Chief Cook. Tailors. Head Valet. Soldiers.
Sergeant. Jester. Flunkeys. Court Savant. Courtiers.
Court Poet. Officer. Crowd. General. Heralds.

ACT ONE

A flowery meadow. In the background, the royal castle. Pigs are wandering about the meadow. HENRIK, *the swineherd, is talking. His friend* CHRISTIAN, *the weaver, is lying, stretched out, on the grass, looking pensive.*

HENRIK. Well, there I was, crossing the royal courtyard with a piglet in my arms. It's just been branded with the royal brand-mark — you know — a pig's snout with a crown. The piglet was squealing something awful. And all of a sudden I hear a voice from above: 'Stop tormenting the poor animal, you brute!' I was just about to swear — because, you understand, I wasn't enjoying the piglet's squealing either — but I happened to look up, and. . . oh! I saw the Princess! So charming, so pretty, that my heart turned over inside me. And I resolved, there and then, to marry her.

CHRISTIAN. You've told me this story one hundred-and-one times already in the last month or so.

HENRIK. All dressed in white she was, imagine! So I say to her: 'Princess, come down to the meadow and watch me herding the pigs.' And she says to me: 'I'm frightened of pigs.' And I to her: 'Pigs are tame, you know.' And she to me: 'They keep on grunting.' And I to her: 'That doesn't harm us humans.' Hey, are you asleep?

CHRISTIAN. *(Sleepily)* Yes, I am.

HENRIK. *(Turning to the pigs)* And so, my dear pigs, I began to walk that way every night. The Princess sat in the window, as pretty as a flower, and I would stand below like a post, my hands pressed to my heart. And I kept saying to her: 'Come down to the meadow!' And she: 'Whatever for? There's nothing to see there.' And I: 'There's some very pretty flowers to look at.' And she: 'We've plenty of flowers here.' And I: 'We've got pebbles of every colour.' And she: 'Fancy that! How interesting!' So I go on and on in this way, trying to talk her into it, until they drive me off and separate us. . . but I just couldn't persuade her. In the end I had an idea. 'I've got a

kettle,' I told her, 'a kettle with little bells, a
kettle that sings in a beautiful voice, plays the
violin, the french horn, the flute, and besides all
that, can tell you what anybody's having for
dinner.' 'Bring your kettle here,' she says to me.
'No,' I say to her, 'because the King would take
it away from me.' 'Well, all right then, ' she says,
'I'll come to your meadow next Wednesday, at
midday on the dot.' So I ran straight to my friend
Christian. He's got clever hands, and he made me
the kettle with little bells. . . Ah, my dear pigs,
you've gone to sleep, too! Of course, I've been
boring you with this all day, every day. . . It can't
be helped — I'm in love. . . Ah! she's coming!
(Gives the pigs a prod) Get up, Duchess! Get up,
Countess, get up, Baroness! Christian, Christian!
Wake up!

CHRISTIAN. Eh? What is it?

HENRIK. She's coming! There, look! All in white,
walking up the path.

(He points to the right with his finger)

CHRISTIAN. What's the matter? Where? Ah, I see
now — she's really coming! And not alone — her
suite's coming too. And you all of a tremble! Stop
it! How can you marry her if you're scared of
her?

HENRIK. I'm trembling from love, not from fear.

CHRISTIAN. Henrik, pull yourself together! You
haven't got to tremble so much that you can
hardly stand on your feet — and all from love!
You're not a girl!

HENRIK. The Princess is coming!

CHRISTIAN. If she's coming it means she likes you.
Think how many girls you've loved — and it's
always gone off well. She may be a Princess but
she's also a girl, after all!

HENRIK. The point is. . . she's so white all over! Let
me have a gulp from your flask. And so pretty. . .
and charming. You walk across the courtyard,
and there she is, looking so pretty in the window.
Like a little flower! And I stand like a post,
pressing my hands to my heart. . .

CHRISTIAN. Shut up! The main thing is to be firm.

16

Once you've decided to marry her, don't beat a
retreat. Ah! I'm no longer sure of you. You used
to be a courageous, crafty kind of chap, but
now...

HENRIK. Stop scolding me! She's coming up...

CHRISTIAN. And all her suite!...

HENRIK. I don't see anybody, only her! Ah, how
charming she is! *(Enter the* PRINCESS *and her*
LADIES-IN-WAITING. *The* PRINCESS *walks up
to the swineherd. The* LADIES-IN-WAITING
stop a little way off)

PRINCESS. Good day, Swineherd.

HENRIK. Good day, Princess.

PRINCESS. You're taller than you looked when I saw
you from above, from my window.

HENRIK. Yes, I am taller.

PRINCESS. And your voice is gentler. You used to
shout so when you were standing below, in the
courtyard.

HENRIK. I'm not shouting here.

PRINCESS. You shouted so loudly that all the palace
knows I've come here to listen to your kettle.
Well, how are you, Swineherd?

(She gives him her hand.)

HENRIK. How are you, Princess?

(He takes her hand)

CHRISTIAN. *(Whispers)* Be bolder, bolder, Henrik!

HENRIK. Princess! You're so sweet that it simply
frightens me.

PRINCESS. Why does it?

HENRIK. So white, so kind, so gentle...

(The PRINCESS *lets out a shriek)*

What's the matter?

PRINCESS. That pig over there is looking daggers at
me!

HENRIK. Which one? Ah, that one! Go away,
Baroness! Off with you, or else... I'll cut your

17

throat tomorrow!

THIRD LADY-IN-WAITING. Ah!

(She faints. All the other LADIES-IN-WAITING *crowd round her)*

INDIGNANT VOICES.

How rude!

He mustn't cut Baroness's throat!

Ignorant fellow!

It just isn't done — cutting Baronesses' throats!

What impudence!

Cutting Baronesses' throats is plain indecency!

FIRST LADY-IN-WAITING. *Solemnly approaches the* PRINCESS) Your Royal Highness! Please forbid this. . . this young swine to insult ladies of the Court.

PRINCESS. In the first place, he's not a swine, he's a swineherd. And in the second place. . .*(To* HENRIK) why do you insult the members of my suite?

HENRIK. Please call me Henrik.

PRINCESS. Henrik? That's interesting! I'm called Henrietta.

HENRIK. Henrietta? Really? And I'm called Henrik.

PRINCESS. Isn't that nice? Henrik!

HENRIK. Fancy that! What a coincidence! Henrietta!

FIRST LADY-IN-WAITING. Dare I remind Your Royal Highness that this. . . this companion of yours intends to cut Baroness's throat tomorrow?

PRINCESS. Oh, yes! Henrik, please tell me why do you want to cut Baroness's throat tomorrow?

HENRIK. Just because I've been feeding her long enough. She's far too fat.

THIRD LADY-IN-WAITING. Ah! *(She faints again)*

HENRIK. Why does this lady keep on tumbling over all the time?

FIRST LADY-IN-WAITING. She is the Baroness whom you've been calling a pig and threatening to kill tomorrow.

HENRIK. Nothing of the sort! *There* is the pig I call the Baroness and which I'm thinking of killing tomorrow.

FIRST LADY-IN-WAITING. You call that pig the Baroness?

HENRIK. Yes, and this one, the Countess.

SECOND LADY-IN-WAITING. Nothing of the sort! I am the Countess.

HENRIK. And that pig over there is the Duchess.

FIRST LADY-IN-WAITING. What impudence! *I* am the Duchess. How dare you give such high titles to pigs? Please, Your Highness, take note of this swineherd's improper behaviour!

PRINCESS. In the first place, he's not just a swineherd, he's Henrik. And in the second place, pigs are his subjects and he has the right to bestow any titles he likes on them.

FIRST LADY-IN-WAITING. And in general, he's behaving improperly. He's holding you by the hand!

PRINCESS. And what is there improper in that? If he were holding me by my foot. . .

FIRST LADY-IN-WAITING. I implore you — be silent! You're so innocent that you might easily say something absolutely dreadful!

PRINCESS. Then stop bothering me. I say, Henrik, why are your hands so hard?

HENRIK. Don't you like that ?

PRINCESS. What nonsense! Why shouldn't I like it? You have very attractive hands.

HENRIK. Princess, I've got to tell you something right now. . .

FIRST LADY-IN-WAITING. *(Determinedly)* Your Highness! We've come here to listen to the musical kettle. If we're not going to listen to the kettle but to what a strange man has to say — and what's more, listen to him with such improper attention — then I shall immediately. . .

PRINCESS. Well, you're not obliged to listen to a strange man, you can stand aside.

FIRST LADY-IN-WAITING.   But he's a stranger to you, as well!

PRINCESS.   What nonsense! I never talk to strangers.

FIRST LADY-IN-WAITING.   Princess, I give you my word that I shall immediately call the King.

PRINCESS.   Leave me alone.

FIRST   LADY-IN-WAITING.   *(Turns towards the castle and shouts)* Ki-ing! Come here quickly! The Princess is behaving disgracefully!

PRINCESS.   Ah! how they bore me! Well, show them the kettle, Henrik, if they must have it.

HENRIK.   Christian, come here! Bring out the kettle.

CHRISTIAN.   *(Takes the kettle out of a sack, quietly)* Well done, Henrik! That's the stuff. Don't let her go. She's up to her ears in love with you.

HENRIK.   You think so?

CHRISTIAN.   There's no question about it. The main thing now is to kiss her. Seize your opportunity. Kiss her, so that she has something to remember when she gets home. Here, Your Highness, here, noble ladies, is the remarkable kettle with little bells. Who's made it? We have. And what for? So that we could amuse the high-born Princess and her noble ladies. The kettle is very plain to look at — just smooth copper, the ass's hide stretched over it, little bells round the edge. But this plain appearance is deceptive. Inside this copper body is hidden the most musical soul in the world. This copper musician can play a hundred and fifty different dances and it can sing one song while it jingles its silver bells. Why so many dances, you may ask? Well, because it's as gay as we are. And why only one song? Because it's as faithful as we are. But this is not all: this miraculous, gay and faithful instrument conceals a nose under its ass's skin!

LADIES-IN-WAITING.   *(All together)* What?

CHRISTIAN.   Yes, a nose. And what a nose! I must tell you, beautiful Princess and noble ladies, that this coarse ass's hide conceals the finest, the most sensitive nose in the world! It's enough to turn it in the direction of any kitchen in any house and

20

our remarkable nose would smell out, whatever the distance, the kind of meal being prepared there. And at once it would describe it, quite clearly, though perhaps with a slightly nasal accent. Well, my noble audience? What shall we start with? With the song, the dances, or the dinners?

FIRST LADY-IN-WAITING. Princess, what do you wish to start with? Ah! I've been so taken up by listening that I hadn't noticed. . . Princess, Princess, Princess! I'm talking to *you!*

PRINCESS. *(In a languorous voice)* To me? Oh, yes, yes. Go on talking.

FIRST LADY-IN-WAITING. What are you doing, Princess? You're permitting him to hold you by the waist. This is most improper!

PRINCESS. What's improper about that? If he were holding me by. . .

FIRST LADY-IN-WAITING. I implore you, be silent! You are so naive that you might easily say something simply frightful!

PRINCESS. Well then, don't pester me. Go and listen to the kettle.

FIRST LADY-IN-WAITING. But we don't know what to start with, the song, the dances or the dinners.

PRINCESS. What do you think, Henrik?

HENRIK. My darling. . . my sweet. . .

PRINCESS. He says it's all the same to him.

FIRST LADY-IN-WAITING. I'm asking *you,* Princess.

PRINCESS. But I've told you — it's all the same to us. Start with dinners if you like.

LADIES-IN-WAITING *(Clapping their hands)* Start with dinners, start with dinners! Dinners!

CHRISTIAN. Noble ladies, I obey! We put the kettle down on its left side and that brings the nose into action. Can you hear it breathing?

(Sounds of heavy breathing are heard)

It's the nose sniffing around.

(Deafeningly loud sneezing is heard)

It's sneezed, so it's about to speak.

21

THE NOSE. *(In a very nasal voice)* I am in the Duchess's kitchen. . .

LADIES-IN-WAITING. *(Clapping their hands)* Oh, how interesting!

FIRST LADY-IN-WAITING. But. . .

LADIES-IN-WAITING. Don't interrupt!

THE NOSE. There's nothing fresh cooking in the Duchess's oven; there are only things being warmed up.

LADIES-IN-WAITING. Why so? Tell us!

THE NOSE. Last night at the King's table she filled her sleeves with food — nine sandwiches with caviar, twelve with salami, five veal cutlets, a whole rabbit, *shashlýk,* a chicken with white sauce, eighteen pies with various fillings, some sauce Tartar with capers and olives, fillet of beef Godard, ice cream with crystallized fruit, coffee ices and a small crust of bread.

FIRST LADY-IN-WAITING. You're lying, impudent Nose!

THE NOSE. Why should I lie? I'm an instrument of precision.

LADIES-IN-WAITING. Bravo, bravo! How interesting! Go on!

THE NOSE. I am now in the Countess's kitchen.

SECOND LADY-IN-WAITING. But. . .

LADIES-IN-WAITING. Don't interrupt.

THE NOSE. The Countess's oven is so cold that. . . *(a sneeze)* I'm afraid I might catch a cold. *(Sneezes again)*

LADIES-IN-WAITING. But why? Why?

THE NOSE. For the whole of last month she's been dining out. She's a very thrifty lady.

SECOND LADY-IN-WAITING. You're lying, shameless Nose!

THE NOSE. Why should I lie? Machines don't lie. I'm in the Baroness's kitchen. It's very warm here. The oven is blazing. The Baroness has an excellent cook. He's preparing dinner for her guests — making chicken rissoles from horsemeat. Now I'm going to

the Marquess's, then to the General's, then
to the President's wife. . .

LADIES-IN-WAITING. *(Shouting all together)*
That'll do, that'll do! You must be tired.

THE NOSE. I'm not in the least tired.

LADIES-IN-WAITING. Yes, you are, you are!
That's enough!

CHRISTIAN. *(Turns the kettle over)* I hope you
are delighted with the performance, noble
ladies?

(LADIES IN WAITING. *Remain silent.)*

If you're not, I'll send the Nose on another
journey round the kitchens.

LADIES-IN-WAITING. We are content, thank
you! Bravo! No more of that, please!

CHRISTIAN. I can see you are really pleased
and happy. And when you're pleased and
happy, the only thing to do is to dance.
Now you'll hear one of the hundred and
forty dances hidden in this wonderful
kettle.

FIRST LADY-IN-WAITING. I hope this dance
is. . . without. . . without words?

CHRISTIAN. Oh, yes, Duchess, it's a perfectly
harmless dance. Here, I'm turning the kettle
over on its right side — and. . . do you
hear?

*(The kettle begins to play, the bells jingle.
HENRIK dances with the PRINCESS,
CHRISTIAN with the Duchess, the Countess
with the Baroness. The OTHER LADIES-
IN-WAITING join hands, forming a ring
round the dancing couples, and begin their
own dance. After a while the music stops.)*

LADIES-IN-WAITING. What a niçe dance!
Encore, encore!

CHRISTIAN. Now, Henrik! Time to act! Here's
your pretext!

PRINCESS. Yes, Henrik! Please start the kettle
off again. I never knew I loved dancing so
much.

23

CHRISTIAN. This kettle, Your Royal Highness, has one dreadful property.

PRINCESS. What is it?

CHRISTIAN. Despite possessing a musical soul, it doesn't do anything for nothing. The first time it played in gratitude for your coming down to our humble meadow from your royal palace. If you wish it to play again. . .

PRINCESS. I must come down again. But how can I do that? To come again I must first go away, and I would much rather not!

HENRIK. No, no, don't go away — it's far too early! You've only just come!

PRINCESS. But the kettle won't play if I don't — and I would so much like to have another dance with you. What must I do? Tell me! I'm ready to do it.

HENRIK. You must. . . *(very quickly)* you must kiss me ten times.

LADIES-IN-WAITING. Oh!

PRINCESS. Ten times?

HENRIK. Because I'm very much in love with you. Why do you look at me like that? Well, if not ten times, then at least five.

PRINCESS. Five times? No.

HENRIK. If you knew how happy it'd make me, you wouldn't argue. Well, kiss me three times if you like. . .

PRINCESS. Three times? No. I refuse.

LADIES-IN-WAITING. You're quite right, Princess, to act in this way.

PRINCESS. Ten, five, three times! Who are you offering this to? You forget that I'm the King's daughter! I'll kiss you eighty times!

LADIES-IN-WAITING. Oh!

HENRIK. How — eighty?

PRINCESS. You can kiss me eighty-two times! I'm a Princess, after all!

LADIES-IN-WAITING. Oh! Oh!

FIRST LADY-IN-WAITING. Your Highness! What are you doing? He's going to kiss you on the lips! It's most improper!

PRINCESS. What's improper about that? He's going to kiss me on the lips and not on. . .

FIRST LADY-IN-WAITING. I implore you, be silent! You're so innocent that you might say something quite dreadful!

PRINCESS. Well then, don't pester me!

HENRIK. Quickly now! Hurry up!

PRINCESS. Yes, Henrik. I'm quite ready.

FIRST LADY-IN-WAITING. Princess, I beg you not to do it. If you're really so keen on having another dance, let him kiss me. . . a hundred times if you 'like.

PRINCESS. Kiss you? That would be really improper, you know. He didn't ask to kiss *you*. Now you're offering a man to kiss you. . .

FIRST LADY-IN-WAITING. But you yourself. . .

PRINCESS. Nothing of the kind! He's forcing me. I see what you're aiming at. A hundred times! Of course, he's so charming, he's got curly hair and such a pleasant-looking mouth. . . In a way she's right, Henrik. You may kiss me a hundred times. And please don't argue, Duchess, or else. . . I'll tell them to lock you up in the castle dungeon.

FIRST LADY-IN-WAITING. But the King might see you from the palace window!

PRINCESS. Stand around us! Do you hear? Stand around us! Shield us with your skirts. Quickly! How dare you interfere with people who want to kiss one another? Henrik, come here!

FIRST LADY-IN-WAITING. But who's going to count the kisses, Your Highness?

PRINCESS. That doesn't matter. If we lose count, we'll start again from the beginning.

FIRST LADY-IN-WAITING. Ladies, please count.

(HENRIK *and the* PRINCESS *kiss)*

LADIES-IN-WAITING. One.

(The kiss is prolonged)

FIRST LADY-IN-WAITING. Your Royal Highness, I really think that's enough for the first kiss!

(The kiss is prolonged)

If you go on like this, we won't finish until tomorrow.

(The kiss continues)

CHRISTIAN. Don't worry him, Madam, he can't hear you anyway. . .He's like that. . . I know him.

FIRST LADY-IN-WAITING. But this is dreadful!

(The KING leaps out of the bushes. He is wearing a crown and an ermine cloak)

The King!

KING. Who has some matches? Let me have some matches!

(General consternation. HENRIK and the PRINCESS stand with their eyes downcast)

LADIES-IN-WAITING. Your Majesty!

KING. Silence! Who's got matches?

CHRISTIAN. I, Your Maj. . .

KING. Silence. Hand them over!

CHRISTIAN. What for, Your Majesty?

KING. Silence!

CHRISTIAN. If you don't tell me, I won't give them to you, Your. . .

KING. Silence! I want matches to light the fire on which I'll burn the ladies-in-waiting. I've got a lot of dry wood all ready in those bushes.

(LADIES-IN-WAITING faint)

KING. What a dreadful thing! My daughter kissing a swineherd! Why are you doing it?

PRINCESS. I just felt like it.

KING. Felt like kissing?

PRINCESS. Yes.

KING. Very well. Tomorrow I'll marry you off to the

King, our neighbour.

PRINCESS. Never!

KING. And who's asking you?

PRINCESS. I'll pluck his beard out for him.

KING. He's clean-shaven.

PRINCESS. I'll tear all the hair off his head.

KING. He's got a bald head.

PRINCESS. Then I'll knock out all his teeth.

KING. He has no teeth. I mean, he's got artificial teeth.

PRINCESS. And so you want to marry me off to a toothless ruin of a man?

KING. It's the man that you're going to live with, not his teeth! Oh, you women! *(In a stentorian voice)* Get up!

(The ladies get up)

Fine, very fine! Just because I was delayed — couldn't find a safety pin to pin up my cloak — you've managed to start an orgy down here! No, it's not enough to burn you at the stake! First I'll burn you, then I'll cut your heads off, and finally I'll hang you all along the highway.

(The ladies weep)

Stop blubbering! No, even that's not enough! I've got an idea: I won't burn you or hang you. I'll let you live and I'll scold you, scold you and nag you for the rest of your lives. Eh? How d'you like that?

(The ladies weep)

In addition to this I'll cancel your pay.

(The ladies faint)

Get up! As for you, Swineherd, I'll send you and your friend into exile beyond the boundaries of my kingdom. You're not all that guilty. The Princess is really so charming that it's hard not to fall in love with her. Where's the kettle? I'll take the kettle into my possession.

(Seizes the kettle)

THE KETTLE *(Sings)*

27

With my heart aflame
I roam the world, free,
I love my Princess
And she loves me.
Wide as the steppes
Is my love so true,
To no one, my Princess,
Shall I surrender you.
For our love we'll fight
And we'll surely win through,
Then we'll go home to live
Together — just us two!
With my heart aflame,
I roam the world, free,
I love Henrietta
And she loves me!

KING. Is this the kettle singing?

HENRIK. Yes, Your Majesty.

KING. It sings well but the words of the song are abominable. It asserts that you intend to marry the Princess despite everything.

HENRIK. Yes, Your Majesty. I will marry the Princess despite everything.

PRINCESS. That's right, that's right!

KING. *(To the* LADIES-IN-WAITING*)* Take her away.

PRINCESS. *(To* HENRIK*)* Au revoir, Henrik. I love you.

HENRIK. Don't worry, Princess, I'll marry you.

PRINCESS. Yes, Henrik, please do. Au revoir, au revoir!

   (She is led away)

HENRIK. Au revoir, au revoir!

KING. Hey, you! Listen to me!

HENRIK. Au revoir, au revoir!

KING. I'm talking to you. *(He turns him round so that they face each other)* Does your kettle sing only one song?

HENRIK. Yes, only one.

KING. Can you make it sing my kind of song?
   (Sings in a croaky voice) 'She's not for you, get out of here!'

HENRIK. No, it can't sing a song like that and never shall.

KING. You'd better not make me angry — you saw how fierce I can be.

HENRIK. Yes, I did see it.

KING. Didn't you tremble?

HENRIK. No, I did not.

KING. Well, you've been warned!

HENRIK. Good-bye, King.

KING. Where are you off to?

HENRIK. I'm going to the King, your neighbour. He's so stupid that I'll have no trouble in outwitting him. There's no man more daring than me. I've kissed your daughter, and I'm not afraid of anything from now on. Good-bye!

KING. Wait a moment! I've got to count the pigs. One, two, three, fifteen, twenty. . . That's all right. You can go.

HENRIK. Good-bye, King. Come on, Christian. *(They go off, singing)*

> As a forest deep,
> Is my love so true,
> To no one, my Princess,
> Shall I surrender you.

KING. Trouble is brewing, I can see that. However, I'm not such a fool myself. I'll write abroad for a governess, as savage as a dog, and I'll send her along with the Princess. And I'll send my chamberlain with her as well. But I won't send any ladies-in-waiting, I'll keep them for myself. Just look at those fellows! Marching along and singing! You can march and sing as much as you like, my boys! I won't let you get away with it!

CURTAIN

(In front of the curtain appears the MINISTER OF TENDER FEELINGS)

MINISTER. I am His Majesty's Minister of Tender Feelings. I have a terrible lot of work to do just now — my King is about to marry a Princess from the

29

neighbouring kingdom. I've come out here in
order first to arrange an appropriately sumptuous
reception for the Princess. And in the second and
the third place, in order to solve two very delicate
problems. The point is that my gracious Sovereign
suddenly conceived a dreadful thought. Gendarmes,
come here!

(Enter two bearded GENDARMES)

GENDARMES. *(Together)* What is your wish, your
Excellency?

MINISTER. See that I'm not being overheard. I am
going to speak about most secret matters of
State importance.

GENDARMES. *(Together)* Certainly, your Excellency!

*(The two walk in opposite directions and take their
stand by the portals)*

MINISTER. *(Dropping his voice)* Well, last Tuesday my
Sovereign suddenly had a dreadful thought. He
was in the act of taking his midday meal when
suddenly he stopped dead while chewing on a piece
of sausage. We rushed towards him, exclaiming:
'Your Majesty! What's the matter with you?'
But he just groaned with his teeth clenched: 'What
a dreadful thought! Dreadful! Dreadful!' The Court
physician then helped the King to recover his
senses, and then we heard what it was that had the
privilege of so upsetting His Majesty. It was indeed
a dreadful thought. Gendarmes!

GENDARMES. *(Together)* What is your wish, your
Excellency?

MINISTER. Stop your ears.

GENDARMES. *(Together)* We obey, your Excellency.
(They stop their ears)

MINISTER. The thought that came into the King's
head was: what if the mother of Her Royal
Highness, the betrothed of the King, what if her
mother was. . .well, of a playful disposition? What
if the Princess is not a King's daughter but a
young lady of unknown origin? This is the first
problem I've got to solve. And the second problem
is this. His Royal Majesty was bathing. . .he was
in a happy mood, giggling and saying frolicksome
things. Then suddenly he exclaimed: 'A second

dreadful thought!' and began to sink in quite
shallow water. It came out that his second
dreadful thought was. . . *(whispers)* what if the
Princess herself was also of a playful disposition
and before her engagement to the King also had
some adventures, and. . .well, you understand! We
rescued the King from drowning, and he, there and
then, still in the sea, gave me the necessary orders.
I've come here, therefore, with the purpose of
finding out the whole truth about the Princess, her
origin and her behaviour, and — I swear by my
knightly honour that I will find out everything
there is to know about Her Royal Highness.
Gendarmes! Gendarmes! What is the matter? Have
you gone deaf? Ah, yes! Of course, I've told them
to stop their ears. There's discipline for you! The
King's sent all his best gendarmes to watch out in
all the villages along the Princess's route. They
instruct the population in the art of rapturous
welcome. They are picked men. *(Goes up to the
GENDARMES and pulls their hands away from
their ears)* Gendarmes!

GENDARMES. *(Together)* What is your Excellency's
wish?

MINISTER. Go and see whether the Princess is
coming.

GENDARMES. We obey, your Excellency. *(They go out)*

MINISTER. My problems are hard, aren't they? But I
know exactly how to solve them. One small pea
and twelve bottles of choice wine are going to
help me in this. I'm a very clever man.

(The GENDARMES return)

GENDARMES. Your Excellency! Far, far away, where
the sky seems to blend with the earth, there's a
high pillar of dust whirling above the hills. Through
that dust we can see now and again a glimmer of a
steel halberd, of a gold coat-of-arms, or a glimpse
of a horse's head. That must be the Princess on the
way to us, your Excellency.

MINISTER. Let's go and see if everything's ready for
her reception.

(They go out.

Gentle hills covered with vineyards. In the foreground

31

an inn, a smallish house of two storeys. Before it, a courtyard with some tables. The MAYOR *of the village, accompanied by young men and girls, rushes around the courtyard. Shouts of: 'She's coming, she's coming!' Enter the* MINISTER OF TENDER FEELINGS)

MINISTER.   Mayor! Stop fussing around! Come here!

MAYOR.   Me? Yes. Here he is. What? No!

MINISTER.   Get a dozen bottles of very strong wine ready at hand.

MAYOR.   What? Bottles? What for?

MINISTER.   We'll need them.

MAYOR.   Ah! I understand. For the Princess's reception.

MINISTER.   Exactly.

MAYOR.   She's given to drink?

MINISTER.   Have you gone out of your mind? The wine's needed for the supper you're going to serve to the Princess's companions.

MAYOR.   Ah! Her companions! That's much more agreeable. . . Yes, yes. . . No, no. . .

MINISTER.   *(Guffaws. Aside)* Isn't he stupid? I'm very fond of stupid people: they're so amusing. *(To the* MAYOR) Get ready the bottles of wine, prepare some roast sucking pigs, some legs of bear. . .

MAYOR.   Ah, so!. . . No!. . . I mean, yes. Hey you, take the keys of the cellars! Give me back the keys of the loft! *(He runs off)*

MINISTER.   *(Calls)* Musicians!

THE CONDUCTOR.   We're here, your Excellency.

MINISTER.   Have you got everything straight?

CONDUCTOR.   The first violin stuffed itself with grapes, your Excellency, and lay down in the sun. The grape juice began to ferment in the bloodstream of the first violin, your Excellency, and turned into wine. We've kept on trying to wake it, but it just kicks back at us and sleeps on.

MINISTER.   Outrageous! What's to be done, then?

CONDUCTOR.   Everything's been arranged, your

32

Excellency. The second violin's going to play the first violin, and the double bass will play the second violin. We tied the violin to a pole, the musician will stand it up like a double bass, and everything will be better than perfect.

MINISTER. But who's going to play the double bass?

CONDUCTOR. Ah! How dreadful! I haven't thought of that.

MINISTER. Put the double bass in the middle. Let anyone who happens to have his hands free for a moment saw away at it.

CONDUCTOR. I obey, your Excellency. *(Runs away)*

MINISTER. What a clever, inventive, resourceful fellow I am!

(Enter the two GENDARMES)

GENDARMES. Your Excellency, the Princess's carriage has just entered the village.

MINISTER. Attention! The orchestra! Mayor! Girls! People! Gendarmes! See that the boys throw their hats up as high as they can!

(Above the fence of the courtyard appears the top of the carriage with trunks on the roof. The MINISTER *rushes towards the gate to meet the carriage. The orchestra plays.* GENDARMES *shout "Hurrah!" Caps fly up into the air. Enter* THE PRINCESS, THE CHAMBERLAIN, *and* THE GOVERNESS)

MINISTER. Your Highness. . . The emotion your arrival arouses in this modest little village is nothing in comparison with the turmoil it stirs up in the heart of my Sovereign who's in love with you. . . Nevertheless. . .

PRINCESS. That's enough. Chamberlain! Where are my handkerchiefs?

CHAMBERLAIN. Eh! Hem! Ugh! Oh, oh! Presently, Your Highness, I'll get a hold on myself and ask the Governess. Mm-mm. . . *(Growls, then calms down)* Madame the Governess, where the handkerchiefs of the Princess may have been lying put in?

GOVERNESS. The handkerchiefs must be lying put in

33

a trunk, *Hottentotenpotentatentanteateenter.*

CHAMBERLAIN. *Oder. (Growls)* The handkerchiefs
are in the trunk, Princess.

PRINCESS. Get them out. Don't you see that I feel
like crying? Get the handkerchiefs out and bring
them here. *(The trunks are brought in)* And tell
them to get my bed ready. It'll be dark soon.
(Aside) I'm dreadfully tired. Dust, heat, holes in
the road. . . I'll go to sleep fast, very fast! I'll
dream of my dear Henrik. I'm so tired of all these
complete strangers who look like monkeys to me.
(Goes into the inn)

(The CHAMBERLAIN *rummages in the trunk)*

MINISTER. Isn't the Princess going to have supper?

CHAMBERLAIN. *(Growls)* Eh-hem, ugh, oho-ho! No!
She hasn't eaten anything for three weeks. She's
so stirred up by the prospect of marriage.

GOVERNESS. *(Pounces on the* MINISTER OF
TENDER FEELINGS) Take your hands of your
pockets out! Improper it is so do! *Entweder!*

MINISTER. What does this lady want from me?

CHAMBERLAIN. *(Growls)* O-oh-ooh! *(Calms down.
To the* GOVERNESS) Control yourself, *encore!*
He no pupil of yours, not! *(To the* MINISTER)
Excuse me, you don't speak foreign languages?

MINISTER. No. From the day His Majesty the King
had declared our nation to be the greatest in the
world, we've been ordered to forget completely
all foreign languages.

CHAMBERLAIN. This lady is a foreign governess, the
fiercest in the whole world. She's been bringing up
naughty children all her life, and it's made her
very callous. She now pounces on everyone and
tries to educate them.

GOVERNESS. *(Pounces on the* CHAMBERLAIN) Stop
scratching yourself! Not to!

CHAMBERLAIN. You see? Ooh-oh! She forbids me to
scratch myself, when I'm not scratching myself at
all but just adjusting my shirt-cuffs. *(Growls)*

MINISTER. What's the matter with you, Mr
Chamberlain? Have you a cold?

34

CHAMBERLAIN. No. It's just that I haven't been hunting for a whole week. I'm full of bloodthirsty thoughts. Halloo! The King knows that if I don't hunt, I turn into a wild beast myself. That's why he sent me to accompany the Princess. Excuse me, Mr Minister, I must go and see what the Princess is doing. *(Roars)* Yoicks! Yoicks! *(Calms down)* Madame Governess, direct your steps to! The Princess finds herself without supervision since long.

GOVERNESS. Wish we go. *(Goes. As she passes the* MINISTER, *barks at him)* Must breathe nose through! Bad boy are you, *ani-bani-tri-kontori!*

(Goes with the CHAMBERLAIN)

MINISTER. Extremely suspicious! Why did the King-father send such fierce people to accompany the Princess? There must be a reason. But I'll find out everything. Everything! Twelve bottles of strong wine will force these fierce guardians to spill the beans. Everything! Oh, how clever I am, how agile, how resourceful, how shrewd! In less than two hours I shall have all the Princess's past laid out before me as on the palm of my hand.

(Twelve GIRLS *enter carrying feather-beds. Each girl carries two feather-beds)*

Aha! Now we shall take care of the pea. *(To the first girl)* Can I have a word with you, my beauty?

(The girl pushes him away. The MINISTER *jumps aside. He goes up to another girl)*

My pretty darling, can I have a word with you?

(The second girl responds in the same way as the first. All the twelve GIRLS *push the* MINISTER *away and disappear into the inn)*

MINISTER. *(Rubbing his side)* What ill-mannered, coarse-minded girls! What shall I do about the pea, then? Gendarmes!

(GENDARMES *come up to the* MINISTER)

GENDARMES. What is your Excellency's wish?

MINISTER. Bring me the Mayor.

GENDARMES. We obey, your Excellency.

MINISTER. I'll have to take that fool into my
confidence. There's no one else.

(The GENDARMES *bring in the* MAYOR)

Gendarmes, stand by and watch that we're not
overheard. I'm going to discuss matters of State
importance with the Mayor.

GENDARMES. We obey, your Excellency. *(They take
their stand beside the* MINISTER *and the*
MAYOR)

MINISTER. Mayor, your girls. . .

MAYOR. Aha! I understand. Yes. You've got it,
too?

MINISTER. What?

MAYOR. Our girls. . . You're rubbing your side. Aha!
Yes.

MINISTER. What are you babbling about?

MAYOR. Well, you pestered the girls and they shoved
you off. Yes I know. I'm a bachelor, too.

MINISTER. Wait a moment!

MAYOR. No. They love, yes, yes. But only young men.
Funny girls. I love them. . . Well, well. . . But they
don't love me. Not me. Nor you. I can't help you.

MINISTER. That's enough! I haven't called you here
for that. Your girls misunderstood me. I wanted
to entrust them with a secret matter of State
importance. Now you will have to carry out this
task.

MAYOR. A-ha! Well, well. . . Yes, yes.

MINISTER. You'll have to steal into the Princess's
bedroom. . .

MAYOR *(Bursts out laughing)* My goodness! What a. . .
Very nice. . . But no! I'm a man of honour.

MINISTER. You misunderstand me. You'll have to go
in there for a second only, just after the girls have
finished making Her Highness's bed. And you'll
have to put this small pea on the wooden planks of
the bedstead under all those twenty-four feather-
beds. That's all.

MAYOR. Whatever for?

MINISTER. That's not your business. Take this pea and go.

MAYOR. I won't go. Yes. . . For nothing in the world.

MINISTER. Why not?

MAYOR. There's something fishy about this. And I'm a man of honour. Yes, Yes. No, no. I'll go sick presently — and you won't be able to force me. No, no! Yes, yes!

MINISTER. Damn it, what a fool! Well then, I'll tell you everything. But remember that this is a secret matter of State importance. The King ordered me to find out whether the Princess is really of noble origin. What if she isn't the King's daughter?

MAYOR. She is. She looks very much like him. Yes, yes.

MINISTER. That doesn't mean anything. You can't imagine how cunning women can be. Only this pea can give us a definite answer. Persons of true royal origin are distinguished by a particularly tender and sensitive skin. The Princess, if she is a real princess, would feel this pea through all the twenty-four feather-beds. She won't be able to sleep at all the whole night, and tomorrow would complain to me about it. But if she does sleep through the night that would be a very bad sign. D'you understand? Now go!

MAYOR. Ah-ha! *(Takes the pea from him)* Well, well. . . I'm beginning to find this interesting. . . So like her father — And yet. . . True, her father's got a beard. . . But her little mouth. . . And her little nose. . .

MINISTER. Go along!

MAYOR. Her little eyes. . .

MINISTER. Go along, I tell you!

MAYOR. Her little forehead. . .

MINISTER. Don't waste any more time, you blockhead!

MAYOR.   I'm going right now! Her figure, too, is very
  like her father's. Ai, ai, ai! *(Goes out)*

MINISTER.   Thank goodness!

MAYOR.   *(Returning)*   And her little cheeks. . .

MINISTER.   I'll cut your throat!

MAYOR.   I'm going, I'm going. *(Goes out)*

MINISTER.   Well, I'll clarify the question of her origin!
  Now I've only to call back the Chamberlain and
  the Governess, make them properly drunk, and
  then find out from them all there is to know
  about the Princess's past behaviour.

  (The GIRLS, *who carried in the feather-beds,
  run through, screaming. They are followed
  by the* CHAMBERLAIN *who is rubbing his
  side)*

  Mr Chamberlain, I can see from the movements of
  your hands that you've tried to converse with these
  girls.

CHAMBERLAIN.   Yes, I've tried a bit of hunting. . .
  (Growls) They kick and prod like wild goats.
  Stupid girls!

MINISTER.   Mr Chamberlain, when women spurn a man,
  wine consoles.

CHAMBERLAIN.   Not in the least. As soon as I've had
  a drink, I start craving for women.

MINISTER.   Ah! never mind! Have a drink with me,
  Chamberlain. A wedding's in prospect. We've got
  some excellent wine to cheer you up. Shall we
  stay up tonight? Eh?

CHAMBERLAIN.   *(Growls)* Ah, how I'd like to!
  Halloo! But no, I can't. I swore to the King that
  as soon as the Princess goes to bed, I'd lie down
  outside her door and guard her, and never close
  my eyes for a moment. I'll stay outside her door
  and the Governess beside her bed — and we'll guard
  her like that all night. We'll have our sleep on the
  road in the carriage. Yoicks!

MINISTER.   *(Aside)* This is very suspicious indeed! I
  simply must make him drunk. Mr Chamberlain. . .

  (Screaming and shouting is heard upstairs. The

MAYOR *bursts in, followed by the enraged*
GOVERNESS)

MAYOR.   Help, help, save me! She'll gobble me up!
She'll murder me!

CHAMBERLAIN.   What's happened, *entweder, oder,
aber?*

GOVERNESS.   This old *hoorda-moorda* into Princess's
bedroom go try did. And I have to bite off his big
silly head, *hottentotenpotentatentanteatenanteter!*

CHAMBERLAIN.   This impertinent fellow crept into
Princess's bedroom? Yoicks! Halloo!

MINISTER.   Wait a moment! I'll explain everything.
Mayor, come here! *(Quietly)* Did you put in the
pea?

MAYOR.   Ugh! Yes, I did. . . She pinches something
awful. . .

MINISTER.   Who pinches?

MAYOR.   The Governess. I put in the pea. Yes. . . I
look at the Princess and it surprises me. . . She's so
like her father. . . Her little nose, her little mouth. . .
Suddenly she pounces on me. . . The Governess.

MINISTER.   You'd better go. *(To the* CHAMBERLAIN)
Everything's clear. The Mayor merely wanted to
find out whether he could be of help to the
Princess in any way. The Mayor offers to make
amends for this by standing us twelve bottles of
strong wine.

CHAMBERLAIN.   Halloo!

MINISTER.   Listen. Chamberlain! Stop bothering
about it, for Heaven's sake. Eh? What's the point?
You've crossed the frontier now. The King
wouldn't know anything about it. Let's have a
good time! We'll invite the Governess, too. Let's
do it here, on this table. I give you my word of
honour, by God! As for guarding the Princess, I'll
send these two fine gendarmes upstairs. They're
the most loyal, the most hand-picked dogs in the
kingdom. They won't let anyone in or out of the
Princess's bedroom. Eh, Chamberlain? Halloo?

CHAMBERLAIN.   *(To the* GOVERNESS) They offer
us *schnapps trinken* on table here. They two

39

gendarmes upstairs sent have. The gendarmes are
sort of dogs *goomty-doomty-doberman-boberman*.
Even fiercer than us. *Una-duna-tres?*

GOVERNESS.   Staircase here one?

CHAMBERLAIN.   One.

GOVERNESS.   *Kvinter-baba-jess.*

CHAMERBLAIN.   *(To the* MINISTER) Well, I'm game.
Let's have a drink. Send the gendarmes up.

MINISTER.   Gendarmes! Upstairs with you! Stand
outside the Princess's door and guard her. At the
double!

GENDARMES.   We obey, your Excellency. *(They run
upstairs)*

MINISTER.   Mayor! Bring the wine, hams of bear,
sausages. . . *(Guffaws. Speaking aside)* Straight
away now! Immediately! I'll find out all there is
to know. How clever I am! How quick! What a
fine chap I am!

*(The light goes out in the lower part of the stage.
The upper part of the stage is lit up. The
PRINCESS's bedroom. The* PRINCESS, *wearing a
night bonnet, is lying on top of twenty-four
feather-beds)*

PRINCESS.   *(Sings quietly to herself)*

> As a forest deep
> Is my love so true,
> To no one, my Princess,
> Shall I surrender you.

What *is* the matter with me? Night after night I've
been falling asleep so easily, as I sang this song to
myself. I sang it, and at once I felt relaxed. At
once I felt convinced that Henrik really wouldn't
give me up to that fat, old King. And sleep came to
me. And in my sleep Henrik came. But it's not
working tonight. Something seems to stick right
into my body through all these twenty-four
feather-beds, and just won't let me go to sleep. I
expect a feather got mixed up with the down, or
perhaps a twig worked itself between the planks
of the bedstead and mattresses. I'm sure I'm
covered in bruises by now. . . Oh, what an unfortunate Princess I am! I've been looking out of the

window: outside, girls are strolling about with their boy friends, and here I lie, no use to anybody! I made a note today of the things I'll ask Henrik when I dream about him. Otherwise I might forget again. Here's my note. First, had he loved other girls before he met me? Second, when did he realize he'd fallen in love with me? Third, when did he notice that I'd fallen in love with him? I've been thinking about these things all the time on the way here. Just imagine — we've only had time to kiss each other once — and we were forced to part! We hadn't even time to have a talk. So I'm obliged to talk to him in my dreams. But sleep just won't come. Something keeps rolling about under the feather-beds. How dreadfully unfortunate I am! Well, I'll try to sing myself to sleep again. *(Sings)*

> With my heart aflame,
> I roam the world, free. . .

(Two male voices join in)

VOICES. *(Sing)*

> I love Henrietta
> And she loves me.

PRINCESS. What's this? Am I dreaming already?

VOICES. *(Sing)*

> Wide as the steppes
> Is my love so true,
> To no one, my Princess,
> Shall I surrender you.

PRINCESS. Oh, how interesting! I can't understand it; I feel frightened. . . and yet, it's so pleasant!

VOICES. *(Sing)*

> For our love we'll fight
> And surely win through,
> Then we'll go home to live
> Together — just us two!

PRINCESS. I'll get off this bed and look out of the window. I'll wrap myself in a blanket and look out. *(Climbs down from the top of the feather-beds)*

VOICES. *(Sing)*

> With my heart aflame,
> I roam the world, free,

I love my Princess
And she loves me.

PRINCESS. Where are my slippers? Here they are!
Could these voices come from just outside the
door?

*(She flings the door open. The two GENDARMES
are standing there)*

Who are you?

GENDARMES. We're gendarmes of His Majesty the
King.

PRINCESS. What are you doing here?

GENDARMES. We're guarding Your Royal Highness.

PRINCESS. And who was singing just now?

GENDARMES. It was the man who swore to marry
Your Highness, come what may. He fell in love with
you because you are so sweet, so kind, so tender.
He's not snivelling, or blubbering, or wasting his
time. He's circling around you, waiting to save you
from your accursed bridegroom. He was singing to
remind you of himself, and his friend was singing
with him.

PRINCESS. But where is he?

*(GENDARMES silently, with long strides, march into
her room)*

Why don't you answer me? Where's Henrik? Why do you
look so sadly at me? Perhaps you've come to cut my
throat?

GENDARMES. Pull our beards.

PRINCESS. Your beards?

GENDARMES. Yes, our beards.

PRINCESS. What for?

GENDARMES. Don't be afraid, just pull.

PRINCESS. But — I don't really know you!

GENDARMES. Henrik asks you to pull us by the
beard.

PRINCESS. Very well, then. *(Pulls)*

42

GENDARMES. Harder!

(*The* PRINCESS *pulls as hard as she can. The*
GENDARMES' *beards and whiskers remain in her*
hands. In front of her stand HENRIK *and*
CHRISTIAN)

PRINCESS. Henrik! (*Rushes towards him, then stops*)
But I'm not dressed. . .

CHRISTIAN. Never mind, Princess — you'll soon be his
wife, you know.

PRINCESS. It isn't because I think it indecent — I
just don't know whether I look pretty, like this.

HENRIK. Henrietta! You're so charming that I'd
sooner die than leave you. Don't worry, we're
following you all the time. Yesterday we made your
gendarmes drunk, tied them up, hid them, and
drove up here. Remember: we think only of one
thing, we have only one aim in life — to free you
and take you away with us. We may fail the first
time, but we'll succeed the next. If we fail on the
second attempt, we'll try a third time. Nothing
succeeds at once. To succeed, you must try today
and tomorrow, and the day after tomorrow. Are you
prepared to?

PRINCESS. Oh, yes! But tell me, Henrik, have you
loved other girls before me?

HENRIK. I hated all of them.

CHRISTIAN. Poor Princess, how much thinner she
looks!

PRINCESS. Henrik, please tell me, have you. . .

CHRISTIAN. Later on, my poor Princess — you'll
be able to talk later on. Now you must listen to us.

HENRIK. We'll try to run away with you today.

PRINCESS. Oh, thank you, Henrik!

HENRIK. But we might not succeed. . .

PRINCESS. Nothing succeeds the first time, my sweet
Henrik.

HENRIK. Take this piece of paper.

PRINCESS. (*Takes it*) Did you write this? (*Kisses it,*
then reads) Go to hell. (*Kisses the paper*)

43

Shut your big mouth, you windbag. *(Kisses the paper again)* What does that mean, Henrik?

HENRIK. If our escape doesn't come off, you must learn this and repeat it to your fiancé, the King. You don't know how to swear properly, so you'd better learn this. Then you could swear at him to your heart's content.

PRINCESS. With pleasure, Henrik. *(Reads)* I wish the devil would gore you with his horns. Very good! *(Kisses the paper)*

HENRIK. There's a pea under your feather-beds. That's why you couldn't go to sleep. Tomorrow tell them that you've had a very good night. Then the King will turn you down. You understand?

PRINCESS. I don't understand a thing, but I'll say what you tell me to. How clever you are, Henrik!

HENRIK. If he doesn't turn you down, don't lose heart all the same. We'll be close to you all the time.

PRINCESS. Very well, Henrik. I'll sleep well even on top of that pea, if it's so necessary. How many feather-beds have you at your home?

HENRIK. Just one.

PRINCESS. I'll train myself to sleep on top of just one feather-bed. But then, where would you sleep, my poor darling? However, we might. . .

CHRISTIAN. Don't go on, I implore you, Princess! You're so innocent that you might say something quite dreadful!

HENRIK. Put your things on, Princess, and let's go. That crowd downstairs are dead drunk. We'll run away.

CHRISTIAN. But if we don't run away, the pea would help us later on.

HENRIK. And even if the pea doesn't help, we'll be close beside you, and we'll get you out of this. We'll snatch you away from the very altar. Come on, my poor darling!

PRINCESS. Listen, my dear friends. You won't be cross if I ask you something?

HENRIK. No, of course not. Go on, ask us. I'll do

anything for you!

PRINCESS.   Well, then. . . even though it's going to
delay us a lot — be so kind, kiss me.

(HENRIK *kisses her. The light in the upper part of
the stage goes out. The courtyard of the inn is lit
up. The* MINISTER OF TENDER FEELINGS, *the*
GOVERNESS *and the* CHAMBERLAIN *are sitting
round a table. They are all drunk, the* MINISTER
more than anybody)

MINISTER.   I'm so smart, Chamberlain. . . D'you
hear? I'm so clever! The King ordered me to find
out. . . told me 'find out quietly' — has the Princess
had any adventures?. . . You understand? Troll-la-la!
'Find out delicately,' he told me. Any other man
would have made a mess of it. . . wouldn't he?
But I've had an idea! I hit upon the idea of making
you drunk, so that you'd spill the deans. . . peans. . .
beans. . . What? Clever, wasn't it?

CHAMBERLAIN.   Halloo!

MINISTER.   Well, then. . . Come on, tell me! You
won't succeed in hiding things from me! Never!
You've got to still. . . spill. . . the dea. . .pea. . .
beans. . . What can you tell me about the Princess?

CHAMBERLAIN.   We chased her with the hounds. . .
(Falls under the table. Emerges again)

MINISTER.   Why?

CHAMBERLAIN.   She's got such a fine tail. Halloo!

MINISTER.   *(Falls under the table. Gets out and up
again)* A tail? Has she got a tail, then?

CHAMBERLAIN.   Of course. Yoicks!

MINISTER.   But why — a tail?

CHAMBERLAIN.   Because it's her nature. Halloo!

MINISTER.   You mean — the whole family? And her
father — has he got a tail?

CHAMBERLAIN.   Certainly. Her father has a tail, too.

MINISTER.   So you've got a King with a tail?

CHAMBERLAIN.   Why, no! Our King's a tail-less chap.
But *her* father has a tail.

MINISTER.   So the King is not her father?

45

CHAMBERLAIN. Who told you he was? Of course not.

MINISTER. Hurrah! *(Falls under the table. Climbs out again)* Spilled the dea. . . beans. . . And who's her father, then?

CHAMBERLAIN. A he-fox, of course. Yoicks! Halloo!

MINISTER. Who, did you say?

CHAMBERLAIN. A he-fox. A vixen has a he-fox for a father.

MINISTER. What vixen you're talking about?

CHAMBERLAIN. That one, you and I've been talking about. *(He gives the GOVERNESS a prod with his elbow. They both guffaw, very drunk)*

GOVERNESS. If only he know could, this *gogol-mogol,* how she mutually kissed with the swineherd! Take your elbows from table! *Auf!* Blinking your eyes stop!

CHAMBERLAIN. Yoicks! Halloo!

GOVERNESS. Wooden head are you!

MINISTER. What are they saying?

CHAMBERLAIN. Halloo!

MINISTER. The swine! Friends. . . comrades don't behave like that. I'll bash you up. . . *(Falls over the table, head on arms)* Mayor, Mayor! Bring more wine! *(Falls asleep)*

GOVERNESS. This stupid idiot gone to sleep! Oh, happy man! Look, he down lies and sleeps. And I sleep can not. I sleep not several nights. *Under-munder. (Falls asleep)*

CHAMBERLAIN. Halloo! A stag! A stag! *(Starts running, falls down and goes to sleep)*

MAYOR. *(Comes in)* Here. More wine. Yes, yes. The Minister! Asleep! The Chamberlain! The lady Governess! Asleep. Well, I'd better sit down. Yes, yes. They'll wake up some time. No, no. *(Dozes off)*

(The door opens quietly. Enter CHRISTIAN. He looks around, then signals. Enter the PRINCESS and HENRIK. They creep towards the exit. The MAYOR notices them and jumps up)

46

MAYOR. Where are you off to? What... eh? Gendarmes! They shaved off their beards! Strange... Come back!

HENRIK. I'll kill you!

MAYOR. But I'll shout for help! I'm a brave man.

CHRISTIAN. Take this money and let's go.

MAYOR. Oh, no! I'm a man of honour. I'll give the alarm at once.

PRINCESS. Let me speak to him. Mayor, please, have pity on me. I may be a Princess but I'm also a girl. *(The* MAYOR *snivels)* If you give me away, they'll take me along and force me to marry a strange old man. *(The* MAYOR *snivels again),* That isn't a good thing, is it? Your King is a capricious type. And I'm not at all strong. *(The* MAYOR *weeps)* Can you imagine me living in captivity? I'd die straight away!

MAYOR. *(Bawls at the top of his voice)* Oh-oh! Run away quickly! Run or you'll die. *(Screams).* Run! O-oh!

(Everyone jumps up, except the MINISTER. *The* GOVERNESS *seizes the* PRINCESS *and carries her upstairs. The* CHAMBERLAIN *whistles, lets out hunting cries. Soldiers run in.* HENRIK *and* CHRISTIAN *fight their way through to the exit. Everyone runs after them. The sound of horses' hoofs is heard, then singing).*

VOICES. As wide as the steppes
Is my love so true,
To no one, my Princess,
Shall I surrender you.

CHAMBERLAIN. *(Comes in)* They've got away, blast them! It's a harder task to get a King's daughter safely to her betrothed than to bring a hundred stags to bay! *(Looks at the* MINISTER). And that one's still asleep. Sleep on, you! Build up your strength! Our quiet young lady will lead you a fine dance, you'll see! Halloo!

ACT TWO

*A reception hall separated by a velvet curtain from the
bedroom of the* KING. *The hall is full of people. By the
curtain stands the King's* HEAD VALET *who pulls the
cord of a bell which is behind the curtain, in the
bedroom. Next to the* HEAD VALET *two* TAILORS *are
hurriedly putting the final stitches to the King's garments.
Next to the* TAILORS *the King's* COOK *is whipping up
the cream for the King's cup of chocolate. A little apart
from them the King's* BOOT-POLISHERS *are cleaning
his boots. The bell rings. Knocking on the door is heard.*

THE BOOT-POLISHERS. Please, Chief Cook, someone's
 knocking on the door of the reception hall.

CHIEF COOK. Please, Tailors, someone's knocking on
 the door of the reception hall.

THE TAILORS. Please, Head Valet, someone's knocking
 on the door.

THE HEAD VALET. Someone's knocking? Tell them
 to come in.

 (The knocking continues, increasing in volume)

TAILORS *(To the* COOK) Let them come in.

CHIEF COOK *(To the* BOOT-POLISHERS) They can
 come in.

BOOT-POLISHERS. Come in!

 (Enter HENRIK *and* CHRISTIAN, *dressed as
 weavers. They are wearing grey hair wigs and grey
 beards. They look around them, then bow to the*
 HEAD VALET)

CHRISTIAN and HENRIK. Good morning, Mr
 Bellringer. *(Silence.* HENRIK *and* CHRISTIAN
 exchange glances. They bow to the TAILORS).
 Good morning, Tailors. *(Silence)* Good morning,
 Mr Cook. *(Silence)* Good morning, Boot-
 Polishers.

BOOT-POLISHERS. Good morning, Weavers.

CHRISTIAN. They've replied! A miracle! But tell us —
 what's the matter with these other gentlemen — are
 they deaf or dumb?

BOOT-POLISHERS. Neither. But in accordance with the Court etiquette you should have spoken first to us. We'll report what you have to tell us to the next person above us. Well, what is it you wish?

HENRIK. We are the most remarkable weavers in the world. Your King is the best dressed man, the greatest dandy in the world. We should like to serve His Majesty, your King.

BOOT-POLISHERS. Aha! Mr Chief Cook, these remarkable weavers wish to serve our most gracious Sovereign.

CHIEF COOK. Aha! Messrs Tailors, some weavers have arrived.

TAILORS. Aha! Mr Head Valet, the weavers!

HEAD VALET. Aha! Good morning, Weavers.

HENRIK and CHRISTIAN. Good morning, Mr Head Valet.

HEAD VALET. So you want to serve? Very well. I'll report on you direct to the Prime Minister, and he'll report to the King. For weavers we have an extra-speedy reception. His Majesty is getting married. He needs weavers very badly. For that reason he'll receive you very quickly indeed.

HENRIK. Very quickly! Indeed! We've already wasted two hours before we could get as far as this place. That's a fine way of doing things, I must say!

(The HEAD VALET *and all the others shudder and look behind them)*

HEAD VALET. *(Quietly)* Messrs Weavers, listen! You're respectable old men. With all the respect due to your grey hairs, I must warn you: not a single word must you say about our ancient, national traditions, sanctified by the Creator Himself. Our State is — the most exalted in the world! If you have any doubts of this, you shall. . . despite your great age. . . *(Whispers into* CHRISTIAN's *ear)*

CHRISTIAN. Impossible!

HEAD VALET. It's a fact. So that you don't produce children with a tendency to critical thought. Are you Arians?

CHRISTIAN. We've been so for ages.

49

HEAD VALET. I'm pleased to hear it. Sit down. Strangely enough I've been ringing the bell for a whole hour, but the King still hasn't woken up.

CHIEF COOK. *(Shivering)* I'll have a g-go at he-he-helping you. *(Runs out)*

CHRISTIAN. Tell me, Mr Head Valet, why does Mr Chief Cook shiver as if he had a fever, although this room is terribly hot?

HEAD VALET. Mr Chief Royal Cook hardly ever takes a step away from his ovens. He's so accustomed to the heat that he got the tip of his nose frost-bitten last year in full sunshine, in July.

(A dreadful roaring noise is heard)

What's this?

(The CHIEF COOK runs in, followed by the KITCHEN BOYS carrying a large covered dish. From it issues the roar)

What is this?

CHIEF COOK. *(Shivering)* This is the great sturgeon, Mr Head Valet. We'll p-put it in the King's b-bedroom. S-she'll go on roaring and s-s-she'll wake up the K-King.

HEAD VALET. Impossible.

CHIEF COOK. But why not?

HEAD VALET. Impossible. Don't you see?. . . the great sturgeon. . . forgive my saying so. . . is. . . a kind of *red* fish. And you know how the King feels about that. . . Take it away!

(The KITCHEN BOYS run away with the dish)

It's better that way, Mr Chief Cook. Hey, there! Call a detachment of soldiers and tell them to fire volley after volley outside the King's bedroom window. It might help.

CHRISTIAN. Does His Majesty always sleep so soundly?

HEAD VALET. Well, no. About five years ago he used to wake up very readily. It was enough for me to clear my throat — and off his bed he'd fly!

HENRIK. Really?

HEAD VALET. Yes, bless my heart! He had a lot of worries then. He kept on invading his neighbours

50

and having battles with them.

CHRISTIAN. And now?

HEAD VALET. Now he has no worries at all. His neighbours grabbed all the lands they could grab from him. So now he sleeps a lot and dreams about how he'd revenge himself on them.

(Loud drum beats are heard. Enter a detachment of SOLDIERS, *led by a* SERGEANT)

SERGEANT. *(Shouts)* 'Shun!

(The SOLDIERS *stand rigidly to attention)*

(Shouts) Draw a deep breath of devotion to the King as you enter his palace! *(The* SOLDIERS *draw in breath with a groan)* Picture to yourselves his great power and tremble with reverence! *(The* SOLDIERS *spread their arms wide and tremble)* Hey you, clod! You're not trembling properly! Look at your fingers! Your fingers! That's right! I can't see your stomach quiver! That's all right now. 'Shun! Think of your luck—being the King's soldiers— think of it and—dance! Dance from sheer joy!

(The SOLDIERS *dance to the drum beat, each one like the other, absolutely in line)*

'Shun! Rise on tip-toe. On tip-toe — march! Right! R-right! Keep in line with His Majesty's Grand-father's portrait! With its nose! The Grandfather's nose! Straight on! *(They march out.)*

CHRISTIAN. Is it possible that the King was defeated with such excellently disciplined soldiers?

HEAD VALET. *(With a gesture of bewilderment)* Yes . . . can you believe it?

(Enter PRIME MINISTER, *a fussy old man with a long white beard)*

PRIME MINISTER. Good morning, Inferior Servants.

ALL. *(Together)* Good morning, Prime Minister.

PRIME MINISTER. Well, how are things? Is everything in order? Eh? The truth, Head Valet! I want the whole brutal truth!

HEAD VALET. Everything's absolutely right, your Excellency.

PRIME MINISTER. But the King's still sleeping? Answer me frankly. Brutally.

51

HEAD VALET.   He's still sleeping, your Excellency.

(A volley of rifle fire off stage)

PRIME MINISTER.   A-ha! Tell me straight — this
firing means the King's about to get up?
Tailors! How are you getting on? I want the
truth! Even if it kills me!

FIRST TAILOR.   We're putting in the last stitches, Mr
Minister.

PRIME MINISTER.   Show me. *(Looks)* Calculate
carefully. You know our requirements. The
last stitch must be put in just before the King
begins to dress. The King puts on an absolutely
new garment every day, just as it comes off the
tailor's bench. If a minute passes after you put in
your last stitch — he won't wear your garment at
all, I must tell you brutally. You're aware of this?

FIRST TAILOR.   Yes, your Excellency.

PRIME MINISTER.   I hope you're using gold needles?

FIRST TAILOR.   Yes, your Excellency.

PRIME MINISTER.   You must hand him his garments
straight on, sewn with golden needles. Straight
and openly. Cook! Have you whipped up the
cream for the King's chocolate?

CHIEF COOK.   Y-yes, your Excellency.

PRIME MINISTER.   Show me. That'll do. But. . .
Head Valet! Who on earth is this? Don't
hesitate! Without equivocation. Tell me!

HEAD VALET.   These are weavers, your Excellency,
offering their services.

PRIME MINISTER.   Weavers? Show me. Aha! Good
morning, Weavers.

HENRIK and CHRISTIAN.   Good morning, your
Excellency.

PRIME MINISTER.   The King needs weavers — I'm
telling you straight, without any hind thoughts.
It's simple enough. Today arrives his bride. Hey,
Cook! What about breakfast for Her Highness? Is
it ready? Eh?

CHIEF COOK.   Y-yes. . . It's ready, your Excellency.

PRIME MINISTER. What is it? Eh? Show me.

CHIEF COOK. Hey, you! Bring the little pies I prepared for Her Highness.

PRIME MINISTER. They're bringing them. Meanwhile, I'll go in and have a look whether the King, by any chance, hasn't opened his eyes. And no nonsense. *(Goes behind the velvet curtain)*

CHIEF COOK. Princess Henrietta didn't eat anything for a whole three weeks.

HENRIK. The poor dear! *(Quickly writes something on a bit of paper)*

CHIEF COOK. But they say that now she eats all the time.

HENRIK. May she enjoy it!

(KITCHEN BOYS *bring in a dish of little pies)*

Ah! What lovely pies! I've attended many courts but I've never seen anything like it! What an appetizing fragrance! How nicely browned they are! How soft they look!

CHIEF COOK. *(Flattered, smiling)* Y-yes. They're so soft that even a hard stare leaves a mark on them.

HENRIK. You're a genius.

CHIEF COOK. Take one.

HENRIK. I daren't.

CHIEF COOK. Yes, d-do take one! You're obviously a connoisseur! One hardly ever meets such people!

HENRIK. *(Takes a pie, pretends to bite it, but quickly puts the note inside it, instead)* Ah! I'm quite overwhelmed! There's no other chef in the whole world to equal you!

CHIEF COOK. But my art, alas! will perish with me!

HENRIK. *(Pretending to chew)* But why?

CHIEF COOK. My book *That's How You Must Prepare Your Food, Gentlemen* has been destroyed.

HENRIK. How? When?

CHIEF COOK. *(In a whisper)* When we started the fashion of burning books in public squares. In the

53

first three days we burned all really dangerous books. But the fashion continued. Then they began burning all the books that came to hand. Now we have no books at all. We burn straw.

HENRIK. *(Hisses loudly)* But this is terrible! Isn't it?

CHIEF COOK. *(Looking behind him, also hisses loudly)* You're the only man I'll admit it to. Yes. Terrible!

(During this brief conversation HENRIK manages to put the pie with his note back on the dish, right on the top of other pies)

HEAD VALET. Quiet! I think the King's sneezed.

(All listen attentively)

HENRIK. *(To CHRISTIAN, quietly)*. Christian, I put a note inside a pie.

CHRISTIAN. All right, Henrik. Don't get excited.

HENRIK. I'm afraid the note'll get all greasy.

CHRISTIAN. Shut up, Henrik. We'll write another.

(The PRIME MINISTER emerges from behind the curtain)

PRIME MINISTER. Our Sovereign's opened one eye. Get ready. Call the chamberlains! Where are the ladies-in-waiting? Hey, trumpeters!

(Enter TRUMPETERS, CHAMBERLAINS and other COURTIERS. They take their places in a curved line at both ends of the velvet curtain. The HEAD VALET, fixing the PRIME MINISTER with his eyes, grasps the cord of the curtain)

PRIME MINISTER. *(In a desperate whisper)* All ready? The truth!

HEAD VALET. Yes, your Excellency!

PRIME MINISTER. *(With abandon)* Pull away! On my head be it!

(The HEAD VALET pulls at the cord. The curtain parts in the middle. All that can be seen is a mountain of feather-beds the top of which is concealed by the arch of the ceiling)

CHRISTIAN. But where's the King?

CHIEF COOK. He sleeps on one hundred and forty-eight feather-beds — that shows how noble he is! You can't see him. He's right under the ceiling.

PRIME MINISTER. *(Peering under the arch)* Silence! Get ready! He's turned over. He's scratched his eyebrow. He's screwing up his face. He's sat up. Trumpets, blow!

(A trumpet blast. All shout together: 'Hurrah, the King!' three times. Silence. After a pause, a peevish voice is heard from the top of the feather-beds)

KING. O-oh! O-oh! What is it now? Whatever for? Why did you wake me up? I was dreaming of a nymph. . . What a dirty trick — waking me like this. . .

HEAD VALET. Dare I remind Your Majesty that the Princess, the bride of Your Majesty, arrives today?

KING. *(Peevishly, from above)* Ah! What's all this about? You're just provoking me. Where's my dagger? I'll cut your throat straight away, you naughty man! Where's that dagger now? Haven't I told you a hundred times to put it under my pillow?

HEAD VALET. But it's half-past-ten already, Your Majesty.

KING. What! And you haven't called me before? There! Take that, you ass!

(A dagger is flung from above. It sticks into the floor close to the HEAD VALET's feet. A pause)

Well? Why aren't you screaming? Haven't I wounded you?

HEAD VALET. No, Your Majesty.

KING. Perhaps I've killed you?

HEAD VALET. No, Your Majesty.

KING. Not even killed you? Damn and blast! How unlucky I am! I can't throw straight any more! This won't do, it won't do at all! Now, stand out of my way! I'm getting up, don't you see?

PRIME MINISTER. Get ready! Our Sovereign's

55

standing bolt upright on his bed. He's taking a step forward. He's opening his parasol! Trumpets!

(A trumpet blast. The KING appears from under the arch. He descends with an open parasol, using it as a parachute. The COURTIERS shout 'Hurrah'. On reaching the floor, the KING throws away the parasol which the HEAD VALET catches in the air. The KING is wearing a gorgeous dressing-gown and a crown fixed on his head with a ribbon, which is tied in a big bow under his chin. The KING is about 50. He is plump and seems in the best of health. He does not look at anyone although the room is full of people. He behaves as if there were no one but himself in the room)

KING. *(To the HEAD VALET)* I'm telling you, it won't do! It won't do at all! Well, why don't you say anything? Don't you see your Sovereign's in a bad mood? And you can't think of anything to do! Pick up that dagger!

(He examines with a thoughtful air the dagger the HEAD VALET hands over to him, then puts it in the pocket of his dressing-gown) You sluggard! You don't even deserve to die by the royal hand. Did I tip you with a gold coin yesterday?

HEAD VALET. Yes, Your Majesty.

KING. Hand it back to me. I'm displeased with you. *(Takes the money from the HEAD VALET)* I'm quite disgusted. . . *(Walks up and down, brushing the COURTIERS who stand around, petrified with reverence, with the skirts of his dressing-gown)* I dreamed of a noble and charming nymph, of extremely good descent and very pure blood. To begin with, she and I conquered our neighbours in battle, and after that we were happy together. I wake up — and what do I see? This abominable valet! What was it I said to the nymph? Sorceress! Enchantress! He who is in love with you cannot help loving you! *(With conviction)* I was very eloquent! *(Peevishly)* Why did I have to wake up? Whatever for? Eh? Hey, you! Tell me, why?

HEAD VALET. In order to wear a perfectly new garment, Your Majesty, with the last stitch just about to be put in.

KING. Blockhead! How can I get dressed if I'm in a bad

mood? Cheer me up first! Call the jester, quickly!
Bring the jester here!

HEAD VALET.   Bring His Majesty's Jester!

(The JESTER *steps out of the immobile line of*
COURTIERS. *He is a respectable-looking man in*
spectacles. He approaches the KING *with a*
hopping gait)

KING.   *(Assuming a brisk, jaunty manner, loudly)* Good
morning, Jester.

JESTER.   *(In the same manner)* Good morning, Your
Majesty!

KING.   *(Dropping into an armchair)* Cheer me up! But
be quick about it. *(Peevishly and plaintively)* It's
time for me to get dressed, but I'm in such a bad
mood, such a bad mood! Come on! Begin!

JESTER.   *(Gravely)* Here's a very funny story, Your
Majesty. A tradesman of sorts. . .

KING.   *(Captiously)* The name?. . .

JESTER.   Petersen. A tradesman, called Petersen, walked
out of his shop and. . . stumbled over a stone, and
down he went, squashing his nose on the cobbles!

KING.   Ha-ha-ha!

JESTER.   And a house-painter happened to be passing.
He was carrying a pot of paint, and he stumbled
over the tradesman and spilled the paint all over an
old woman. . .

KING.   Really? Ha-ha-ha!

JESTER.   And the old woman had a fright and stepped
on a dog's tail. . .

KING.   Ha-ha-ha! You don't say! Ah-ha-ha! *(Wiping*
tears of laughter) On a dog's tail?

JESTER.   Yes, a dog's tail, Your Majesty. And the dog
bit a very fat man that happened to be passing
by.

KING.   O-oh! Ha-ha-ha! Enough, enough!. . .

JESTER.   And the fat man. . .

KING.   Enough, enough! I can't take any more, I'll
burst. You can go now — you've cheered me up.
I'll begin to dress. *(Unties the ribbon under his*

57

chin) Take my night crown. Bring the day-time
one. That's it. Call the Prime Minister.

HEAD VALET.   His Majesty wants his Excellency the
Prime Minister!

(The PRIME MINISTER *runs up to the* KING)

KING.   *(Jauntily)* Good morning, Prime Minister.

PRIME MINISTER.   *(In the same manner)* Good
morning, Your Majesty.

KING.   Well, old man? What have you got to tell me?
Ha-ha-ha! Isn't my Jester marvellous? The dog's
got the old woman by the tail! Ha-ha-ha! What I
like about my Jester is his pure humour. Without
any hidden pricks or innuendoes. . . The tradesman
bites the fat man! Ha-ha-ha! Well, what's the news,
old man? Eh?

PRIME MINISTER.   Your Majesty! You know that I'm
an honest old man, an absolutely straight old man.
I tell the truth straight to a man's face even when
the truth happens to be unpleasant. You see, I've
been standing here all the time, I saw you waking
up, I heard you — to put it crudely — laughing at
things, and so on. Allow me to tell you straight,
Your Majesty. . .

KING.   Yes, yes, go on, tell me. You know I'm never
cross with you.

PRIME MINISTER.   Permit me to tell you straight to
your face, brutally, in my old man's way — you're
a great man, Sire!

KING.   *(Very pleased)* Now, now. . . Why should you?

PRIME MINISTER.   No, Your Majesty, no, I just can't
contain myself! I must repeat this — forgive my
lack of self-control — you're a giant! A blinding
light!

KING.   Oh-oh! What a fellow! You really mustn't. . .!

PRIME MINISTER.   For instance, Your Majesty ordered
your Court Savant to draw — excuse my saying it —
the pedigree of the Princess. To find out everything —
putting it very crudely — about her ancestors.
Forgive my frankness, Your Majesty — that was a
marvellous idea.

KING.   Go on with you! Not at all!

PRIME MINSTER. Well, the Court Savant is here. I'm
          telling you this without any tricks or beating about
          the bush. Shall I call him? Oh, Sire! *(Shakes his
          finger at the King)* Oh, clever, clever Majesty!

KING. Come here, you truthful old man! *(Moved)* Let
          me kiss you. And don't you ever be afraid of
          telling me the truth straight to my face. I'm not
          like other kings. I love truth, even when it happens
          to be unpleasant. Has the Court Savant come?
          Never mind. Please! Call him in here. I'll be putting
          on my clothes and drinking chocolate, and he can
          talk on. Give orders for dressing and the chocolate,
          my honest old man.

PRIME MINISTER. *(Jauntily)* I obey. *(Calls)* Flunkeys!

          *(FLUNKEYS carry in a screen to the sound of
          trumpets. The KING disappears behind it, so that
          only his head shows)*

          Tailors!

          *(The trumpets sound even more solemnly. The
          TAILORS, putting in the last stitches as they
          walk up to the screen, station themselves beside
          it)*

          Cook!

          *(CHIEF COOK marches up to the screen to the
          accompaniment of trumpet blasts. He hands a cup
          of chocolate to the HEAD VALET, walks
          backwards and disappears in the crowd of
          COURTIERS)*

          The Savant!

          *(The COURT SAVANT, holding an enormous
          book, places himself in front of the screen, facing
          it)*

          Silence! *(Looks round him)*

          (Everyone is dead still)

          Are you ready? *(In a commanding voice)* Begin!

          *(The trumpets stop and a light, rhythmical music
          follows. It is like the sound of a musical box. The
          TAILORS disappear behind the screen. The HEAD
          VALET spoons the chocolate into the KING's
          mouth)*

KING. *(Having swallowed several spoonfuls, shouts jauntily)* Good morning, Court Savant!

SAVANT. Good morning, Your Majesty.

KING. Start talking. But no, wait a moment. Prime Minister! Let the courtiers listen, too.

PRIME MINISTER. Messrs Courtiers! His Majesty's noticed that you are here.

COURTIERS. Hurrah, King! Hurrah, King! Hurrah, King!

KING. And I see the girls are here, too. Ladies-in-waiting. Coo-coo!

(Hides behind the screen)

FIRST LADY-IN-WAITING. *(An elderly, energetic-looking woman, in a bass voice)* Coo-coo, Your Majesty.

KING. *(Re-appearing)* Ha-ha-ha! *(Jauntily)* Good morning, my little rascals!

FIRST LADY-IN-WAITING. Good morning, Your Majesty.

KING. *(Playfully)* Whom did you see in your dreams last night, my sweet?

FIRST LADY-IN-WAITING. You, Your Majesty.

KING. Me? Brave girl!

FIRST LADY-IN-WAITING. Glad to serve Your Majesty.

KING. And you, girls, what did you dream about?

ALL THE OTHER LADIES-IN-WAITING. About you, Your Majesty.

KING. Brave girls!

ALL THE LADIES-IN-WAITING. Glad to serve Your Majesty.

KING. Fine! First Lady-in-Waiting, you've succeeded in militarizing the girls very well. They answer me very smartly today. I graciously acknowledge my satisfaction. What's your grade?

FIRST LADY-IN-WAITING. A Colonel, Your Majesty.

KING. I make you a General.

FIRST LADY-IN-WAITING. I humbly thank Your
Majesty.

KING. You deserve it. You've been my leading beauty
for thirty years now. Every night you see me — only
me — in your dreams. You're my little bird, General.

FIRST LADY-IN-WAITING. Glad to serve Your
Majesty.

KING. *(Getting sentimental)* My little sweeties! Don't
go too far from me, my darlings! The Professor's
going to be as dry as dust. I'll need refreshing. Well,
Court Savant, come, spit it out!

SAVANT. Your Majesty! With the assistance of
Professor Brochhaus and Lecturer Effron, I have
compiled an absolutely exact pedigree of our
high-born visitor.

KING. *(To the* LADIES-IN-WAITING) Coo-coo!
He-he-he...

SAVANT. First of all, about her coat-of-arms. A
coat-of-arms, Your Majesty, is a symbolic
representation, yes, a symbolic representation
which is passed from generation to generation and
designed in accordance with certain rules, yes,
rules.

KING. I know what a coat-of-arms is, Professor.

SAVANT. From immemorial times certain symbolic
designs, yes, designs, came into use and were cut
on signet rings...

KING. *(To the* LADIES-IN-WAITING) Tew-tew! *(as to
birds)*

SAVANT. They were also painted on weapons, banners
and other things, yes, other things.

KING. *(To the* LADIES-IN-WAITING) Chuck-chuck!
My little birds!

SAVANT. These designs represented the results...

KING. Enough about the designs! Come to the point!
(To the LADIES-IN-WAITING) Coo-coo!

SAVANT. Yes, they represented the outcome of a wish to separate oneself from the general mass of people, yes, to separate oneself. . . To give oneself a sharp distinction which would be noticeable even in the heat of battle. Yes! Of battle!

(The KING comes out from behind the screen. He is gorgeously attired)

KING. Come to the point, Professor!

SAVANT. Coats-of-arms. . .

KING. To the point, I tell you! Be brief!

SAVANT. Even from the time of the Crusades. . .

KING. *(Raising his dagger at him)* I'll kill you like a dog! Cut the cackle, or else. . .

SAVANT. In that case, Your Majesty, I'll begin to blazonize. . .

KING. Eh? What will you begin?

SAVANT. Blazonize, Your Majesty.

KING. I forbid it! What abomination is this? What's that word?

SAVANT. But, Your Majesty. . . to blazonize means to describe a coat-of-arms.

KING. Then you should say so straight away!

SAVANT. And so, I blazonize. The Princess's coat-of-arms. On a gold field strewn with scarlet hearts there are three royal-blue, crowned partridges, burdened with a leopard.

KING. What? What? Did you say 'burdened'?

SAVANT. Yes, Your Majesty. Round them, a border combining the colours of her kingdom.

KING. All right, all right. . . I don't like it, but let it be so, all the same. Tell me about her pedigree but be briefer.

SAVANT. I obey, Your Majesty. When Adam. . .

KING. How dreadful! Is the Princess a Jewess then?

SAVANT. Your Majesty! How can you!

KING.   But Adam was a Jew, wasn't he?

SAVANT,   This point is still under discussion, Your
Majesty. I have information to show that he was a
Karaim.(*)

KING.   I should think so! I must be sure that the
Princess is of pure blood. This is very fashionable
just now, and I stick to fashion. I'm a man of
fashion, am I not, my little birds?

LADIES-IN-WAITING.   You certainly are, Your
Majesty.

SAVANT.   Yes, Your Majesty. You've always kept in
step with the most modern ideas of the day, Your
Majesty. Yes, most!

KING.   Absolutely! Take the cost of my trousers alone...
Continue, Professor.

SAVANT.   So Adam...

KING.   Leave this delicate subject and pass on to more
recent times.

SAVANT.   The Pharaoh Isametikh...

KING.   Let's leave him alone, too. A very ugly name.
Go on.

SAVANT.   Then, Your Majesty, permit me to pass on
directly to the Princess's own dynasty. The founder
of the dynasty was George the First, named Great
for his exploits... Yes, Great...

KING.   That's fine.

SAVANT.   He was succeeded by his son, George the
Second, whose exploits earned him the name of
Ordinary. Yes, Ordinary.

KING.   I am in a great hurry. Just enumerate her
ancestors. I'll understand without explanation why
they earned their various names. If you don't hurry
up, I'll cut your throat.

SAVANT.   I obey, Your Majesty. Further we have
Wilhelm I, the Gay, Henrik I, the Short, George III,
the Dissolute, George IV, the Pretty, Henrik II, the

(*) A Jewish sect inhabiting the Crimea.

Devil May Care.

KING. Why was he called that?

SAVANT. For his exploits, Your Majesty. Then come
Philip I, the Abnormal, George V, the Funny,
George VI, the Negative, George VII, the Barefoot,
George VIII, the Anaemic, George IX, the Brutal,
George X, the Spindleleg, George XI, the Brave,
George XII, the Antipathetic, George XIII, the
Impudent, George XIV, the Interesting, and finally,
the present reigning monarch, the Princess's father,
George XV, named for his exploits the Bearded. Yes,
the Bearded.

KING. A very rich and varied collection of ancestors,
I'm sure.

SAVANT. Yes, Your Majesty. The Princess has
eighteen ancestors, not counting the coats-of-arms
on her mother's side. Yes, she has.

KING. It's quite sufficient. . . You can go. *(Looks at
his watch)* Oh, how late it is! Call the Court Poet,
quickly!

PRIME MINISTER. The King wants the Poet. At the
double!

(The COURT POET *runs up to the King)*

KING. Good morning, Court Poet.

POET. Good morning, Your Majesty.

KING. Have you prepared the speech of welcome?

POET. Yes, Your Majesty. My inspiration. . .

KING. And the poem on the Princess's arrival?

POET. My muse assisted me in finding five hundred and
eight pairs of most splendid rhymes, Your Majesty.

KING. Why — are you going to read out only rhymes?
And what about the verses?

POET. Your Majesty! My muse has only just had time
to complete a poem on your Majesty's parting
with the Lady-in-Waiting on the right flank. . .

KING. Your muse never manages to keep up with the
pace of events. All she and you can do is to cadge
now a country cottage, then a little house in town,

64

then a cow. It's quite disgraceful! Why, for instance, should a poet need a cow? But when it comes to writing, you're never on time. . . You poets are all the same, all of you!

POET. Nevertheless, my devotion to Your Majesty. . .

KING. I happen to need your poems, not your devotion!

POET. But the speech is quite ready, Your Majesty.

KING. A speech! Indeed, you're all past masters at making speeches! Well, give us the speech, at least.

POET. As a matter of fact, it isn't even a speech but a conversation. Your Majesty says things and the Princess replies. A copy of her replies was sent to the Princess on her journey by a special messenger. May I make the contents public?

KING. You may.

POET. Your Majesty says: 'Princess! I am so happy that you ascend my throne like the rising sun. The light of your beauty illuminates everything around you.' To this the Princess replies: 'The sun is you, Your Majesty. The brilliance of your exploits has eclipsed all your rivals.' And you retort to this: 'I am so happy that you are capable of appreciating my true worth.' The Princess replies: 'Your virtues are a pledge of our future happiness.' And you: 'You understand me so well that all I can say is that you are as intelligent as you are beautiful.' The Princess then says: 'I am so happy that Your Majesty likes me.' And you: 'I feel that we love one another, Princess. Permit me to embrace you.'

KING. That's very good.

POET. The Princess says: 'I'm overcome with confusion, but. . .' Just then there's a salvo of cannon fire, the soldiers shout 'Hurrah!' , and you kiss the Princess.

KING. I kiss her? Ha-ha! That's not bad! On the mouth?

POET. Exactly so, Your Majesty.

KING. That's rather clever! You can go. Ha-ha! *(To* PRIME MINISTER) It's a pleasant prospect, old man. Yes! Yes, indeed! *(In his excitement seizes the* FIRST LADY-IN-WAITING *by the waist)* Who else is waiting for an audience? Eh? Speak out, my truthful old man!

PRIME MINISTER. Your Majesty, I won't conceal from you that two weavers are still waiting for an audience.

KING. Ah! Why aren't they admitted? Quickly! Send them to me at the double!

PRIME MINISTER. Weavers! The King calls you! At a gallop!

(HENRIK *and* CHRISTIAN *skipping jauntily run out to the centre of the stage)*

KING. How old they look — they must be very experienced. And how agile — I bet they're good workers. Good morning, Weavers.

HENRIK and CHRISTIAN. We wish good health to Your Majesty.

KING. What have you got to say? Eh? Well? Why don't you speak?

(CHRISTIAN *sighs with a moan)*

What are you saying?

(HENRIK *sighs with a moan)*

What?

CHRISTIAN. Poor King! O-oh!

KING. Are you trying to scare me, you fools? What's the matter? Why do you call me 'poor King'?

CHRISTIAN. Such a great King, and look — how he's dressed!

KING. How am I dressed? Eh? Tell me!

HENRIK. Most ordinarily, Your Majesty.

CHRISTIAN. Like anybody.

HENRIK. Like any of the kings, your neighbours.

CHRISTIAN. O-oh, Your Majesty, o-oh!

KING. What's this? What are they saying? How can it

66

be? Unlock my wardrobes! Bring me the cloak
number 4009, part of my lace suit. Look at it, you
fools. Pure silk. Bordered with guipure lace in front.
Round the collar lace d'Alençon, round the hem
Valencienne lace. This goes with my all-lace suit for
outdoor functions. . . And you tell me I dress
like anybody! Bring me the boots. Look, the boots,
too, are trimmed with Brabant lace! Have you
ever seen anything like it?

HENRIK.   We have indeed!

CHRISTIAN.   Many a time!

KING.   Damn and blast! Bring my dinner suit, then!
No, not that one, you ass! Number 8498. Look at
it, you! What is this?

HENRIK.   A pair of trousers.

KING.   Made of?. . .

CHRISTIAN.   Need I tell you? Of gra-de-naples.

KING.   Have you no conscience? Do you mean to say
that gra-de-naples is nothing special? And what
about this coat? Pure gro-de-tour, with sleeves of
of gros-grain. And the collar of pou-de-soie. And
the cloak in turquoise silk with vertical stripes
of reps along the surface. Come on, admire it!
Why are you turning away?

HENRIK.   We've seen enough of such things.

KING.   Stockings of drap-de-soie?

CHRISTIAN.   We've seen enough of that, too.

KING.   Feel them, you fool!

HENRIK.   I don't need to. . . I know.

KING.   You know! Bring me my trousers for the wedding
ball! What's this?

CHRISTIAN.   Broadcloth.

KING.   Correct, but of what quality? Where else in the
world will you find such quality? And the coat of
Cheviot cloth with the Boston collar? And the
cloak? Made of the best Jersey cloth! Have you
ever seen such garments, you fool?

HENRIK. Yes, Your Majesty. Indeed, any fool's seen plenty of garments like these.

CHRISTIAN. Whereas we can make such cloth that. . . O-ho! Such stuff that only clever people would be able to see it. We'd make you a fabulous wedding suit, Your Majesty.

KING. Indeed? They all say that! Have you got references?

CHRISTIAN. We worked a whole year for the Turkish Sultan. He was quite indescribably pleased with our work. That's why he didn't write anything to recommend us.

KING. A Turkish Sultan! Fancy that!

HENRIK. The Great Mogul of India thanked me personally.

KING. Fancy that! The Great Mogul! Don't you know that our nation is the greatest in the world? All other nations are mere rubbish — only ourselves are fine fellows. Haven't you heard that?

CHRISTIAN. I must add that our fabric possesses one truly marvellous property.

KING. Just imagine! What is that?

CHRISTIAN. I've already mentioned it, Your Majesty. Only clever people would be able to see it. Our cloth is invisible to people who are unfit for their jobs or who are complete and utter fools.

KING. *(Getting interested)* Go on, go on. How's that?

CHRISTIAN. Our fabric cannot be seen by persons who are unfit for their jobs or who're plain stupid.

KING. Ha-ha-ha! O-oh, o-oh, o-oh! You're killing me! I'm damned! D'you mean that my Prime Minister here won't see it if he's unfit for his job?

CHRISTIAN. Correct, Your Majesty. Such is the miraculous property of that fabric.

KING. Ah-ha-ha! *(He is weak with laughter)* D'you hear, old man? Prime Minister! I'm speaking to you!

PRIME MINISTER. Your Majesty, I don't believe in

68

miracles.

KING. *(Threatening him with his dagger)* What? You don't believe in miracles? A man so close to the throne doesn't believe in miracles? Then you're a materialist? You scoundrel! To the dungeons with you!

PRIME MINISTER. Your Majesty! Allow me, an old man, to put you right on this. You didn't hear me out to the end. I was going to say: 'I don't believe in miracles, saith the fool in his heart.' A fool says this. . . as for ourselves, we owe our very existence to a miracle!

KING. Ah, that's what you meant? Well, it's all right then. Wait a moment, Weavers. What remarkable cloth it must be! You mean, it'll enable me to see who of my staff is not fit for his job?

CHRISTIAN. Exactly so, Your Majesty!

KING. And I'll grasp at once who is clever and who stupid?

CHRISTIAN. It won't take you a moment, Your Majesty.

KING. The stuff is of silk?

CHRISTIAN. Pure silk, Your Majesty.

KING. Stay here. I'll talk to you again after the Princess's reception.

(A trumpet blast)

What's that now? Eh? Find out, old man.

PRIME MINISTER. It's the Minister of Tender Feelings who's just arrived.

KING. A-ha! A-ha! A-ha! Fine, fine! Quickly bring the Minister of Tender Feelings in! Be quick, I tell you!

(Enter the MINISTER OF TENDER FEELINGS*)*

Have you good news? I see by your face the news is good! Good morning, Minister of Tender Feelings!

MINISTER. Good morning, Your Majesty.

KING. Well, well, my dear man? I'm listening.

MINISTER. Your Majesty! Alas! The Princess is

absolutely without reproach as far as her morals are concerned.

KING. He-he! But why 'alas' ?

MINISTER. The purity of her blood, alas! Your Majesty, the Princess failed to feel the pea through twenty-four feather-beds. More than that, since that night she slept on one feather-bed only through the rest of her journey.

KING. Why are you grinning then, you ass? It means there'll be no wedding! And I was so much in the mood for it! What a let-down! What a disgusting trick! Come here! I'll cut your throat for this!

MINISTER. But Your Majesty, I felt I had no right to conceal this unpleasant truth from you!

KING. I'll show you an 'unpleasant truth' right away! *(Chases him with a dagger)*

MINISTER. *(Screams)* O-oh! A-ah! I won't do it again! Spare me! *(Runs out of the room)*

KING. Get out! Get out all of you! You've upset me! You've offended me! I'll stab all of you to death! Bury you alive in my dungeons! Sterilize you! Get out!

(Everyone, except the PRIME MINISTER, *rushes out of the reception hall)*

KING. *(Pounces on the* PRIME MINISTER) Drive her out! Immediately! The Princess is to be chased away! She might be a Semite! She might be a Hamite! Out! Away!

PRIME MINISTER. Your Majesty! Do hear an old man out! I'll tell you straight away, rudely, like a bear. If you drive her away because she's — reputedly — not of pure blood. . . well, her father would take offence.

KING. *(Stamping his foot)* Let him take offence!

PRIME MINISTER. That'll start a war.

KING. What do I care?

PRIME MINISTER. It might be much better if you meet the Princess and then tell her gently, delicately, that — let's say — her figure doesn't quite please you. Let me tell you in my crude, straightforward way that you, Your Majesty, are quite an expert in these matters. It's quite hard to please you. And in this way, gently, quietly, we'll get rid of the Princess. I can see — yes, indeed, I can — the King's beginning to see my point! Oh, clever, clever Majesty! He agrees with me!

KING. Very well, I agree, old man. Go, get everything ready for the reception, and after that I'll get rid of her. She'll have first to be received at Court.

PRIME MINISTER. Oh, what a King! What a genius! *(Goes out)*

KING. *(Peevishly)* How dreadful it all is, really! Again they've upset me. Jester! Bring the Jester here, quickly! Talk to me, buffoon! Cheer me up.

(The JESTER runs in, hopping up and down)

JESTER. A certain tradesman...

KING. *(Aggressively)* His name?...

JESTER. Ludvigsen. A certain tradesman was crossing a bridge — and suddenly — flop! straight into the river!

KING. Ha-ha-ha!

JESTER. And he fell on a boat that was passing under the bridge, and hit the oarsman on the head with the heel of his boot.

KING. Ha-ha-ha! On the head? Ho-ho-ho!

JESTER. The oarsman, too, tumbled over into the water, but he grabbed an old woman that was passing along the bank by her skirt. She, too, tumbled into the river.

KING. Ha-ha-ha! You're killing me! O-oh! O-oh! Ha-ha-ha! Ha-ha-ha!

(Wipes his tears, fixing the JESTER with eyes full of admiration) Well?

JESTER. And the old woman...

CURTAIN

71

The courtyard of the royal palace, paved with multi-coloured tiles. By the back wall stands a throne. On the right a barrier to keep the populace within bounds.

THE MINISTER OF TENDER FEELINGS. *(Enters, limping slightly. Shouts)* O-oh! Come here, Mr Chamberlain! O-oh!

CHAMBERLAIN. Why are you groaning? Are you wounded? Ah! Halloo!

MINISTER. Ah! No, not wounded! Murdered! Here! Carry the sedan chair of the Princess in here. O-oh!

MINISTER. You'll see in a moment. *(Runs out)*

> *(A sedan chair bearing the PRINCESS is carried in. The GOVERNESS and the CHAMBERLAIN walk beside it)*

CHAMBERLAIN. *(To the PORTERS)* Put the sedan chair down and clear out. Don't you dare come near the window, you scoundrels! Yoicks!

GOVERNESS. Tell them: take hands of pockets out! Noses not touch! Straight stand!

CHAMBERLAIN. Ah, I can't be bothered with manners! I look out that no *gogol-mogol* notes over handed your-mine Princess. *(To the PORTERS)* What are you listening for? You don't understand any foreign language anyway. Get out!

> *(The PORTERS run away)*

(To the GOVERNESS) It's like a heavy load my shoulders off, *ein, zwei, drei!* We'll get *diese* Princess off our hands and on to the King's And — *una, duna, res!*

GOVERNESS. *(Cheerfully)* Kvinter, baba, jess. And mine is glad!

CHAMBERLAIN. *(To the PRINCESS)* Get ready, Your Highness. Presently I'll go and report your arrival to the King. Your Highness! Are you asleep?

PRINCESS. No, I was just thinking.

CHAMBERLAIN. Ugh! Well, never mind! *(To the GOVERNESS)* You go and stand by that gate, *lobi-tobi.* And keep your eyes skinned! I go speak *avec* the King.

GOVERNESS. *Und! (She places herself by the entrance to the courtyard)*

PRINCESS. Everything is so foreign here — the ground all covered with stones — not a blade of grass! The walls are watching me as a wolf watches a lamb. I'd feel very afraid if I hadn't received a note from my charming, curly-haired, kind, affectionate, handsome Henrik, my own dear Henrik! I am so glad, that I can even smile. *(Kisses the note)* Oh, how nicely it smells of nuts! Oh, how prettily it's gone all greasy! *(Reads)* 'We are here. I am wearing white hair and a white beard. Swear at the King. Tell him that he's abominably dressed. Henrik.' I don't understand it at all. But oh, how clever he is! I wonder where he is. If only I could see him for a second!

(The sounds of singing are heard from behind the wall. Two male voices sing quietly)

> For our love we'll fight
> And surely win through,
> Then we'll go home to live
> Together — just us two.

PRINCESS. Ah, it's his voice! It means he'll come out presently. That's how it happened last time — he sang a song, then he came!

(Enter the PRIME MINISTER and stands stock still, as if struck by the PRINCESS's beauty)

It's he! With white hair and white beard!

PRIME MINISTER. Allow me to tell you, Your Highness, tell you in my crude, old man's, paternal way — I'm quite overcome by your beauty.

PRINCESS. *(Runs up to him)* Well?

PRIME MINISTER. *(Puzzled)* Yes, Your Highness.

PRINCESS. Why don't you tell me to pull you by the beard?

PRIME MINISTER. *(Appalled)* Whatever for, Your Highness?

PRINCESS. *(Bursts out laughing)* Oh, you! You won't take me in this time! I've recognized you at once!

73

PRIME MINISTER.   Good God!

PRINCESS.   Now I know how to pull! *(She pulls his beard with all her force)*

PRIME MINISTER.   *(Shrilly)* Your Highness!

(The PRINCESS *pulls him by the hair and pulls off his wig. He is quite bald)*

PRIME MINISTER.   *(Shrilly)* Help!

(The GOVERNESS *runs up to him)*

GOVERNESS.   What is he do to her, the foreign old man? La! *Pas-de-trois!*

PRIME MINISTER.   But me — the Prime Minister of His Majesty!

GOVERNESS.   Princess, why do you *bitte-dritte* him?

PRINCESS.   I want him to go to hell or some such similar place!

GOVERNESS.   Take those drops, *vass-iss-dass.*

PRINCESS.   I smashed the bottle, and you can go to hell yourself, you bitch!

PRIME MINISTER.   *(Laughs loudly, enjoying it. Aside)* But she's stark mad! This is wonderful! It'll be perfectly easy to get rid of her. I must go and report to the King. No, I'd better not — he doesn't like unpleasant reports. Let him see for himself. *(To the* PRINCESS) Your Highness, permit me to tell you straight out, in my old man's way: you're so playful that my heart rejoices at you! Our ladies-in-waiting will fall in love with you at first sight. By God, they will! May I call them in? They'll help you to freshen yourself up after the journey, they'll show you this and that, while we get ready here for the reception. Girls!

(LADIES-IN-WAITING *enter in military formation)*

Permit me, Princess, to introduce the ladies-in-waiting to you. They're very glad to meet you.

PRINCESS.   So am I. Very glad. I feel so lonely here, and now I see they are — most of them — as young as I. Are you really glad to see me?

FIRST LADY-IN-WAITING.   Allow me to report to you, Your Highness.

74

PRINCESS. What?

FIRST LADY-IN-WAITING. Your Highness! During
my hours of duty nothing special occurred. Four
ladies-in-waiting are here. Four are not attending
on Your Highness. One is on duty in the neighbour-
hood. Another on point-duty. Two are having fits
of hysterics on account of the impending
marriage. *(She salutes)*

PRINCESS. Are you a soldier, Lady-in-waiting?

FIRST LADY-IN-WAITING. No, Your Highness, I'm a
General. Please enter the palace, Princess. Girls!
Listen to my command! Steady! Ready? March!
(They go in)

PRINCESS. But this is dreadful!

(They all disappear inside the palace)

PRIME MINISTER. Hey, you there! Bring in the
soldiers. I'm off to fetch the crowd. *(Goes out)*

(Enter SOLDIERS and an OFFICER)

OFFICER. In anticipation of meeting the King, get
weak in the knees with emotion!

(The SOLDIERS bend their knees)

With knees bent — forward march!

(The SOLDIERS march with bent knees)

Left! Right! To the wall! Stand still!

*(Enter the CROWD. The PRIME MINISTER
leads them behind the barrier)*

PRIME MINISTER. *(To the CROWD)* I know that
you're his Majesty's most loyal subjects, but I
must remind you that in the grounds of his Majesty's
palace you mustn't open your mouth except to
shout 'hurrah' or to sing a hymn of praise.
Understand?

THE CROWD. Yes, we understand.

PRIME MINISTER. I see you don't, not properly.
You're already in the precincts of the palace.
But instead of shouting 'hurrah', you're saying
something quite different. Well?

THE CROWD. *(Apologetically)* Hurrah!

PRIME MINISTER. Just think of it — the King! Do
you grasp it? The King himself is quite close
beside you. He's wise, he's very special! Not
like other men at all. And think — such a wonder
of Nature is not much more than two paces
away from you. Amazing, isn't it?

THE CROWD. *(Reverently)* Hurrah!

PRIME MINISTER. You must stand here in silence
until the King comes out. Then sing the hymn of
praise and shout 'hurrah' until the King tells
you to 'stand at ease'. After that, keep silent.
Only when his Excellency gives the sign to the
Royal Guards to shout, you may shout, too.
You understand?

THE CROWD. *(Soberly)* Hurrah!

*(Shouting is heard, increasing in volume as it
gets nearer: 'The King is coming! The King is
coming! The King is coming!' The* KING *enters
with his suite)*

OFFICER. *(Commands)* Overcome with delight at the
sight of the King — faint!

(The SOLDIERS *fall down)*

PRIME MINISTER. *(To the* CROWD) Sing the hymn!

THE CROWD. *(Sings)*

> Lo! our King! What a King!
> Lo! Lo! Oh la!la!
> Let us sing
> Oh! la-la
> To our King
> Hurrah!
> Lo! Lo! Our King! Such a King!
> Oh, la, la! Hurrah!

KING. Stand at ease!

(The CROWD *falls silent)*

OFFICER. *(Commands)* Recover!

(The SOLDIERS *get up)*

KING. Well, where is she? How annoying! What a bore!
I want my lunch as soon as possible, and I've got
to. . . waste time on that hybrid girl.

Where is she? We must get rid of her quickly.

PRIME MINISTER. She's coming, Your Majesty.

(Enter PRINCESS with the LADIES-IN-WAITING)

OFFICER. *(Commands)* At the sight of the beautiful young Princess — jump with joy!

(The SOLDIERS jump up and down.

From the moment the PRINCESS appears the KING begins to behave in an enigmatic way. His face reflects complete bewilderment. He speaks in a hollow voice like a hypnotized person. He gazes at the PRINCESS with this head lowered, like a bull's. The PRINCESS mounts the dais)

OFFICER. *(Commands)* Calm down!

(The SOLDIERS stop jumping)

KING. *(Speaking like a sleep-walker)* How are you, Princess?

PRINCESS. Go to hell!

(The KING gazes at her for a few moments as if trying to grasp the meaning of her words. Then with a strange smile, he unrolls the written speech of welcome and clears his throat)

OFFICER. *(Commands)* Look struck dumb with attention!

KING. *(In the same sleep-walker's voice)* Princess! I am happy to see you ascend my throne like the rising sun! The light of your beauty illuminates everything.

PRINCESS. Shut up, you stupid windbag!

KING. *(In the same manner)* I am happy, Princess, that you appreciate my true worth. . .

PRINCESS. Silly ass!

KING. *(In the same manner)* You understand me so well, Princess, that all I can say is that you're as intelligent as you are beautiful.

PRINCESS. You're an idiot!

KING. I feel that we love one another, Princess.

Will you allow me to kiss you? *(He takes a step forward)*

PRINCESS.   Get out, you son of a bitch!

(Salvoes of cannon fire. Joyous shouts of 'Hurrah'. The PRINCESS descends from the dais. The KING, walking strangely, without bending his knees, advances to the footlights. LADIES-IN-WAITING crowd round him. The PRIME MINISTER supports him by the elbow)

FIRST LADY-IN-WAITING.   Your Majesty! Allow me to pinch the impertinent girl!

PRIME MINISTER.   Your Majesty, shall I call the doctor!

KING.   *(Speaking with difficulty)* No, not the doctor. . . No. . . *(Shouts)* Call the weavers!

PRIME MINISTER.   They're here, Your Majesty.

KING.   *(Shouts)* Make me a wedding suit! Immediately!

FIRST LADY-IN-WAITING.   But didn't you hear, Your Majesty, how she broke the discipline?

KING.   No, I didn't hear! I only saw! I'm up to my ears in love! She's wonderful. I'll marry her! Marry her at once! How dare you look so surprised? I don't care a damn about her origin! I'll change all the laws — she's so pretty! No! Write this down! I grant her, here and now, the most noble, most pure-blooded origin! *(Roars)* I'll marry her even if the whole world is against me!

CURTAIN

A corridor in the palace. A door leading into the weavers' room. The PRINCESS stands, pressing herself against the wall. She is looking very sad. Loud drum-beats are heard from outside.

PRINCESS.   It's very hard to live in a foreign land. Here everything is mili. . . what's the word? Militarized! Everything's done to the beating of drums. The trees in the garden are lined up like

78

a detachment of soldiers. The birds fly in batallions. And in addition to all that, they have these dreadful traditions, made sacred by centuries of use. You can't breathe for them. At dinner they serve first chops, then orange jelly, then soup. This has been an established practice from the ninth century. Flowers in the garden are dusted with white powder. Cats' fur is shaved off, leaving only whiskers and a tuft on the end of the tail. And none of this can be changed, or else — the State will go to ruin! I could be very patient if Henrik were with me. But Henrik has disappeared, vanished without a trace! How can I find him when the ladies-in-waiting follow me about everywhere in close formation! Only when they're led away to be drilled can I come alive. . . It was very difficult to track down all the bearded men and pull their beards. So often when I caught one in the passage and pulled hard — nothing happened. The beard held firm, as if stitched on, the man screamed for help. . . It was no joke! I've heard the new weavers have beards. . . The ladies-in-waiting are outside in the town square, marching, preparing for the wedding parade. . . The weavers are working in this room. Shall I go in and pull their beards? Oh, I'm so scared! What if Henrik is not there, either? What if he had been caught and had his head chopped off in the public square, to the beating of drums — in accordance with the eighth century traditions? No, I really feel. . . I feel I'll have to cut this King's throat, however disgusting I might find it. I'll go in to the weavers. I'll put on my gloves. . . My hands have gone rough with all this beard pulling. *(She takes a step towards the door when the* LADIES-IN-WAITING *enter the corridor in military formation)*

FIRST LADY-IN-WAITING. Permit me to report, Your Highness. . .

PRINCESS. Turn about!

(The LADIES-IN-WAITING *turn round)*

March!

(The LADIES-IN-WAITING *march out. The* PRINCESS *takes a step to the door. The*

LADIES-IN-WAITING *return)*

FIRST LADY-IN-WAITING.   The wedding dress. . .

PRINCESS.   Turn about — mar-rch!

(The LADIES-IN-WAITING *take several strides, then return)*

FIRST LADY-IN-WAITING.   Is ready, Your Highness.

PRINCESS.   Turn about — mar-rch!

(The LADIES-IN-WAITING *turn round and march. They meet the* KING *and the* PRIME MINISTER *who enter)*

FIRST LADY-IN-WAITING.   'Shun! Stand still!

KING.   Ah, my sweet girls! And, oh! She's here, too! Looking exactly as I saw her in my dream, only much more cross. Princess! Darling Princess! He who's in love with you can't help loving you!

PRINCESS.   Go to hell! *(Runs away, followed by the* LADIES-IN-WAITING)

KING.   *(Laughs uproariously)* Her nerves are on edge. I understand her so well. I, too, am at the end of my tether — I can hardly wait. Never mind! Tomorrow's the wedding! In a moment I'll see that remarkable cloth. *(Goes towards the door, then stops)*

PRIME MINISTER.   Your Majesty, as usual, is taking the right direction. It is here, yes, just here.

KING.   Wait a minute, though. . .

PRIME MINISTER.   The weavers are working — if I may put it so crudely — they're working just here.

KING.   I know, I know. *(Walks up to the footlights)* Yes. . . that material is very special. . . Of course, I've nothing to worry about. First of all, I'm intelligent. Secondly, I'm absolutely no good for any place except the royal throne. Even on the throne I'm never quite satisfied, I'm always getting annoyed with something. In any other occupation I'd be simply terrible. And yet. . . It might be better if someone else first paid a visit to the weavers. For instance, the Prime Minister. He's an honest, clever old man — but he's

certainly less intelligent than I. If he would see
that material, I'd be sure to see it, too. Prime
Minister! Come here!

PRIME MINISTER.   I'm here, Your Majesty.

KING.   I've just remembered that I must slip round to
my treasury, to select diamonds for the bride.
You go and have a look at that stuff, and
report to me afterwards.

PRIME MINISTER.   Your Majesty, forgive my rudeness. . . but. . .

KING.   No, I won't forgive. Go! And be quick about
it! *(Runs out)*

PRIME MINISTER.   Y-yes. . . It doesn't matter. . .
All the same. . . *(Calls)* Minister of Tender
Feelings!

(Enter the MINISTER OF TENDER FEELINGS)

MINISTER.   Good day!

PRIME MINISTER.   Good day. Listen – I'm expected
at my office this moment. Go in to the weavers
and afterwards report to me how they're
getting on. *(Aside)* If this fool finds he can see
the stuff, I'm sure to see it, in my turn. . .

MINISTER.   But, Mr Prime Minister, I'm supposed to
go immediately to the barracks of the ladies-in-
waiting and persuade them not to weep at the
King's wedding tomorrow.

PRIME MINISTER.   Plenty of time for that! Go in
to the weavers! At once! *(Runs out)*

MINISTER.   Y-yes. . . Of course, I. . . However. . .
(Calls) Court Poet!

(Enter COURT POET)

MINISTER.   Go in to the weavers and then report
to me how they're getting on. *(Aside)* If this
fool can see that cloth, I'm sure to see it, too.

COURT POET.   But, your Excellency, I'm engaged in
completing the poem on the Princess's departure
from her country to take the road to our
Kingdom!

81

MINISTER. What use is that to anybody? The Princess
          arrived here a fortnight ago. Go now! Quickly!
          (Runs out)

POET. I'm sure I'm not a fool. . . But. . . Ah! I'll risk
          it! Come to the worst, I can tell a lie. It wouldn't
          be the first time!

CURTAIN

*The weavers room. Two large hand looms are pushed
against the wall. In the middle of the room two large
empty frames. A large table. On the table a pair of
scissors, a pin cushion with gold pins and a folding yard
measure.*

CHRISTIAN. Henrik, Henrik, cheer up! Here, in this
          sack we have the finest silk thread they gave us
          for weaving the cloth. I'll weave it into a
          marvellous dress for your bride. And in this sack
          we've got gold. We'll ride home on the best horses
          we can get. Cheer up, Henrik!

HENRIK. I'm very cheerful. I'm silent because I'm
          thinking.

CHRISTIAN. What about?

HENRIK. About myself and Henrietta strolling together
          by the river near my home.

          (Knocking on the door is heard. CHRISTIAN
          *seizes the scissors and pretends to be cutting
          something out as he bends over the table.*
          HENRIK *draws on the table with a piece of chalk)*

CHRISTIAN. Come in!

          (Enter COURT POET)

POET. Good day, Court Weavers.

CHRISTIAN. *(Without leaving his work)* Good day,
          Court Poet.

POET. Listen, Court Weavers. I've been sent here on a
          very important errand. I must examine and report
          on your cloth.

CHRISTIAN. Certainly, Mr Poet. Henrik, what do
          you think of this design? Shall we make the roses
          with the petals pointing upwards or downwards?
          Or perhaps with the foliage at the top?

HENRIK. *(Narrowing his eyes)* Yes, I think, yes. I
think with the petals pointing upwards. The
gleam on the silk shows best that way. The petals
would move as if they were alive with every breath
the King draws.

POET. I'm waiting, Court Weavers.

CHRISTIAN. What for exactly, Mr Poet?

POET. What do you mean — 'what for exactly'?
I'm waiting for you to show me the fabric you've
made for the King's wedding garments.

(HENRIK *and* CHRISTIAN *stop working. They
stare at the* COURT POET *in utter amazement.
Alarmed, he continues)*

Now, now! Haven't you heard me? Why are you
staring at me so? If I've slipped up over something,
tell me — don't try to muddle me up! My work is
nerve-racking anyway. I must be treated with care.

CHRISTIAN. But we are so surprised, Mr Poet!

POET. Surprised — at what? Tell me at once!

CHRISTIAN. But the cloth is before you. Here it is, on
these two frames, stretched for drying. And here
on the table there's a pile of other materials.
Look, what lovely colours, what fine designs!

POET. *(Clears his throat)* Of course, there they are...
On the table... What a large pile! *(Recovers his
confidence)* But I was telling you to show me the
silks. To show and explain which would be used
for the waistcoat, which for the cloak, the coat,
and so on.

CHRISTIAN. Certainly, Mr Poet. On this frame you
see three kinds of silk. *(The* POET *writes in his
note book)* This one, with a rose design, will be
used for the waistcoat. It'll look very pretty.
The petals would move like real ones as the King
breathes. Here, in the middle, the silk with the
King's coat-of-arms. It's for the King's cloak. On
this other silk we've woven the pattern of forget-
me-nots. It's for the King's trousers. The plain
white silk on that frame will be used for the King's
underclothes and for his stockings. This satin is
for the King's shoes. And on the table there are
lengths of silk of all kinds.

POET. But tell me — I'm just curious to know — what name do you give in your common language to this silk here, the one with the rose pattern?

CHRISTIAN. In our common language we call the ground of this design green. And in your language?

POET. We call it green, also.

HENRIK. Quite a cheerful colour, isn't it, Mr Poet?

POET. Oh, yes! Ha-ha-ha! Very cheerful indeed! Yes! Thank you, Weavers. You know — there's no other subject of conversation in the whole of the palace other than your wonderful cloth. Everyone's quivering with eagerness to make sure that everyone else is a fool. The Minister of Tender Feelings will be here in a moment. Good-bye, Weavers.

CHRISTIAN and HENRIK. Good-bye, Court Poet.

(The POET *goes out)*

HENRIK. Well, our affairs are improving, Christian.

CHRISTIAN. Yes. Now I'll make the Minister of Tender Feelings bounce.

HENRIK. How — bounce, Christian?

CHRISTIAN. Like a ball, Henrik.

HENRIK. And you expect him to oblige, Christian?

CHRISTIAN. I'm absolutely sure of it, Henrik.

(Knocking on the door. Enter the MINISTER OF TENDER FEELINGS. *In his hand he holds the pages from the* POET's *note book. With great assurance he goes up to the first frame)*

MINISTER. What wonderful roses!

CHRISTIAN. *(Lets out a wild shout)* Ah!

MINISTER. *(Jumps)* What's the matter?

CHRISTIAN. Forgive me, Mr Minister, but can't you see? *(Points at the floor)*

MINISTER. What is it I can't see? What the devil have I got to see?

CHRISTIAN. You're standing on the silk we've put on the floor to cut the King's waistcoat out from.

MINISTER. Ah, yes, I see! I see! *(Takes a step sideways)*

HENRIK. Ah! Now you're treading on the King's cloak.

MINISTER. Oh, damn it! I'm so absent-minded. *(Jumps well to the right)*

CHRISTIAN. Ah! That's the King's underclothes!

(The MINISTER jumps far to the left)

HENRIK. Ah! The King's stockings!

(The MINISTER takes a gigantic leap towards the door)

CHRISTIAN. Ah! The King's shoes!

(The MINISTER jumps out of the room. Pokes his head in through the half-open door)

MINISTER. *(Through the door)* Oh, what excellent work! Unfortunately, we Ministers of the Crown are obliged by the nature of our duties to hold our heads up. For that reason, I can't properly see anything that's low down, or on the floor. But all that is displayed on the frames — the roses, forget-me-nots, coats-of-arms — all that is most beautifully done! Carry on, Weavers, carry on! The Prime Minister will be here to see you, shortly. *(Exit, closing the door)*

CHRISTIAN. Well, who was right, Henrik?

HENRIK. You were, Christian.

CHRISTIAN. As for the Prime Minister, I'll call him a fool straight to his face.

HENRIK. Straight to his face, Christian?

CHRISTIAN. Yes, absolutely straight, Henrik.

(The PRIME MINISTER opens the door and pokes his head through. CHRISTIAN, pretending not to notice him, goes behind the empty frames)

PRIME MINISTER. Hey, Weavers! Why don't you tidy up your floor a bit? Such precious cloth — and you let it trail in the dust! Ai,ai,ai! The King'll be coming to see you presently.

HENRIK. I obey, your Excellency. *(Pretends to be picking up the cloth and folding it on the table)*

(The PRIME MINISTER *comes in. Cautiously stops just inside the door.* CHRISTIAN, *on the other side of the frame, takes a bottle from his pocket and drinks)*

PRIME MINISTER.   Hey you, how dare you drink vodka at work?

CHRISTIAN.   What fool is bawling out there?

PRIME MINISTER.   What! Have you gone blind, you ass? It's me, the Prime Minister!

CHRISTIAN.   Forgive me, your Excellency, I can't see you from behind this cloth, and I didn't recognize your voice. But you saw *me* — that's what I can't understand!

PRIME MINISTER.   Yes... I mean, no — I recognized the smell of the stuff! I hate vodka. I can smell the damned stuff a mile off!

(CHRISTIAN *comes out from behind the frame)*

CHRISTIAN.   But this isn't vodka at all — it's water, your Excellency.

PRIME MINISTER.   Stop pushing your filthy bottle under my nose! Go back to your loom! The King'll be here shortly. *(Goes out)*

(Singing is heard off stage. The KING *approaches, singing)*

KING.   *(Off)* I'm coming to look at it, I'm coming to look at it! Troll-la-la! Troll-la-la!

(Gaily enters the room, followed by his COURTIERS)

Troll-la-la, troll-la-la... *(His voice trails off in dismay)* Troll-la-la... *(A pause. Smiling vaguely, he makes a very wide gesture with his hand)* Well? What do you think of it? Eh?

COURTIERS.   Marvellous, truly remarkable cloth!

MINISTER OF TENDER FEELINGS.   The cloth is most noble and luxurious, Your Majesty.

COURTIERS.   So true! What a fitting description! Most noble and luxurious!

86

KING. *(To the* PRIME MINISTER) And what do you say, my honest old man? Eh?

(The KING *is dismayed but does his best not to show it. While talking to the* PRIME MINISTER, *he glances at the table and the frames, obviously still hoping to see the wonderful cloth. There is a fixed smile on his face)*

PRIME MINISTER. Your Majesty, this time I'll tell you such absolutely pure truth as the world's never heard before. It may surprise you, Your Majesty, you may be amazed, but all the same, I'm going to tell you the truth!

KING. Yes, yes.

PRIME MINISTER. You must forgive me, but now and again I feel like being absolutely direct. Nowhere will you find cloth, Your Majesty, even remotely like this. It is gorgeous and full of colour.

COURTIERS. Oh, how true! Gorgeous and full of colour! How well he puts it!

KING. Yes, the weavers have done well! I see, you have... you've got most of it more or less ready?....

CHRISTIAN. Yes, Your Majesty. I hope Your Majesty won't find us at fault as far as the colour of these roses is concerned?

KING. No, I won't find you at fault. Definitely not.

CHRISTIAN. We decided that red roses were too common: everyone sees enough of them on bushes all over the place.

KING. Sees them on bushes... Yes. Fine, fine!

CHRISTIAN. For that reason we wove them on silk in sa... *(coughs)* si... *(coughs)*

COURTIERS. Satin! How clever! How original! Most noble and luxurious!

CHRISTIAN. In silver, Courtiers, Sirs!

(A pause)

MINISTER OF TENDER FEELINGS. Bravo, bravo!
(Claps his hands, the COURTIERS *do the same)*

87

KING. I was just about to thank you for making them silver. Silver's my favourite colour. I was literally on the point of . . . Well, I express my royal gratitude to you.

CHRISTIAN. And you don't think, Your Majesty, that the cut of this waistcoat is too bold?

KING. No, not too bold. No. But we've talked enough. Come, let's start trying things on. I still have many things to attend to.

CHRISTIAN. I must ask the Minister of Tender Feelings to hold the King's waistcoat for a few moments.

MINISTER. I'm not sure I'm worthy of. . .

KING. You are worthy. Yes. Well? *(Braces himself up)* Let him hold this beautiful waistcoat. Prime Minister, help me to undress. *(Undresses)*

CHRISTIAN. Ah!

MINISTER OF TENDER FEELINGS. *(Jumps and looks at the floor)* What is it?

CHRISTIAN. The way you're holding the waistcoat, your Excellency!

MINISTER. It's how I'd hold a sacred object!. . . Why?

CHRISTIAN. But you're holding it upside down!. . .

MINISTER. I was so taken up by the beauty of the design. *(Turns about the non-existing waistcoat in his hands)*

CHRISTIAN. Would the Prime Minister be so kind as to hold the King's trousers?

PRIME MINISTER. I've just come out of my office, my friend. I've got ink on my hands. *(To one of the* COURTIERS) You take them, Baron.

FIRST COURTIER. I left my spectacles at home, your Excellency. Perhaps the Marquess here. . .

SECOND COURTIER. I'm too excited. . . my hands are trembling. Perhaps the Count here. . .

THIRD COURTIER. In our family we consider it a bad omen — to hold the King's trousers. . .

KING. What's all this about? Come, dress me quickly! I'm in a hurry.

CHRISTIAN. I obey, Your Majesty. Henrik, come here!
Your leg, please Your Majesty. A little to the left,
please. Now to the right. I'm afraid your Courtiers
would have helped you with a greater skill. We feel
embarrassed in the presence of so great a King.
Now the trousers are on. Mr the Minister of Tender
Feelings, the waistcoat, please. Excuse me, but
you're holding it back to front! Ah! You've dropped
it now! Allow me, then. . . Henrik, bring the
cloak. That's all. The charm of this cloth is that
it is so light. Your shoulders don't feel the weight
of it at all. The underclothes will be ready
tomorrow morning.

KING.   It's a little tight round the shoulders. *(Turns
about in front of a looking-glass)* The cloak's a
bit on the long side. But on the whole the
costume suits me well.

PRIME MINISTER.   Your Majesty, forgive my
rudeness. You're a very handsome man as it is,
but in this costume you're twice as handsome.

KING.   Really? Well, take it off now.

(The weavers undress the KING *and put his own
clothes back on him)*

Thank you, Weavers. You're a fine couple of
fellows. *(Goes to the door)*

COURTIERS.   *(Together)* Fine fellows, Weavers!
Bravo! Noble and luxurious! Splendid and full of
colour! *(They slap the weavers on the shoulders)*
Now we won't let you go. You'll have to dress all
of us.

KING.   *(Stops in the doorway)* You can ask anything
you like of me. I'm very pleased.

CHRISTIAN.   Your Majesty, allow us to accompany
you in your wedding procession. That would be
our best reward.

KING.   I give my permission. *(Exit with his suite)*

HENRIK and CHRISTIAN.   *(Sing)*

All you Courtiers, we're stronger than you!
All you time-servers, we're braver than you!
Because for your jobs you fear —
Your consciences aren't clear!
As for us — we fear nothing!

We've worked long and hard on our stuff
And we've made it stronger than steel,
So strong that pigs and piglets will
Be struck with terror by it!
As for us — we fear nothing!

If we bring our foe to the ground,
Our own trumpets we'll sound,
If he proves stronger than us,
Then the hangman'll get us!
Still we fear nothing!

The CURTAIN *comes down for a few moments. When
it rises again it is the same room the following morning.
The noise of the crowd is heard from outside. The*
KING *is being dressed behind a screen. The* PRIME
MINISTER *stands, facing the audience.*

PRIME MINISTER.   Now, why did I take on the Prime
Minister's job? Whatever for? As if there weren't
plenty of other jobs! Today's affair will end badly —
I feel it in my bones! Fools will see the King
naked! This is terrible! Really terrible! The whole
of our national system, all our traditions are
founded on unshakeable stupidity. What'll happen
if the fools tremble at the sight of their Sovereign
stark naked? Our very foundations will be shaken,
the walls will crack, smoke will rise from the
ruins of our State! No, we mustn't let the King go
out naked! Splendour is the great prop of the
throne. I had a friend once — a Colonel of the
Guards. He retired, and on one occasion he
came to see me — out of uniform. And all of a
sudden I saw that he wasn't a Colonel at all —
just a fool. It was dreadful. All his prestige,
all his charm, vanished with the glitter of his
uniform. No! I'll go to the Sovereign and tell
him straight — he mustn't go out! No! He must not!

KING.   *(Calling)* My honest old man!

PRIME MINISTER.   *(Runs to him)* Here I am — to
put it crudely!

KING.   Do these underclothes become me?

PRIME MINISTER.   They're sheer beauty — I'm
telling you straight.

KING.   Thank you. You may go.

90

PRIME MINISTER. *(Comes forward again)* No! I can't do it! I can't tell him anything. The words freeze on my lips. I've lost the habit in my twenty years of service. Shall I tell him? Shall I not tell him? What'll happen? What'll come of it!

CURTAIN

A square. In the foreground a richly carpeted dais. On either side of the dais a road covered with carpets. The road on the left leads to the gates of the royal palace, that on the right towards backstage. A barrier draped in luxurious materials separates the crowd from the roads and the dais. The CROWD *sings, whistles and makes a lot of noise. When the noise abates somewhat, separate conversations are heard.*

FIRST WOMAN. Oh, I'm so excited about the King's new clothes! I had a heart attack twice last night from sheer excitement.

SECOND WOMAN. And I was in such a state of nerves that my husband fainted.

A BEGGAR. Help, help! I've been robbed!

VOICES. What's the matter? What's happened?

BEGGAR. Someone stole my purse.

A VOICE. But you only had a few coppers in it, surely?

BEGGAR. A few coppers? What cheek! A few coppers in the purse of an old hand, a clever old beggar like me? I had ten thousand Thalers in it! Ah! Here it is, my purse! It's slipped inside my coat lining. Thank Heaven! Give to an old man, for Christ's sake!

A CLEAN-SHAVEN MAN. What if the King-father is late?

A BEARDED MAN. Didn't you hear the salute from the cannon? The King-father's already arrived. He'll come with the Princess, our King's bride, straight from the harbour. The King-father travelled by sea. Over-land travel by carriage makes him sea-sick.

THE CLEAN-SHAVEN MAN.   And the sea doesn't?

THE BEARDED MAN.   It's not quite so vexing on the
    sea.

A BAKER AND HIS WIFE.   Allow me, gentlemen,
    allow me! You're here just for the spectacle but
    my wife and I are on business.

VOICES.   We're all here on the same business.

THE BAKER.   No, not all of us. The wife and I've
    been arguing for fifteen years. She says *I*'m a fool,
    and I say she is. At last we'll get our argument
    settled today — by means of the King's clothes.
    Let us through!

VOICES.   No, we won't. We're all here with our wives,
    we all argue, we all have business!

A MAN WITH A CHILD ON HIS BACK.   Make way
    for the child! Make way for the child! He's only
    six, but he can read and write, and he knows his
    tables. I promised to show him the King as a
    reward. Boy, how much is seven times eight?

THE BOY.   Fifty-six.

THE MAN.   D'you hear? Make way for the child, make way
    for my clever son! And how much is six times eight?

THE BOY.   Forty-eight.

THE MAN.   D'you hear, gentlemen? And he's only six!
    Make way for the clever boy, my clever son!

ABSENT-MINDED MAN.   I left my spectacles at home, so
    I won't be able to see the King. Damn my short sight!

A PICKPOCKET.   I can easily cure you of your short sight.

ABSENT-MINDED MAN.   Really? How?

PICKPOCKET.   With massage. Here, straight away.

ABSENT-MINDED MAN.   Oh please, do! My wife
    told me to take a good look and then describe
    everything to her in detail. . . And here I am,
    without my glasses. . .

PICKPOCKET.   Open your mouth, shut your eyes and
    count loudly up to twenty.

    (The ABSENT-MINDED MAN *counts aloud
    without shutting his mouth. The* PICKPOCKET

takes his watch, his purse, his wallet, and disappears in the crowd.)

ABSENT-MINDED MAN. *(Having finished counting)* But where's he gone? He's run away. And I can't see any better! Worse, if anything. I can't see my watch, my purse or my wallet.

THE MAN. Make way for my boy! Make way for my clever son! How much is six times six?

THE BOY. Thirty-six.

THE MAN. D'you hear? Make way for my son! Make way for a child-genius!

(Drum beats are heard. There is a great movement in the crowd. People climb up telegraph poles, stand on kerbstones, get on to one another's shoulders)

VOICES. He's coming! He's coming! Here he is! Isn't he goodlooking! Well-dressed, too! I say, you've squashed my watch! . . . You're sitting on my neck! Why don't you come in your own carriage if you want more room? Look at him! Wears a helmet, too! Look at him! Got glasses on, too!

(Enter SOLDIERS led by a GENERAL)

GENERAL. *(Commands)* Push the crowd back! Farther from the barrier!

SOLDIERS. Back you go! Farther away! Away, away! *(They push the crowd back)*

GENERAL. *(Commands)* Turn your backs to the crowd!

(SOLDIERS *turn their backs to the crowd and face the dais. Trumpets blare out. HERALDS march in)*

HERALDS. Off with your caps! Off with your caps! Off with your caps to his Majesty the King-father!

(They go into the palace. From the right enter KING-FATHER, richly dressed and the PRINCESS in wedding apparel. They mount the dais. The crowd falls silent)

PRINCESS. Father, do believe me for once in your

93

life! The bridegroom is an idiot!

KING-FATHER.   A king can't be an idiot, my child.
Kings are always wise.

PRINCESS.   But he's so fat!

KING-FATHER.   Child, a king can't be 'fat'. You
ought to say he 'has presence'.

PRINCESS.   I think he's deaf, too. When I swear at
him, he doesn't hear — he just neighs.

KING-FATHER.   A king doesn't 'neigh'. He only
smiles graciously. But do stop bothering me! Why
are you looking at me with such pathetic eyes?
I can't do anything. Turn away at once! There
now! I brought you the music kettle. The King
won't be with you the whole day, after all. When
he's not there, you might listen to music, to the
little bells ringing. And when there's no one near,
you could even listen to the song the kettle sings.
A princess can't be allowed to marry a swineherd,
you know. It's simply not allowed!

PRINCESS.   He's not a swineherd — he's Henrik.

KING-FATHER.   That makes no difference. Don't be
a silly, don't undermine respect for kingship. If
you do, our neighbour kings would smile
contemptuously at you.

PRINCESS.   You're a tyrant!

KING-FATHER.   I'm nothing of the sort. There —
look! The Minister of Tender Feelings is running
to tell us something. Cheer up, child! Isn't he a
funny sight?

MINISTER.   Your Majesty and Your Highness! My
Sovereign will come out in a minute. At this
moment he's graciously engaged in pursuing the
Second Chamberlain with a dagger. The wretched
man dared to smile when he saw the new costume
our most gracious master had just put on. As
soon as the impudent knave is punished, our
Sovereign will come out. *(A trumpet blast)* The
Chamberlain's been punished!

(HERALDS *come out)*

HERALDS.   Off with your caps, off with your caps, off
with your caps to his Majesty!

94

(From the palace come out TRUMPETERS,
followed by the LADIES-IN-WAITING *in
military formation, then by the* COURTIERS *in
richly embroidered uniforms. After them comes
the* PRIME MINISTER)

PRIME MINISTER.   The King is coming! The King is
coming! The King is coming!

(He looks round. The KING *is not there)*

Halt! *(He runs back to the palace, returns and
says to the* KING-FATHER) In a moment! Our
Sovereign's — to put it bluntly — been delayed in
front of a looking-glass. *(Shouts)* The King is
coming! The King is coming! The King is coming!
(Looks round. The KING *is still not there.
He runs into the palace, returns. To the* KING-
FATHER) They're bringing him! *(Loudly)*
The King is coming! The King is coming! The King
is coming!

(A sedan chair is brought in with the KING
*sitting inside. Smiling graciously, he looks out of
the window. The* SEDAN CARRIERS *stop. The*
CROWD *shouts 'Hurrah!' The* SOLDIERS
*fall down on their faces. The door of the sedan
opens and the* KING *leaps out. He is stark naked.
The welcoming shouts cease abruptly)*

PRINCESS.   Ah! *(She turns away)*

GENERAL.   *(Commands)* Recover!

(The SOLDIERS *get up, glance at the* KING *and
fall again, face downwards, horrified)*

GENERAL.   *(Commands)* Recover!

(The SOLDIERS *get up again with an obvious
effort)*

GENERAL.   Turn away!

(The SOLDIERS *turn away. The* CROWD *is
silent. The* KING, *smiling a self-satisfied smile
and fixing the* PRINCESS *with his eyes, slowly
moves towards the dais. He comes up to the*
PRINCESS)

KING.   *(Gallantly)* Not even the most sumptuous
garments can hide the fierce flame burning in my
heart!

95

PRINCESS. Papa! You see now what an idiot he is!

KING. Greetings, Cousin!

KING-FATHER. Greetings, Cousin! *(Whispers)* What are you doing, Cousin? Why do you appear like this before your subjects?

KING. *(Whispers)* What's that? So you, too? Ha-ha-ha!

KING-FATHER. What do you mean — me, too?

KING. You, too, are either a fool or unfit for your job. Anyone who can't see this wonderful stuff is either a fool or unfit for his job.

KING-FATHER. Anyone who says he can see this stuff is a fool, you idiot!

KING. Who's an idiot?

KING-FATHER. Speak quietly or the mob'll hear you. Speak quietly and smile. *You* are an idiot.

KING. *(With a forced smile)* I?

KING-FATHER. Yes, you!

(The KING *is silent for a few moments, bursting with indignation, then asks in a voice which betrays his waning confidence)*

KING. Why?

KING-FATHER. *(Hisses angrily while still smiling)* Because you've come out into a square full of people with your trousers off!

KING. *(Slaps himself on the leg)* And what's this?

KING-FATHER. A leg.

KING. A leg?

KING-FATHER. Yes! A leg!

KING. No!

KING-FATHER. A bare leg!

KING. Now, why are you lying? I give you my word of honour that I'm dressed like a picture.

KING-FATHER. You're naked, stark naked!

KING. Now, why are you saying such disgusting things? Why? Courtiers! Am I wearing clothes?

COURTIERS. Wonderful, most colourful clothes! Splendid, really noble-looking clothes!

KING. *(To* KING-FATHER*)* So a fig for you! Prime Minister! Am I wearing clothes?

PRIME MINISTER. *(In his ordinary manner)* Forgive my being blunt, your Majesty. *(Fiercely)* You're stark naked, you old fool! D'you understand? Stark naked!

(The KING *lets out a strange scream, more like a hiccup than a cry. His scream is full of amazement)*

PRIME MINISTER. Just look at the people! Just look at them! They seem to be thinking! They *are* thinking, you miserable buffoon! Traditions are about to crumble! The State is going up in smoke! *(The* KING *lets out the same kind of scream)* Be quiet, you idiot! General! Come here! *(The* GENERAL *runs up to the steps of the dais)* Can you rely on the troops? Will they defend the King in case of anything happening? You hear how silent the people are!

GENERAL. It's the weather that's let us down, Prime Minister, Sir!

KING. What's that?

GENERAL. The weather, Your Majesty. It looked like rain this morning, and many people brought umbrellas with them, in case. . .

KING. Umbrellas?

GENERAL. Yes, Your Majesty. They're armed with umbrellas. If only the crowd were unarmed. . . but they've got umbrellas!

KING. Umbrellas?

GENERAL. Quite frankly — I can't vouch for the soldiers. They might retreat from the field of battle. *(Whispers)* The rot's set in among them. . . *(The* KING *emits the same shriek)* I, too, am surprised, Your Majesty. There aren't any books, or leaflets, or agitators to be seen; the discipline is excellent, yet the rot is spreading day by day. I tried to order them to stop rotting. But it doesn't work.

97

MINISTER OF TENDER FEELINGS. Well, I don't
    know. . . It can't go on like this. . . I'm not too
    happy myself. . . I'll go over to the people.

PRIME MINISTER. Silence!

MINISTER OF TENDER FEELINGS. Oughtn't we
    to convene a provisional committee on the
    safety of courtiers?. . .

PRIME MINISTER. Silence! We mustn't waste any
    time. We must dazzle the crowd by acting
    daringly. We must go on with the wedding
    ceremony as if nothing had happened.

PRINCESS. But I. . .

PRIME MINISTER. *(With a bow)* Silence!

KING-FATHER. He's right. Come on then!

MINISTER OF TENDER FEELINGS. My ladies-in-
    waiting are militarized. They would defend our
    committee.

PRIME MINISTER. Your ladies-in-waiting! What
    nonsense! Sire, take the Princess's hand. *(Makes
    a sign to the* HERALDS)

HERALDS. Silence! Silence! Silence!

A BOY'S VOICE. Papa, look — he's got nothing on!

    (A pause, then an uproar)

MINISTER OF TENDER FEELINGS. *(Runs towards
    the palace, shrieking)* My mother's a locksmith,
    my father a laundress! Down with the monarchy!

THE BOY. He's naked, and he's fat!

VOICES. D'you hear what the child's saying? *He*
    can't be unfit for his job! He's not employed by
    anybody! He's clever — he knows his tables!
    The King is naked! He's got a wart on his belly —
    and yet he forces us to pay taxes! He's got a
    belly like a water-melon — and yet he orders us
    about! Look, he's got a pimple! . . . A pimple!
    And he dares to have us sterilized!

KING. Shut up, all of you! I do all this on purpose.
    Yes! I do everything on purpose! From now on I
    decree that everyone should get married with
    nothing on! Everyone! *(The* CROWD *whistles)*

You, miserable fools! *(More whistling. The* KING *rushes back into the palace.* PRIME MINISTER *and the rest of the* COURTIERS *rush after him.* KING-FATHER *and the* PRINCESS *are left standing on the dais)*

KING-FATHER. We must flee! Look at the eyes of those people behind the barrier! They saw the King naked. Now they're undressing me with their eyes. In a moment they're going to pounce on me!

HENRIK and CHRISTIAN. *(Jumping on the dais, shouting)* Boo!

KING-FATHER. Ah! It's started! *(Holding up his cloak, he runs out along the road on the right)*

PRINCESS. Henrik!

HENRIK. Henrietta!

CHRISTIAN. *(To the* CROWD) Dear friends! You've come to celebrate a wedding but the bridegroom's run away. But this is still an occasion for celebration. How can it be otherwise? A young girl has been at last re-united with her dear, beloved Henrik! She was to be married to an old man, but the power of love has overcome all obstacles. We welcome your just anger against these gloomy walls! We greet you, so greet us in return! Greet our love, our friendship, laughter, joy!

PRINCESS. *(Sings)* Darling Henrik, my beloved,
Curly-haired and very nice,
Marching steadily in time,
Will get me home in a trice!

THE CROWD. *(Sing)* Let all our land rejoice!
We drove the King out,
We've made our choice!
Let all our land rejoice!
(They dance)

HENRIK. *(Sings)* He who has a sound mind
Will always get ahead,
Marching steadily in time,
He'll be happy in the end!

THE CROWD. *(Sings)* Let all our land rejoice!
We drove the King out,
We've made our choice!
Let all our land rejoice!

CURTAIN

1934

THE SHADOW

'And the Savant grew very angry, not so
much because his Shadow had gone from
him but more because he recollected a
well-known story about a man without a
shadow, a story which everyone knew in
his own country. If he returned home now
and told them the story, everyone would
say that he had started imitating others.'

from 'The Shadow' by Hans Andersen

'A theme from another man's story seemed
to enter my flesh and blood; I recreated
it, and only then let it loose on the world.'

from Chapter VIII of *The Fairy-Tale of
My Life* by Hans Andersen

CHARACTERS

The Savant
His Shadow
Pietro
Annunziata
Yulia Djuly
The Princess
The Prime Minister
The Minister of Finance
Cesar Borgia
A Secret Counsellor
Doctor
Majordomo
Courtiers. Holiday-Makers. Flunkeys. Nurses. Citizens.
Girl in a Mask. Man in Evening Dress. Old Man with
a Star.

ACT ONE

A smallish room in an inn, in a southern country. Two doors, one leading into a passage, the other on to a balcony. It is twilight. The Savant is reclining on a divan. He is a young man, aged about 26. He is groping over a table, searching for his spectacles.

SAVANT.   When you lose your spectacles, it's unpleasant of course, but at the same time it's beautiful, too. In the twilight the whole of my room looks quite different from the usual. This rug, thrown over a chair, takes on the appearance of a very nice and kind princess. I am in love with her and she has come to visit me. She's not alone, of course. A princess is not supposed to go out without her suite. This tall, narrow clock in its wooden case is not, of course, a clock. It's the princess's constant attendant, the Secret Counsellor. His heart beats very evenly, like a pendulum. His advice changes with the require-ments of the moment and he gives it always in whispers. It's not for nothing that he's a *Secret* Counsellor. And if the counsels of the Secret Counsellor prove to be disastrous, he completely denies afterwards that he's given them. He asserts that people just didn't hear what he said, and this is, of course, very practical on his part. And who could be that? Who is that stranger, well-built, yet slender, dressed all in black with a white face? Why does it suddenly enter my head that he's the princess's betrothed? After all, it's I who am in love with her! I'm so much in love with her that it'll be simply monstrous if she marries another! The charm of all these fantasies is in that as soon as I put on my spectacles, everything will get back into its place. The rug will become a rug, the clock a clock, and this sinister stranger will vanish. *(Passes his hand over the table)* Well, here they are, my spectacles. *(Puts on his spectacles and gives a sudden cry)* What's this? *(In the armchair a very good-looking, luxuriously-dressed girl, wearing a mask, is sitting. Behind her stands a bald-headed old man in a morning coat, adorned with a star. And*

*against the wall leans a tall, thin, pale-faced man
in black evening dress and blindingly white linen.
He has a diamond ring on his finger)*

SAVANT. *(Muttering, as he lights a candle)* What are
these marvels? I'm just a modest scholar. How
can I have such important visitors? But all the
same. . . How do you do, gentlemen? I'm very
glad to see you, but won't you explain to me why
I'm being so honoured? You're silent? Ah, I
understand! I've just dozed off. This is a dream.

GIRL IN A MASK. No, it's not a dream.

SAVANT. Really? What is it then?

GIRL IN A MASK. It is a fairy-tale. Au revoir, Mr
Savant. We shall meet again.

MAN IN EVENING DRESS. Au revoir, Savant. We
shall meet again.

OLD MAN WITH A STAR. *(In a whisper)* Au revoir,
Honoured Savant. We shall meet again, and everything might end respectably if you behave
wisely.

*(There is a knock on the door and all three
visitors vanish)*

SAVANT. How extraordinary!

(Knocking is repeated)

SAVANT. Come in!

*(Enter ANNUNZIATA, a black-haired young girl
with large dark eyes. Her face expresses great
energy but her manner and voice are soft and
hesitant. She is about 17 and is very beautiful)*

ANNUNZIATA. Forgive me, Sir. You have visitors. . .
Ah!

SAVANT. What's the matter with you, Annunziata?

ANNUNZIATA. But I clearly heard voices in your
room!

SAVANT. I fell asleep and was talking in my sleep.

ANNUNZIATA. But forgive me, I heard a woman's
voice!

SAVANT. I dreamt about a princess.

104

ANNUNZIATA. And an old man was muttering
    something in a subdued voice. . .

SAVANT. I dreamt about a Secret Counsellor.

ANNUNZIATA. Also some man or other. . . it
    seemed to me he shouted at you.

SAVANT. That was the princess's fiancé. Well?
    You see now that it was a dream. You don't
    think that such unpleasant visitors could come to
    me in real life?

ANNUNZIATA. Are you joking?

SAVANT. Yes.

ANNUNZIATA. Thank you for telling me. You're
    always so kind to me. I daresay I heard voices
    in the room next door to yours and mixed it all
    up. But. . . you won't be annoyed with me? May
    I tell you something?

SAVANT. Of course, Annunziata.

ANNUNZIATA. I wanted to warn you quite a long
    time ago. You're a scholar and I'm a simple girl.
    But. . . I could tell you something I know
    which isn't known to you. *(She curtseys)*
    Forgive me for being impertinent.

SAVANT. Please go on. Teach me. I'm a scholar, and
    scholars go on learning all their lives.

ANNUNZIATA. Are you joking?

SAVANT. No, I'm absolutely in earnest.

ANNUNZIATA. Thank you for telling me. *(Looks
    round at the door)* In your books about our
    country they write a lot about the healthy
    climate, pure air, beautiful views, hot sun. . .
    Well, in a word, you know yourself what they
    write in books about our country.

SAVANT. Of course I do. That's just the reason why I
    came here.

ANNUNZIATA. Yes. You know what is written about
    us in books, but you don't know some things that
    aren't written about us in books.

SAVANT. That does happen to scholars sometimes.

105

ANNUNZIATA. You don't know that you're living
at present in a very special country. All they tell
you in fairy-tales, all that is just an invention
where other people are concerned, happens
here in reality every day. For instance, the Sleeping
Beauty used to live a five hours' walk from the
tobacconist's, the shop that's on the right of the
fountain. Only now the Sleeping Beauty is dead.
But the man-eating ogre is still alive and is working
in the town, at the Municipal Loan Bank, as a
valuer. And Tom Thumb married a very tall
woman nicknamed the Grenadier, and their
children are people of ordinary height, just like
you and me. And do you know what is surprising?
That woman, nicknamed the Grenadier, is
completely under the thumb of Tom Thumb.
She even takes him to the market with her. Tom
Thumb sits in the pocket of her pinafore and
bargains fiercely like the devil. However, they
live together on very good terms. The wife is so
considerate to her husband. Every time they
dance the minuet on feast days, she puts on extra
strong spectacles, so that she doesn't tread on
her husband by accident.

SAVANT. But all this is extremely interesting! Why
didn't they write of this in books about your
country?

ANNUNZIATA. *(Glancing back at the door)* Not
everybody likes fairy-tales.

SAVANT. Really?

ANNUNZIATA. Yes, really! Would you believe it?
(Glances round at the door) We're terribly afraid
that if everyone finds out about this, they'll
stop coming to our country. That would be so
unprofitable. Don't give us away, please.

SAVANT. No, I won't tell anybody.

ANNUNZIATA. Thank you for this. My poor father
is very fond of money and I would be in despair
if he earned less than he expects. When he's
upset he swears horribly.

SAVANT. All the same, it seems to me that the
number of visitors is likely to increase when they
hear that in your country fairy-tales are true.

ANNUNZIATA. No. If children were our visitors that would be so, but grown-ups are cautious people. They know perfectly well that many fairy-tales end sadly. That is just what I wanted to talk to you about. Be careful.

SAVANT. How can I be careful? To avoid catching cold one must dress warmly. To avoid falling down one must look where one is going. But how can one avoid a fairy-tale with a sad ending?

ANNUNZIATA. Well... I don't know... You mustn't talk to people you don't really know.

SAVANT. Then I'll have to be silent all the time as I'm a stranger here.

ANNUNZIATA. No, please, do be careful! You are a very nice man, and it's just your kind that gets into trouble.

SAVANT. How do you know that I am a good man?

ANNUNZIATA. Well, I'm very often in the kitchen. And our cook has eleven women friends. And they all know everything what is, what was, and what will be. Nothing can be hidden from them. They know what is happening in every family as if houses had walls of glass. In the kitchen we laugh, and weep, and feel horrified. On the days when some particularly interesting things happen, everything in the oven gets ruined. These friends of the cook all say in a chorus that you're an excellent person.

SAVANT. Was it they who told you that in your country fairy-tales come true?

ANNUNZIATA. Yes.

SAVANT. You know, in the evening, without my spectacles I'm quite ready to believe it. But in the morning when I come out of the house, I see things quite differently. Your country, alas! is like any other country in the world. Wealth and poverty, eminence and slavery, death and misfortune, wisdom and stupidity, saintliness, crime, conscience, shamelessness, all these are so intermingled that one simply stands aghast. It would be very difficult to disentangle it all, to sort it out and arrange it so that no living

107

creature is harmed. In fairy-tales it is all so very
much simpler.

ANNUNZIATA. *(Curtseying)* Thank you.

SAVANT. What for?

ANNUNZIATA. For talking to me so beautifully.
To me, a simple girl.

SAVANT. Never mind, this kind of thing does happen
to scholars. But tell me, did my friend, Hans
Christian Andersen, who used to live here in
this room before, did he know about the fairytales?

ANNUNZIATA. Yes, he had found out about it
somehow.

SAVANT. And what did he say about it?

ANNUNZIATA. He said: 'I suspected all my life that
I was writing pure truth.' He was very fond of our
house. He liked the quiet here.

(There is a deafening detonation)

SAVANT. What's that?

ANNUNZIATA. Oh, don't pay any attention. That's
my father. He must have quarrelled with someone.
He's very quick-tempered, and at the slightest
provocation he fires his pistol. But he's so highly-
strung that he always misses.

SAVANT. I understand. This phenomenon is quite
familiar to me. If he didn't miss, he wouldn't
fire so often.

(A voice roars backstage, calling: 'Annunziata!')

ANNUNZIATA. *(Mildly)* I'm coming, Daddy darling.
(To the SAVANT*)* Au revoir. Ah! I quite forgot
why I came. What would you like me to bring
you? Coffee or milk?

*(The door flies open with a bang. A well-built,
young-looking, broad-shouldered man rushes into
the room. His features resemble* ANNUNZIATA's.
*He is morose and does not look people in the eye.
He is the owner of the furnished rooms,* ANNUN-
ZIATA's *father,* PIETRO)

PIETRO. Why don't you come when you're called?
Go at once and re-load my pistol. Didn't you

108

hear? Your father was shooting. I've got to explain everything to you, push your head into everything! I'll murder you!

ANNUNZIATA. *(Calmly and bravely goes up to her father and kisses him on the forehead)* I'm going, Daddy. Au revoir, Sir. *(Goes out)*

SAVANT.   It seems your daughter's not afraid of you, Señor Pietro.

PIETRO.   No, I'll be damned. She treats me as if I were the tenderest father in the town.

SAVANT.   Perhaps it is in fact so.

PIETRO.   It's not her business to know it. I can't bear anyone to make guesses about my feelings or thoughts. Silly little girl! I get nothing but upsets. Just now the lodger in room number 15 again refused to pay me. In my fury I fired at the lodger in number 14.

SAVANT.   Doesn't he pay either?

PIETRO.   He does pay. But he, number 14, is a miserable little man. Our Prime Minister can't bear him. But that accursed fellow in number 15, who doesn't pay, works on our abominable, revolting, disgusting newspaper. Oh, I wish the whole world would fall through the ground! I twist around like a corkscrew trying to wring money out of the lodgers in my miserable inn, and still I can't make ends meet. As well as this, I've got to do a job outside, otherwise I'd die of starvation.

SAVANT.   Have you really got a job outside?

PIETRO.   Yes.

SAVANT.   Where is it?

PIETRO.   I work as a valuer at the Municipal Loan Bank.

(Suddenly music begins to play. Sometimes it is hardly audible, and sometimes it sounds as if it were inside the room itself)

SAVANT.   Tell me. . . Tell me please where does this music come from?

PIETRO.   From the house opposite.

SAVANT.   And who lives there?

PIETRO.   I don't know. People say some accursed princess.

SAVANT.   A princess?

PIETRO.   So they say. But I came to you on business. This accursed number 15 asks you to see him. This newspaper fellow. This thief, who's trying to live in my beautiful room without paying. Can he come?

SAVANT.   With pleasure. I'll be very glad.

PIETRO.   Don't be glad in advance. Au revoir. *(Goes out)*

SAVANT.   The owner of the inn a valuer at the Municipal Loan Bank? A cannibal? Just imagine! *(He opens the door which leads on to the balcony. The wall of the opposite house becomes visible. The street is narrow. The balcony of the house opposite almost touches the balcony of the SAVANT's room. As soon as he opens the door, the noise of the street bursts in. Out of the general hubbub different voices separate themselves)*

VOICES.   Water melons, water melons! Sold by the piece!
   Water, water! Icy cold water!
   Here, knives for murderers!
   Who wants knives for murderers?
   Flowers, flowers! Roses! Lillies! Tulips!
   Make way for an ass! Make way for an ass!
   Stand aside, men! Here comes an ass!
   Give alms to a poor dumb fellow!
   Poisons, poisons, fresh poisons!

SAVANT.   Our street is simmering like a veritable cooking pot. How I like it here! If I didn't feel so restless all the time, if it didn't seem to me that the whole world is unhappy just because I haven't yet found out how to save it, I'd feel very content indeed. And when the girl who lives opposite comes out on to her balcony, I feel as if I need to make one, only one little effort, and everything will become clear to me.

(A very good-looking young woman enters the room. She is beautifully dressed. She looks round, narrowing her eyes. The SAVANT does not notice her.

110

He continues his monologue)

SAVANT. If there is harmony in the sea, in the mountains, in the forests and in oneself, then it must mean the world is designed more wisely than...

WOMAN. This isn't going to be successful.

SAVANT. *(Turning round)* Excuse me...?

WOMAN. No, it won't! What you're muttering doesn't contain the slightest crumb of wit. Is this your new article? But where *are* you? What's the matter with you today? Don't you recognize me?

SAVANT. Forgive me, I do not.

WOMAN. Stop making fun of my short-sight. This is inelegant. Where are you then?

SAVANT. I'm here.

WOMAN. Come nearer.

SAVANT. Here I am. *(Comes up to the stranger)*

WOMAN. *(She is genuinely surprised)* Who are you?

SAVANT. I am a visitor and I live here, in this inn. That's who I am.

WOMAN. Forgive me... My eyes have again let me down. Isn't this number 15?

SAVANT. No, I regret to say it isn't.

WOMAN. What a nice, kind face you have! Why aren't you in our Circle yet? In the Circle of Real People.

SAVANT. But what is that Circle?

WOMAN. Oh, a Circle of artists, writers, courtiers... Even a Minister comes to join us sometimes. We are elegant, without prejudices and we understand everything. Are you famous?

SAVANT. No.

WOMAN. What a pity! It isn't our custom, but I feel as if I were ready to forgive you that. I like you so much. Are you angry with me?

SAVANT. No, of course not. Why should you think so?

WOMAN. I'll sit down and stay with you a little. May I?

SAVANT. Of course.

WOMAN. Suddenly it seemed to me that you're the man I've been looking for all my life. It has happened to me before — I hear a voice, the way a man speaks. . . and I think — here he is! But he comes nearer — and I see I was quite wrong. . . But then it's too late to retreat. . . He's come too near. It's a terrible thing to be good-looking and short-sighted. Am I boring you?

SAVANT. No, of course not.

WOMAN. How simply and calmly you answer me! But *he* irritates me.

SAVANT. Who?

WOMAN. The man I've come to see. He's an extremely restless man. He wants to be liked by everyone in the world. He's a slave of fashion. For instance, when it was fashionable to get sunburnt, he got sunburnt to such an extent that he became almost black, like a negro. Then suddenly sun-tan went out of fashion, and he decided to have an operation. The skin under his shorts — it was the only white place on his body — was transplanted by doctors on to his face.

SAVANT. I hope this didn't do him any harm?

WOMAN. No. He merely became extremely shameless and he now calls a slap on the face just 'a slap on the bottom'.

SAVANT. Why then do you visit him?

WOMAN. Well, he's a man from our Circle, after all, from the Circle of Real People. And besides, he works on a newspaper. Do you know who I am?

SAVANT. No.

WOMAN. I'm a singer. My name is Yulia Djuly.

SAVANT. You are very famous in this country.

WOMAN. Yes. Everyone knows my songs: 'Mamma, what is love?', 'Maidens hurry to find happiness',

112

'His love's sick longing leaves me cold', and 'Ah, why am I not a meadow?' Are you a doctor?

SAVANT.   No, I'm a historian.

WOMAN.   Are you here for a rest?

SAVANT.   I'm studying the history of your country.

YULIA.   Our country is a small one.

SAVANT.   Yes, but its history is like all other histories. And this makes me glad.

YULIA.   Why?

SAVANT.   It means that there are laws in this world which are common to everyone. When you've been living in the same place for a long time, occupying the same room and seeing the same people, the people you yourself have chosen, or when you have your own children as your friends, the world appears to be very simple. But as soon as you come out of your house, everything becomes extremely diversified. And this. . .

(Outside, behind the door, someone lets out a frightened shriek. It is followed by the sound of broken glass)

SAVANT.   Who's there?

(An elegant young man enters, shaking himself. After him the bewildered ANNUNZIATA)

YOUNG MAN.   Good evening. I was standing just outside your door, and Annunziata took fright at me. Am I really so frightening?

ANNUNZIATA.   *(To the SAVANT)* Forgive me. I broke the glass of milk I was bringing you.

YOUNG MAN.   But you're not asking me to forgive you?

ANNUNZIATA.   But it was your own fault, Sir! Why were you lurking behind someone else's door and standing there so still?

YOUNG MAN. I was eavesdropping. *(To the SAVANT)* Do you like my frankness? All learned men are straightforward. You must like it. Do you? Now tell me! Do you like my frankness? And do you like me?

YULIA. Don't answer him. If you say yes, he'll
despise you, and if you say no, he'll begin to
hate you.

YOUNG MAN. Yulia, Yulia! Wicked Yulia! *(To the*
SAVANT) Allow me to introduce myself. Cesar
Borgia. Have you heard my name before?

SAVANT. Yes, I have.

CESAR BORGIA. Really? Is it true? And what
exactly have you heard about me?

SAVANT. Many things.

C. BORGIA. Was I praised or did they abuse me? And
who was it?

SAVANT. It is just that I have read your critical
and political articles in the local newspaper.

C. BORGIA. They're quite popular. . . But every time
someone's not pleased. You abuse a man, and
he's immediately displeased. I'd like to discover
the secret of complete success. For such a
secret I'm ready to give anything. Do you like
my frankness?

YULIA. Come, let's go. We're the guests of a Savant,
and learned men are always occupied.

C. BORGIA. I warned Mr Savant. Our host had told
him that I was to come. And you, my brilliant
Yulia, did you mistake the room?

YULIA. No, it seems to me that I came just where I
should have come.

C. BORGIA. But weren't you coming to see me? I'm
just about to finish an article about you. You
will like it, but alas! your women friends won't
like it. *(To the* SAVANT) Will you permit me to
call on you again today?

SAVANT. Please do.

C. BORGIA. I want to write an article about you.

SAVANT. Thank you. It will help me in my work on
your archives. They'll treat me there with greater
respect.

C. BORGIA. What a cunning man you are! I know quite well why you came to us. It isn't at all a matter of archives.

SAVANT. What is it then?

C. BORGIA. A crafty man! You're looking all the time at the neighbouring balcony.

SAVANT. Am I really looking that way?

C. BORGIA. Yes, you are. You think that she lives there.

SAVANT. Who?

C. BORGIA. You mustn't be so secretive. After all, you're a historian; you're studying our country, so you must know the testament of our last king, Louis IX, nicknamed The Dreamer.

SAVANT. Forgive me, but I've only got as far as the sixteenth century.

C. BORGIA. Is that so? And you haven't heard anything about the King's will?

SAVANT. I assure you I have not.

C. BORGIA. Strange! Why is it then you asked our host to give you this particular room?

SAVANT. Because my friend, Hans Christian Andersen, used to live in this room.

C. BORGIA. Only for that reason?

SAVANT. I give you my word that this is so. But in what way is my room concerned with the will of the late King?

C. BORGIA. Oh, in a very important way. . . Au revoir! My dazzling Yulia, will you allow me to accompany you?

SAVANT. Permit me to ask, what exactly was written in that mysterious will?

C. BORGIA. Oh, no, I'm not going to tell you. I'm interested in it myself. I want power, I want esteem, and I'm terribly short of money. Don't you realize that I am Cesar Borgia, the name that's known to the whole of my country? And

yet I have to work as a simple valuer at the
Municipal Loan Bank? Do you like my frankness?

YULIA.   Come along! Do come! You're liked by
everybody here. *(To the* SAVANT) He never
goes away at once. You and I will meet again.

SAVANT.   I shall be very glad to.

C. BORGIA.   Don't rejoice in advance. (CESAR
BORGIA *and* YULIA *go out)*

SAVANT.   Annunziata! How many valuers are employed
by your Municipal Loan Bank?

ANNUNZIATA.   A great many.

SAVANT.   And are they all former cannibals?

ANNUNZIATA.   Almost all.

SAVANT.   What is the matter with you? Why are you
looking so sad?

ANNUNZIATA.   Oh, I have asked you to be careful!
They say that the singer, Yulia Djuly, is the same
little girl who stood on a loaf of bread to save
her new shoes.

SAVANT.   But then, that little girl was punished for it,
as far as I can remember.

ANNUNZIATA.   Yes, she fell through the ground but
later she scrambled out again, and from that
time on she goes on trampling on good people.
On her best women friends and even on herself —
and all of it so that she can save her new shoes,
her pretty stockings and her little dresses. I'll
bring you another glass of milk presently.

SAVANT.   Wait a moment. I'm not thirsty. I'd like
to talk to you.

ANNUNZIATA.   Thank you for the honour.

SAVANT.   Tell me please what testament was it that
your late King Louis IX, surnamed The Dreamer,
left.

ANNUNZIATA.   Oh, it's a secret, a terrible secret!
The testament was sealed in seven envelopes
with seven wax seals and it was signed by seven
Secret Counsellors. When the Princess opened and
read it, she was completely alone. Outside her

116

windows and door stood sentinels who stopped
their ears 'in case' — although the Princess was
reading it in silence. What was written in that
mysterious document is known only to the
Princess and the whole of the town.

SAVANT. The whole of the town?

ANNUNZIATA. Yes.

SAVANT. But how could that happen?

ANNUNZIATA. Nobody can explain it. It seems that
all the precautions had been observed. It's a
kind of miracle. Everyone knows what the
testament was about. Even the street urchins.

SAVANT. But then what was in it?

ANNUNZIATA. Don't ask me.

SAVANT. Why not?

ANNUNZIATA. I'm very much afraid that this
testament is the beginning of a new fairy-tale
that'll end sadly.

SAVANT. Annunziata! After all, I'm a visitor here.
The testament of your King doesn't concern me
in any way. Tell me. Otherwise, it isn't really
nice. I'm a scholar, a historian, and suddenly I
find I don't know what is known to every street
urchin. Do tell me, please.

ANNUNZIATA. *(With a sigh)* All right, I will tell
you. When a good man asks me, I can't refuse him.
Our cook says that this will lead me to great
misfortune, but let this misfortune be on my head,
and not on yours. And so. . . but you're not
listening to me!

SAVANT. But of course I am.

ANNUNZIATA. Why then are you looking at the
balcony of the house opposite?

SAVANT. No, no. . . You see, I'm just sitting down
more comfortably, I've lit my pipe and my eyes
are fixed on your face.

ANNUNZIATA. Thank you. And so, five years ago
our King, Louis IX, called The Dreamer, died.
Street urchins called him not 'Dreamer' but

117

'silly little fool'. But it wasn't true. The late King,
I admit, often put his tongue out at them as he
looked out of the window, but the children
themselves were to blame. Why did they have to
tease him? The late King was an intelligent man,
but the duties of a king are such that they damage
a man's character. At the very beginning of his
reign, the Prime Minister whom the King trusted
more than his own father, poisoned the favourite
sister of the King. The King then had the Prime
Minister executed. The second Prime Minister
was not a poisoner, but he lied so much to the
King that the King stopped believing everybody,
even himself. The third Prime Minister was not a
liar, but he was terribly cunning. He kept on
spinning and spinning the thinnest of cobwebs
around the simplest things. As he listened to his
last report, the King was about to say 'I confirm
this', but instead started humming in a very thin
voice, like a fly that's got caught in a spider's
web. The Prime Minister was dismissed on the
demand of the King's chief physician. The fourth
Prime Minister was not cunning. He was straightforward and simple. He stole the King's gold
snuff box and ran away. Then the King just
waved his hand at all matters of administration.
From that time on Prime Ministers started
replacing one another by themselves. And the
King occupied himself with the theatre. This, they
say, is even more difficult to manage than ruling
a kingdom. After years of work in a theatre
world, the King developed a kind of catalepsy.

SAVANT.   What catalepsy?

ANNUNZIATA.   It's very simple. He might be walking
along — and suddenly he'd freeze up with one foot
in the air, and with an expression of despair on
his face. His chief physician explained this by
the fact that the King got completely and
incurably muddled up, trying to understand the
relationship of the theatre workers to one another.
There were so many of them.

SAVANT.   The chief physician was right, I suppose.

ANNUNZIATA.   He offered a simple medicine which
would have undoubtedly cured our poor King. He

suggested that half of the theatre company
should be executed, but the King did not agree to
that.

SAVANT. Why not?

ANNUNZIATA. He couldn't decide which half of
the company deserved execution. And in the end
the King waved his hand at everything and began
having affairs with bad women. They alone did
not deceive him.

SAVANT. Really?

ANNUNZIATA. Yes, that is so. They proved to be
truly bad women. That's exactly what people were
saying about them. And this comforted the King,
but in the end it ruined his health. And he lost
the use of his legs. And from that time on, they
began to wheel him around the palace in a wheel-
chair while he remained silent, and thought, and
thought. . . What he was thinking he didn't tell
anybody. From time to time the King ordered his
servants to wheel him up to a window, and, having
opened a pane, he put his tongue out at the street
urchins, who jumped up and down and shouted:
'Silly little fool! silly little fool!' And then the
King wrote his testament. And after that he died.

SAVANT. At last we've come to the essence of the
matter.

ANNUNZIATA. When the King died, his only daughter,
the Princess, was thirteen years old. 'My dear,' he
wrote to her in his testament, 'I have lived my
life badly, I haven't done anything. You won't do
anything either: you are poisoned by the palace air.
I do not want you to marry a prince. I know all
the princes of the world, every single one of them.
They are all too big fools for such a small country
as ours. When you are 18 years old, go and live
somewhere in the town and search, search,
search. . . Find a kind, honest, educated and
intelligent husband for yourself. Let him be not
a distinguished or aristocratic man. After all, he
might succeed in doing something which none of
the aristocratic or highly born men manage to do.
What if he would know how to rule, and rule well?
Eh? That would be a joke! So do try, please. Dad.'

119

SAVANT. Did he really write this?

ANNUNZIATA. Exactly as I tell you. In the kitchen, they quoted the testament so many times that I memorized it word for word.

SAVANT. And the Princess is living in the town now?

ANNUNZIATA. Yes, but it isn't so very simple to find her.

SAVANT. Why not?

ANNUNZIATA. Crowds of bad women have rented whole floors of houses and pretend to be princesses.

SAVANT. Don't you know your Princess by sight?

ANNUNZIATA. No. Having read the testament, the Princess began to wear a mask so that she's not recognized when she starts in search of a husband.

SAVANT. Tell me, is she... *(He falls silent. On the balcony of the house opposite appears a girl with blond hair, in a dark modest attire)* Tell me, is she... What was it I wanted to ask you?... However... it's nothing...

ANNUNZIATA. Again you're not looking at me!

SAVANT. Am I not? Where am I looking then?

ANNUNZIATA. You're looking over there! Ah! Allow me... I'll close the door of the balcony.

SAVANT. Why? Don't. Only now it has become really cool...

ANNUNZIATA. It's necessary to close windows and doors after sunset. Otherwise you might catch malaria. No, it isn't really malaria that matters. You ought not to look over there. Please! Are you angry with me? Don't be angry. Don't look at that girl! Permit me to shut the door to the balcony. Really, you're just like a little child. For instance, you don't like soup, but what is dinner without soup? Then you send your linen to the laundry without making a list. And I'm sure you'll go to your death with the same kindly, cheerful expression on your face! I'm speaking so daringly that I hardly understand myself what I'm saying. This is impertinent, but it's impossible

120

not to warn you. They say about that girl that
she's a bad woman. . . Wait. . . wait!. . . I don't
think that this is all that frightening. . . But I'm
afraid of something, much, much worse!

SAVANT. You think so?

ANNUNZIATA. Yes. What if this girl is really the
Princess? What then? What will you do then?

SAVANT. Of course, of course. . .

ANNUNZIATA. You didn't even hear what I said to
you!

SAVANT. Didn't I?

ANNUNZIATA. If she really is the Princess, everyone
will want to marry her, and you'll be just crushed
to death in the crowd.

SAVANT. Yes, yes, of course.

ANNUNZIATA. No, I see I can't do anything about
it. What an unfortunate girl I am, Sir!

SAVANT. Aren't you!

(ANNUNZIATA *goes to the exit. The* SAVANT
*walks towards the door that opens on to the
balcony.* ANNUNZIATA *looks round and stops)*

ANNUNZIATA. Good-bye Sir! *(Quietly, with unexpected determination)* I won't allow anyone to
hurt you! Not for anything in the world! Never!

(She goes out.

The SAVANT *looks at the girl standing on the
balcony of the house opposite. She is looking
down into the street. The* SAVANT *begins to
speak quietly, then louder and louder. Towards the
end of the monologue the girl is gazing at him
fixedly)*

SAVANT. Of course, the world is arranged more
wisely than it appears to be. A little more — two
or three more day's work — and I will understand
how to make everyone happy. Everyone will be
happy but not in the same way as I am. Only
here, in the evenings, when you are standing on the
balcony I begin to understand that I can be happy
as no man can be. . . I know you. It's impossible

121

not to know you. I understand you as I understand
fine weather, the moon, the path in the mountains. . .
It's so simple, after all! I can't tell exactly what
you're thinking about, yet all the same, I know for
certain that your thoughts would gladden me just
as your face, your plaits of hair and your eyelashes
make me glad. Thank you for everything. Thank
you for having chosen this house, for having been
born and living at this time, when I am alive! What
would I have done if I didn't happen to meet you?
It's simply terrible to think of it!

GIRL.   Are you saying this because you've learnt it by
heart?

SAVANT. I. . .I. . .

GIRL.   Go on.

SAVANT.   You've spoken to me!

GIRL.   Have you composed all this yourself or did you
commission someone to do it?

SAVANT.   Excuse me, but your voice so startled me
that I don't understand anything.

GIRL.   You're avoiding giving me a straight answer
rather cleverly. Please, did you yourself compose
what you were saying to me? Perhaps you didn't. . .
Well, all right, let's leave it. I'm bored today. How
can you have patience enough to sit in this room
all day long? Is this your study?

SAVANT.   Excuse me. . .?

GIRL.   Is this your study, or a dressing room, or a
drawing room, or one of the ballrooms?

SAVANT.   This is simply my room, my only room.

GIRL.   Are you a beggar?

SAVANT.   No, I'm a scholar.

GIRL.   Well, never mind. You have a very strange
face.

SAVANT.   How — strange?

GIRL.   When you're talking it seems as if you weren't
lying.

SAVANT.   It's quite true, I am not lying.

122

GIRL. Everyone is a liar.

SAVANT. That isn't true.

GIRL. Yes, it is true. Perhaps they don't lie to you —
you have only one room — but to me they lie
perpetually. I am sorry for myself.

SAVANT. What are you saying! Do they hurt you?
Who?

GIRL. You pretend so cleverly to be attentive and kind
that I feel like complaining to you.

SAVANT. Are you so unhappy?

GIRL. I don't know. Yes, I think so.

SAVANT. Why?

GIRL. For no reason. All people are scoundrels.

SAVANT. You mustn't talk like this! Only girls who
have chosen for themselves the most terrible path
in life talk in this way. They kill, crush, plunder,
calumniate without pity. Who can they pity if
everyone is a scoundrel?

GIRL. So you mean that not everyone is?

SAVANT. No, not everyone.

GIRL. That would have been nice if it were so. I'm
terribly afraid of turning into a frog.

SAVANT. Why into a frog?

GIRL. Have you heard the fairy-tale about the princess-
frog? They tell it wrongly. In reality, everything was
different. I know that for certain. The princess who
was a frog is my aunt.

SAVANT. Your aunt?

GIRL. Yes. Once removed. They say that the man who
fell in love with her despite her monstrous appearance kissed the princess-frog. And because of that
the frog was transformed into a beautiful woman.
Isn't that so?

SAVANT. Yes, as far as I can remember.

GIRL. But in reality my aunt was a beautiful girl. She
married a scoundrel who only pretended that he

liked her. And his kisses were cold and so revolting that the beautiful girl very soon turned into a cold and revolting frog. It was very unpleasant for us, her relatives. They say such things happen much more often than you imagine. Only my aunt wasn't able to conceal her transformation. She was extremely uncontrolled. This is terrible, don't you agree?

SAVANT. Yes, it is very sad.

GIRL. You see! And what if this is going to be my fate, too? After all, I'll have to get married. Do you know for certain that not all men are scoundrels?

SAVANT. I know it absolutely for certain. You see, I'm a historian.

GIRL. How nice it would be! However, I don't believe you.

SAVANT. Why not?

GIRL. Because I don't believe anything or anyone, in general.

SAVANT. No, this can't be true! You have such a healthy complexion, such lively eyes. Not to believe anything is death, you know.

GIRL. Ah, I understand everything!

SAVANT. To understand everything is death, too.

GIRL. Everything in the world is the same. These people are right, and those others are right, and in the end I'm indifferent to everything.

SAVANT. To be indifferent to everything — but this is even worse than death! You can't believe this, you can't think like that! No! How you've upset me!

GIRL. It's all the same to me. . . No, it seems it isn't quite the same! Perhaps now you will not look at me any more, every evening?

SAVANT. Yes, I will. Things are not as simple as they seem. I had imagined that your thoughts were as harmonious as you are, but now they are here before me. They are not at all like the thoughts I expected from you, but all the same, I like you.

GIRL. You like me?

SAVANT. I love you.

GIRL. Well, I understood everything, I didn't believe in anything, everything was all the same to me, but now it has all become a muddle. . .

SAVANT. I love you.

GIRL. Go away. Or no. . . Yes, go away and close the door. No, I'll go away. . . But — if tomorrow evening you dare fail to come here, on to the balcony, I. . . I'll order. . . no. . . I'll just be upset. *(Goes to the door, turns round)* I don't even know your name.

SAVANT. My name is Christian-Theodore.

GIRL. Au revoir, Christian-Theodore. . . darling. . . Don't smile, don't imagine that you've cleverly deceived me. No, don't be upset. . . I'm just talking. . . When you told me so suddenly, so directly that you loved me, I felt such warmth, though I've come out on to the balcony in an organdie dress. Don't you dare speak to me! Enough! If I hear one word more, I'll burst into tears. Au revoir! What an unfortunate girl I am! *(Goes out)*

SAVANT. There now! I fancied that in a moment I'd understand everything, and now it seems to me that in a moment I'll be completely confused. I fear that this girl is really the Princess. 'All people are scoundrels, everything in the world is the same, I'm indifferent to everything, I don't believe in anything'. . . what obvious symptoms of pernicious anaemia, so common among pampered people who grow up in a hothouse atmosphere! But despite this, she felt warm when I confessed to her that I loved her. It means that after all she has real blood in her veins! *(Laughs)* I'm certain, I'm quite sure that everything will end beautifully. My shadow, kind, obedient shadow! You lie at my feet so humbly. Your head is looking through the doorway by which the strange girl has gone. What about it, Shadow? Why don't you go after her, into her house? It would cost you nothing. Why don't you just tell her: 'All you've been saying is nonsense. My master loves you, loves you so much that everything will come out beautifully. If you are the princess-frog, he will revive you and transform you into a beautiful woman.' In a word, you know

what you must say. After all, we've grown up together!
(Laughs) Go!

(The SAVANT *goes away from the balcony door.
His shadow suddenly separates from him. It draws
itself out to its full length on the opposite balcony.
It dives through the door which the girl left half-
open as she went in)*

What's this? I have a very strange feeling in my legs
and in the whole of my body. I. . . am I falling ill?. . .
I. . .*(He reels, falls into an armchair, rings the bell.
ANNUNZIATA runs in)* Annunziata! It seems to
me you were right.

ANNUNZIATA. Was that the Princess?

SAVANT. No, I've been taken ill. . .*(He closes his eyes)*

ANNUNZIATA. *(Runs to the door)* Father!

(Enter PIETRO)

PIETRO. Don't bawl! Don't you know that your father
was listening just outside the door?

ANNUNZIATA. I didn't notice.

PIETRO. You don't notice your own father! What have
we come to? Well? What are you blinking for? Are
you going to start blubbering?

ANNUNZIATA. He's fallen ill!

PIETRO. Allow me, sir! I'll help you to get into bed.

SAVANT. *(Gets up)* No, I can manage myself. Don't
touch me, please.

PIETRO. What are you afraid of? I'm not going to eat
you!

SAVANT. I don't know. Suddenly I felt so weak. *(He
goes to the screen behind which is his bed)*

ANNUNZIATA. *(Quietly, in terror)* Look!

PIETRO. What now?

ANNUNZIATA. He has no shadow!

PIETRO. Really? That's quite correct — he hasn't! What
an accursed climate! And how did he manage that?
All kinds of rumours will get around! People will
think it's an epidemic. (*The* SAVANT *disappears*

behind the screen) Not a word to anyone! Do you hear me?

ANNUNZIATA. *(Behind the screen)* He's fainted!

PIETRO. That's better. Run and fetch the doctor. The doctor will keep the fool in his bed for a week or two, and by that time he'll grow a new shadow. And nobody will ever find out anything.

ANNUNZIATA. A man without a shadow — but this is one of the saddest fairy-tales in the world!

PIETRO. I'm telling you — he'll grow a new shadow. He'll extricate himself somehow. Run!

(ANNUNZIATA *runs out)*

PIETRO. The hell of it! It's a good thing that the journalist is busy with his lady and hasn't smelled out anything, and. . .

(Enter CESAR BORGIA)

C. BORGIA. Good evening!

PIETRO. Ah! Here you are! The devil! Where's your woman?

C. BORGIA. She's gone to a concert.

PIETRO. To hell with all the concerts!

C. BORGIA. The Savant has fainted?

PIETRO. Yes, damn him!

C. BORGIA. Did you hear?

PIETRO. What exactly?

C. BORGIA. His conversation with the Princess?

PIETRO. Yes.

C. BORGIA. That's a short answer. Why don't you curse everything and everybody then, fire your pistol and shout at the top of your voice?

PIETRO. When matters are serious I keep quiet.

C. BORGIA. It looks as if that was the real Princess.

PIETRO. Yes, that was her.

C. BORGIA. I see you would like him to marry the Princess?

127

PIETRO.   I? I'll gobble him up at the first opportunity.

C. BORGIA.   Yes, we must gobble him up. Yes, we
must. . . we must! In my view, this is the most
suitable moment. It's the easiest thing to gobble a
man up when he's sick or gone away on holiday.
Then he himself wouldn't know who's gobbled
him up, and you still can preserve an excellent
relationship with him.

PIETRO.   The shadow!

C. BORGIA.   What about the shadow?

PIETRO.   We must find his shadow.

C. BORGIA.   What for?

PIETRO.   It'll help us. It will not forgive him — never in
its life — that it has been his shadow in the past.

C. BORGIA.   Yes, it will help us to gobble him up.

PIETRO.   The shadow is a complete opposite of the
Savant.

C. BORGIA.   But then it might prove to be stronger than
it should be.

PIETRO.   But the shadow will not forget that we helped
it to get on in the world. And we'll gobble him up.

C. BORGIA.   Yes, we must gobble him up. We must, we
must!

PIETRO.   Quiet!

(ANNUNZIATA runs in)

ANNUNZIATA.   Go away from here! What do you want
here?

PIETRO.   Daughter! *(Gets out his pistol)* But. . . all the
same, come along to my place. We'll talk it over
there. Is the doctor coming?

ANNUNZIATA.   Yes, he's coming at a run. He says it's
a serious case.

PIETRO.   Very well. *(He goes out together with* CESAR
BORGIA)

ANNUNZIATA.   *(Peeping behind the screen)* I knew it
in advance! His face is calm and kind as if he were

dreaming that he's walking in the forest under the trees. No, they'll never forgive him for being such a good man! What is going to happen? What is going to happen!

CURTAIN

ACT TWO

*A park. An open space strewn with sand and surrounded
with clipped trees. In the background a pavilion. The*
MAJORDOMO *and his* ASSISTANT *are busy on the
proscenium.*

MAJORDOMO.   Put the table here. And the chairs there.
   Put the chess-board on the table. Yes, like this.
   Now everything is ready for the council.

ASSISTANT.   But tell me, Mr Majordomo, why do the
   ministers sit in council here, in the park and not in
   the palace?

MAJORDOMO.   Because the palace has walls. You
   understand?

ASSISTANT.   No, I don't.

MAJORDOMO.   Because the walls have ears. Do you
   understand?

ASSISTANT.   Yes, now I understand.

MAJORDOMO.   I hope so. Put the cushions on that
   chair.

ASSISTANT.   Is this for Mr Prime Minister?

MAJORDOMO.   No, it's for the Minister of Finance.
   He's seriously ill.

ASSISTANT.   And what is the matter with him?

MAJORDOMO.   He's the richest businessman in the
   country. His rivals hate him something terrible. And
   so one of them went as far as committing a crime
   last year. He resolved to poison Mr Minister of
   Finance.

ASSISTANT.   How terrible!

MAJORDOMO.   Don't get upset in advance. Mr Minister
   of Finance heard about it in time and so he bought
   up all the poisons to be had in the country.

ASSISTANT.   How fortunate!

MAJORDOMO.   Don't rejoice in advance. Then the
   criminal came to see Mr Minister of Finance and
   offered him an unusually high price for the

130

poisons. And Mr Minister acted quite naturally.
After all, he's an adherent of *real politik*. He
calculated the profit and sold all his store of
poisons to that scoundrel. And the scoundrel
poisoned the Minister. The whole family of his
Excellency the Minister died in dreadful torment,
and he himself has barely been alive from that
time on, but he made about twenty per cent clear
profit on the transaction. Business is business. You
understand?

ASSISTANT.   Yes, now I understand.

MAJORDOMO.   Well, so you should. Is everything
ready now? Armchairs, chess-board? Today they're
going to have an especially important consultation.

ASSISTANT.   Why do you think so?

MAJORDOMO.   First of all, only two of the principal
ministers are going to meet. The Prime Minister
and the Minister of Finance. In the second place,
they'll pretend that they're playing chess and not
having a meeting. Everybody knows what that
means. I bet that the shrubs around here are
absolutely chock-a-block with the curious.

ASSISTANT.   And what if the curious are going to hear
what the ministers are saying?

MAJORDOMO.   The curious will not find out anything.

ASSISTANT.   Why not?

MAJORDOMO.   Because the ministers understand one
another from half a word. Who can understand
much from half a word? *(Suddenly bends down in
a deep bow)* They're coming. I've been serving at
Court so long that my back bends by itself
whenever any highly-placed person approaches. I
can't see them yet, nor hear them, but I'm already
bowing. That's why I'm at the top — the Majordomo here. Do you understand? Come on, bow!
Lower than that!

(MAJORDOMO *bends down almost to the ground.
The* ASSISTANT *does the same. From the two
sides of the stage, right and left, the two ministers
come out simultaneously: the* PRIME MINISTER
and the MINISTER OF FINANCE. *The* PRIME
MINISTER *is a short man with a paunch, bald-*

headed and rosy-cheeked. He is about 50. The
MINISTER OF FINANCE *is emaciated, very tall,*
and he looks around in terror as he limps along on
both legs. He is led and supported under the arms
by two tall FLUNKEYS. *The ministers come up to*
the table simultaneously, simultaneously sit down
and at once begin to play chess. The FLUNKEYS,
who led the Minister of Finance in and helped him
into a chair, remove themselves without a sound.
MAJORDOMO *and his* ASSISTANT *remain on the*
stage, standing at attention)

PRIME MINISTER.   Health? . . .

MINISTER OF FINANCE.   Just gha. . .

PRIME MINISTER.   Business? . . .

MINISTER OF FINANCE.   Very b. . .

PRIME MINISTER.   Why?

MINISTER OF FINANCE.   Concur. . .

(They play chess in silence)

MAJORDOMO.   *(In whisper)* You see, I told you they
understood one another from half a word.

PRIME MINISTER.   Have you heard about the Princess?

MINISTER OF FINANCE.   Yes, they rep. . .

PRIME MINISTER.   That visiting Savant's ravished her
heart.

MINISTER OF FINANCE.   Ravished? Just wait!
Flunkey! No, not you! My flunkey! *(Enter one of*
the flunkeys who had brought the Minister in)
Did you lock all the doors when we left the
palace?

FLUNKEY.   Yes, all, your Excellency.

MINISTER OF FINANCE.   The iron one as well?

FLUNKEY.   Yes, your Excellency.

MINISTER OF FINANCE.   And the copper one?

FLUNKEY.   Yes, your Excellency.

MINISTER OF FINANCE.   And the cast iron one?

132

FLUNKEY. Yes, your Excellency.

MINISTER OF FINANCE. And have you placed all the traps in position? You remember that you answer with your life for the smallest, the least important loss?

FLUNKEY. I do remember it, your Excellency.

MINISTER OF FINANCE. You can go.

(The FLUNKEY *goes out)*

MINISTER OF FINANCE. *(To the* PRIME MINISTER*)* I'm listening.

PRIME MINISTER. On the information received from the Secret Counsellor on duty, the Princess looked into a mirror a long time the other day, then began to cry and said. . . *(takes out a note-book and reads from it)* 'Ah, why am I being wasted for nothing?' And for the fifth time that day she sent to enquire after the Savant's health. Having found out that no special change had taken place, the Princess stamped her foot and whispered *(reads)* 'The devil take it!' And today she herself has asked him for a rendezvous in the park. So there! How do you li. . . this?

MINISTER OF FINANCE. I don't li. . . this at all. Who is he, that Savant?

PRIME MINISTER. Ah! we've studied him to the finest detail!

MINISTER OF FINANCE. Is he a blackmailer?

PRIME MINISTER. Worse.

MINISTER OF FINANCE. A thief?

PRIME MINISTER. Even worse than that.

MINISTER OF FINANCE. Adventurer? A crafty fellow? A crook?

PRIME MINISTER. Oh, if only he were!

MINISTER OF FINANCE. But what is he, in the end?

PRIME MINISTER. A simple, naive man.

MINISTER OF FINANCE. Check to the king!

133

PRIME MINISTER.   I'm taking your castle.

MINISTER OF FINANCE.   Check to the Queen!

PRIME MINISTER.   Poor Princess! If he were a
blackmailer, we would have exposed him. If he
were a thief we would have caught him. And we
would have beaten the crook at his game. But this
one. . . the actions of simple and honest men are
sometimes so puzzling.

MINISTER OF FINANCE.   He must be either bou. . .
or ki. . .

PRIME MINISTER.   Yes, there's no other way.

MINISTER OF FINANCE.   Have they already sme. . .
this out in the town?

PRIME MINISTER.   Rather!

MINISTER OF FINANCE.   I was sure of that. That's
why all wise people transfer their gold abroad in
such quantities. One banker transferred even his
gold teeth abroad the other day, and now he
travels all the time back and forth over the frontier.
He has nothing to chew his food with in his own
country.

PRIME MINISTER.   In my opinion, your banker's been
showing excessive nervousness.

MINISTER OF FINANCE.   It's just sensitivity. There
are no organisms in the world more sensitive than
business circles. The testament of the King alone
provoked seven bankruptcies, seven suicides, and
all the gilt-edged securities fell by seven points. And
now. . . Oh, what mightn't happen now! No
changes, Mr Prime Minister! Life must go on
smoothly, like a clock.

PRIME MINISTER.   By the way, what is the time?

MINISTER OF FINANCE.   My gold watch has been
transferred abroad. And if I wear my silver watch,
it'll start a rumour that I've been ruined and cause
panic in business circles.

PRIME MINISTER.   Hasn't any gold been left in the
country?

MINISTER OF FINANCE.   There's more gold here than

is needed.

PRIME MINISTER.   Where does it come from?

MINISTER OF FINANCE.   From abroad. The foreign business circles are disturbed for their own foreign reasons and are transferring gold to us. So we live like that. Well, let us sum up. We'll buy the Savant.

PRIME MINISTER.   Or kill him.

MINISTER OF FINANCE.   How shall we do it?

PRIME MINISTER.   In a most delicate fashion. After all, such an important feeling as love is mixed up with this business! I intend to dispose of the Savant with the help of friendship.

MINISTER OF FINANCE.   Friendship?

PRIME MINISTER.   Yes. For that reason it's necessary to find a man who's a friend of our Savant. A friend would know what he likes and what we could offer him to buy him. The friend would know what he hates and what for him is equivalent to death. I ordered my office to find a friend of his.

MINISTER OF FINANCE.   This is dreadful.

PRIME MINISTER.   Why?

MINISTER OF FINANCE.   But this Savant is a visitor. It means we'll have to get his friend to come from abroad. And in what column am I going to enter this expense? Every disturbance of the accounts provokes bitter tears from my principal bookkeeper. He'd sob like a child, and then he'd fall into a state of delirium. For a while he'd stop issuing money altogether. To everybody. Even to me. Even to you.

PRIME MINISTER.   Really? This is unpleasant. After all, the destiny of the whole kingdom is at stake. What can we do then?

MINISTER OF FINANCE.   I don't know.

PRIME MINISTER.   Who does, then?

ASSISTANT.   *(Stepping forward)* I do.

MINISTER OF FINANCE.   *(Jumping up)* What's this? Has it begun?

PRIME MINISTER. Calm yourself, please. If it is to begin some time or other, it'll not start with the palace servants.

MINISTER OF FINANCE. So it's not a revolt?

PRIME MINISTER. No. It's simply impertinence. Who are you?

ASSISTANT. I'm the man you're looking for. I'm the Savant's friend, his closest friend, in fact. We never left one another from the cradle until the last few days.

PRIME MINISTER. Listen, my dear fellow. Do you know who you're talking to?

ASSISTANT. Yes.

PRIME MINISTER. Then why don't you call me, your Excellency?

ASSISTANT. (*With a deep bow)* Forgive me, your Excellency.

PRIME MINISTER. Are you a visitor?

ASSISTANT. I came into the world in this town, your Excellency.

PRIME MINISTER. And you are nevertheless a friend of the visiting Savant?

ASSISTANT. I am exactly the person you need, your Excellency. I know him as nobody does, and he doesn't know me at all, your Excellency.

PRIME MINISTER. This is strange.

ASSISTANT. If you wish, I'll tell you who I am, your Excellency.

PRIME MINISTER. Yes, do. Why are you looking behind you?

ASSISTANT. Allow me to write on the sand who I am, your Excellency.

PRIME MINISTER. Write then.

(The ASSISTANT *draws something on the sand. The Ministers read it and exchange glances)*

PRIME MINISTER. What would you sa. . .?

MINISTER OF FINANCE. Suit. . . But be very care. . .

136

otherwise he'd put up the pri. . .

PRIME MINISTER. Who got you your job at the palace?

ASSISTANT. Mr Cesar Borgia and Mr Pietro, your Excellency.

PRIME MINISTER. *(To the* MINISTER OF FINANCE) Do you know these men?

MINISTER OF FINANCE. Yes, they're completely reliable cannibals.

PRIME MINISTER. Very well, my man. We'll think it over.

ASSISTANT. Dare I remind your Excellency that you're living in a southern country?

PRIME MINISTER. Well, what of it?

ASSISTANT. Everything grows so fast in the South, your Excellency. The Savant and the Princess had their first conversation together only a fortnight ago and since then they haven't met a single time, but look how their love has grown, your Excellency. We must take care not to be too late, your Excellency.

PRIME MINISTER. But I've told you that we'll think it over. Stand aside. *(The Ministers fall into deep thought)* Come here, my man! *(The* ASSISTANT *obeys)* We have thought it over and we decided to take you into our service, in the office of the Prime Minister.

ASSISTANT. Thank you, your Excellency. In my opinion, one should act concerning the Savant in this way. . .

PRIME MINISTER. What's the matter with you, my man? You want to start acting before your appointment's been formalized? Have you gone mad? Don't you know what an office is?

ASSISTANT. Forgive me, your Excellency.

(There is a burst of laughter backstage)

PRIME MINISTER. The holiday-makers are coming here. They will disturb us. Let's go to the office, and there I'll make your appointment official.

137

After that we'll be prepared to listen to you.

ASSISTANT.   Thank you, your Excellency.

MINISTER OF FINANCE.   Flunkeys! (FLUNKEYS *appear)* Lead me out!

(They go out. The doors of the pavilion fly open and the DOCTOR *comes out, a young man who looks extremely morose and preoccupied. He is surrounded by the* HOLIDAY-MAKERS, *dressed lightly but luxuriously)*

FIRST WOMAN HOLIDAY-MAKER.   Doctor, why have I a feeling on the underside of my knee, a feeling rather like an inclination to dream?. . .

DOCTOR.   Under which knee?

FIRST WOMAN.   Under my right knee.

DOCTOR.   It'll pass.

SECOND WOMAN HOLIDAY-MAKER.   And why when I'm having my meal, do I begin between the 8th and the 9th course, to have melancholy thoughts?

DOCTOR.   What thoughts, for instance?

SECOND WOMAN.   Well, I suddenly feel like going into a desert and praying and fasting there.

DOCTOR.   It'll pass.

FIRST MALE HOLIDAY-MAKER.   Doctor, and why after the fortieth bath do I suddenly stop liking brown-haired girls?

DOCTOR.   And who do you like now?

FIRST MALE HOLIDAY-MAKER.   A fair-haired girl.

DOCTOR.   That'll pass. Ladies and gentlemen, allow me to remind you that the hour of treatment is over. Nurse for Medical Care, you're free to go. Nurse for Recreation, you can begin your duties.

NURSE FOR RECREATION.   Who'd like a ball? Who'd like a skipping rope? Here are some hoops! Hoops, ladies and gentlemen! Who'd like to play rounders? Who'd like to play cat and mouse? The time is passing, ladies and gentlemen! Enjoy yourselves, ladies and gentlemen! Play!

138

(The HOLIDAY-MAKERS *go their different ways, playing. Enter the* SAVANT *and* ANNUNZIATA)

ANNUNZIATA. Doctor, he's just bought a whole hawker's tray of boiled sweets.

SAVANT. But I've given them all to the street urchins.

ANNUNZIATA. It makes no difference. How can a sick person buy sweetmeats?

DOCTOR. *(To the* SAVANT) Stand facing the sun. Yes, like this. Your shadow's grown to normal dimensions. One would have expected this. Everything grows so fast in the South. How are you feeling?

SAVANT. I feel perfectly healthy.

DOCTOR. All the same, I'll make an auscultation. No, you needn't take off your jacket. I have excellent hearing. *(Takes a stethoscope from the table in the pavilion)* So. Breathe deeply, breathe deeper, even deeper than that. Once again. Now sigh with relief. Once again. Look at everything through your fingers. Wave your hand at everything — so. Once again. Shrug your shoulders. Yes. *(Sits down and falls into a reverie. The* SAVANT *takes a bundle of letters out of the side pocket of his jacket. He searches through them)*

ANNUNZIATA. Well, what do you say, Doctor? How is he getting on?

DOCTOR. Badly,

ANNUNZIATA. You see! And he says he's perfectly healthy!

DOCTOR. Yes, he is healthy. But his affairs are going badly. And they'll go even worse unless he learns to look at the world through his fingers, until he waves everything aside, until he learns the art of shrugging his shoulders at things.

ANNUNZIATA. What are we to do then, Doctor? How can we teach him all that? *(The* DOCTOR *silently shrugs his shoulders)* Answer me, Doctor! Please! You know, I won't leave you alone, you know how stubborn I am. What must he do?

139

DOCTOR. Take care.

ANNUNZIATA. And he just smiles!

DOCTOR. Yes, it does happen like this.

ANNUNZIATA. He's a scholar, he's very clever, he's older than me, but sometimes I feel like spanking him. Come, do talk to him!

(The DOCTOR *waves his hand in a gesture of dismissal)*

DOCTOR. You see, he's not listening to me. He's got his nose buried in some bits of paper . . .

ANNUNZIATA. They're the Princess's letters. Sir, the Doctor wants to have a talk with you, and you're not listening.

SAVANT. I'm not listening? I heard everything.

ANNUNZIATA. And what do you say to that?

SAVANT. What I say?. . . What I say. . .

ANNUNZIATA. Sir. . .

SAVANT. Presently. . . I just can't find something here. . .*(mutters)* How did she put it? Did she write 'always with you' . . . or 'forever with you' . . .?

ANNUNZIATA. *(Plaintively)* I'll shoot you!

SAVANT. Yes, yes. . . do please.

DOCTOR. Christian-Theodore! You're a scholar, after all. . . Listen to me, do! After all, I'm a comrade of yours.

SAVANT. *(Putting the letters away)* Yes, yes. Forgive me.

DOCTOR. In the popular legends about a man who's lost his shadow and in the monographs by Shamisso and your friend, Hans Christian Andersen, it is said. . .

SAVANT. Let's not remember things that are said there. Everything will end differently with me.

DOCTOR. Answer me as your physician. Do you intend to marry the Princess?

SAVANT. Of course.

140

DOCTOR.   But I've heard that you dream about making more people happy.

SAVANT.   That is also true.

DOCTOR.   But both these things can't be true.

SAVANT.   Why not?

DOCTOR.   Having married the Princess you'll become a king.

SAVANT.   The whole point is that I won't become a King. The Princess loves me and she'll come away with me. As for the crown, we'll reject it. You'll see how well it'll work out! And I'll explain to everybody who asks me, and persuade even the least curious that royal power is completely senseless and futile, and that for that reason I refuse the throne.

DOCTOR.   And people will understand you, you think?

SAVANT.   But of course! The example of my own life will prove it!

(The DOCTOR *silently waves his remark aside)*

SAVANT.   You can explain everything to a human being. After all, he understands the alphabet and this is very much simpler than the alphabet. The most important thing is that it concerns him so closely.

(The HOLIDAY-MAKERS *run playing across the stage)*

DOCTOR.   *(Pointing at them)* These, too, would understand you, do you think?

SAVANT.   Of course. Every human being has something that's alive in him. You must be able to touch this live part, that's all.

DOCTOR.   You are a child! I know them better than you do. After all, I'm treating them.

SAVANT.   And what is their complaint?

DOCTOR.   Satiety, in an acute form.

SAVANT.   Is that dangerous?

DOCTOR.   Yes, for all those who come in contact

141

with them.

SAVANT.   How is it?

DOCTOR.   An acute form of satiety suddenly takes
hold of even the most honourable people. For
instance, a man earns a lot of money in quite an
honest way. And suddenly he develops a sinister
symptom, the special restless, hungry look of a
man well provided for. That finishes him. From that
moment onwards he is sterile, blind and cruel.

SAVANT.   Haven't you tried to explain it all to them?

DOCTOR.   That's exactly what I wanted to warn you
against. Woe to him who tries to make them
think of anything but money. This really drives
them absolutely mad with fury.

(The HOLIDAY-MAKERS *run through)*

SAVANT.   Look, they are enjoying themselves.

DOCTOR.   Well, it's their rest time.

(YULIA DJULY *enters quickly)*

YULIA.   *(To the* DOCTOR) Here you are at last! Are
you quite well?

DOCTOR.   Yes.

YULIA.   Ah! it's you, Doctor.

DOCTOR.   Yes, it's me.

YULIA.   Why are you looking at me like a rabbit in
love? Off with you!

(The DOCTOR *wants to reply but does not and
goes into the pavilion silently gesturing with his
hand)*

YULIA.   Where are you, Christian-Theodore?

SAVANT.   I'm here.

YULIA.   *(Comes up to him)* Yes, it is you. *(Smiles)*
How glad I am to see you! Well, what has this
miserable doctor told you?

SAVANT.   He told me that I'm quite well. Why do you
call him miserable?

YULIA.   Ah! I loved him some time ago and, as a
rule, I absolutely hate such people afterwards.

142

SAVANT. Was it an unhappy love?

YULIA. It was worse. This doctor here has a monstrously ugly and malicious wife of whom he's frightened to death. It was only possible to kiss him on the back of his head.

SAVANT. Why so?

YULIA. Because he was turning round all the time to see whether his wife was coming. But that's enough about him. I came here in order to warn you, Christian-Theodore. A misfortune threatens you.

SAVANT. Impossible! I'm so happy.

YULIA. But all the same, you're threatened with misfortune.

ANNUNZIATA. Don't smile, Madam, I implore you. If you do, we shan't understand whether you're being serious or joking. And we may even perish because of that.

YULIA. Don't take any notice of my smiling. In our Circle — in the Circle of Real People — we always smile, just in case. If you smile all the time, whatever you say can be turned around this way or that. I'm speaking seriously now, Christian-Theodore. You're threatened by misfortune.

SAVANT. What misfortune?

YULIA. I've told you that a certain Minister visits our Circle.

SAVANT. Yes, you have.

YULIA. That is the Minister of Finance. He visits our Circle because of me. He pays court to me, and all the time he's about to make me an offer of marriage.

ANNUNZIATA. He? But he can't even walk!

YULIA. He's led about by two beautifully-clad flunkeys. You see, he's so very rich! And just now I met him, and he asked where I was going. When he heard your name, he screwed up his face, Christian-Theodore.

ANNUNZIATA. How terrible!

143

YULIA.   In our Circle we have, all of us, one art at our
finger tips. We can read the faces of highly-
placed people amazingly well. And even I,
despite my short-sight, just now read in the face of
the Minister that something is being plotted
against you, Christian-Theodore.

SAVANT.   Well, let them plot.

YULIA.   Ah! You've done me no good in the past
two weeks! Why did I have to come and meet
you? I've been transformed into a sentimental
petty bourgeois! It's too much trouble.
Annunziata, take him away!

SAVANT.   Why?

YULIA.   The Minister of Finance is coming here in a
moment, and I'm going to use all my charm to
try and find out what they're plotting. I shall
even try to save you, Christian-Theodore.

ANNUNZIATA.   How can I thank you, Madam?

YULIA.   Not a word to anybody!. . . if you're really
grateful to me. Now go.

ANNUNZIATA.   Come along, Sir.

SAVANT.   Annunziata, you know quite well that I
must meet the Princess here.

YULIA.   You still have an hour. Go away if you love
the Princess and pity me.

SAVANT.   Au revoir, poor Yulia! How worried you
both are! And only I alone know that everything
will be fine.

ANNUNZIATA.   He's coming. Madam, I implore you. . .

YULIA.   Quiet! Haven't I told you that I'm going to
try?

(The SAVANT *and* ANNUNZIATA *go out. The*
MINISTER OF FINANCE *comes in, led by his*
FLUNKEYS)

MINISTER OF FINANCE.   Flunkeys! Help me to sit
down beside this fascinating woman. Put me into
a posture which disposes for a light and witty
chat. *(The* FLUNKEYS *obey him)* That's right.
Now go. *(The* FLUNKEYS *go out)* Yulia, I want
to make you glad.

YULIA. It's quite easy for you to do so.

144

MINISTER OF FINANCE.   Enchantress! Circe!
    Aphrodite! Just now in the office of the Prime
    Minister we were talking about you.

YULIA.   Naughty boys!

MINISTER OF FINANCE.   I assure you! And we all
    agreed on one thing — you're a clever, practical
    nymph.

YULIA.   Oh, you flatterers!

MINISTER OF FINANCE. And we decided that you're
    just the person to help us in a certain matter.

YULIA.   Tell me, in what matter. If it isn't a difficult
    one, I'm ready to do anything for you.

MINISTER OF FINANCE.   Oh, it's only a trifle.
    You'll have to help us to destroy the visiting
    Savant, called Christian-Theodore. You are
    acquainted with him, aren't you? Will you help
    us? (YULIA *does not reply*) Flunkeys!
    (FLUNKEYS *appear*) Put me into a posture of
    extreme surprise! (FLUNKEYS *obey*) Yulia,
    I'm extremely surprised! Why are you looking at
    me in such a way as if you didn't know what to
    reply?

YULIA.   I really don't know how to answer you. These
    past two weeks have been simply ruining me.

MINISTER OF FINANCE.   I don't understand.

YULIA.   I don't understand myself.

MINISTER OF FINANCE.   Is this a refusal?

YULIA.   I don't know.

MINISTER OF FINANCE.   Flunkeys! (FLUNKEYS
    run in) A posture of extreme indignation!
    (FLUNKEYS *obey*) I'm extremely indignant,
    Madam Yulia Djuly! What does this mean? Have
    you fallen in love with that indigent youngster,
    by any chance? Silence! Stand up! Stand to
    attention! Now it's no longer a man but the
    Minister of Finance who is before you. Your
    refusal shows that you do not sufficiently respect
    our entire State system! Quiet! Silence! I'll put
    you on trial!

YULIA.   Wait a moment. . .

MINISTER OF FINANCE.   I'm not going to wait.

'Ah, why am I not a meadow!' Only now do I
understand what you wanted to convey by this
song. You were hinting that the farmers didn't
have enough land. Eh? What? You'll see what
I'll do to you! Tomorrow the newspapers will
analyze your figure bit by bit, every bone; your
manner of singing, your private life. . .
Flunkeys! I want to stamp my foot!

(FLUNKEYS *stamp their feet*)

Not your feet, blockheads! My foot! (FLUNKEYS
obey) Au revoir now, famous lady that was!

YULIA. But wait a moment!

MINISTER OF FINANCE. I'm not going to wait.

YULIA. Look at me!

MINISTER OF FINANCE. I'd be obliged if you would
call me 'your Excellency'.

YULIA. Look at me, your Excellency!

MINISTER OF FINANCE. Well?

YULIA. Don't you understand that for me you're
always more a man than a Minister of Finance?

MINISTER OF FINANCE. *(Flattered)* Now, now!
Come off it!

YULIA. I give you my word. And can a woman say
'yes' at once to a man?

MINISTER OF FINANCE. Aphrodite! Shall we make it
precise? Do you agree?

YULIA. Now I'll reply 'yes'.

MINISTER OF FINANCE. Flunkeys! Embrace her! *(The
FLUNKEYS embrace YULIA)* Blockheads! *I* want
to embrace her! Yes, like this. Dear Yulia!
Thank you. Not later than tomorrow, by order
of my Chancellery, I'll declare myself your
principal protector. Flunkeys! Let me sit beside
this Aphrodite. Put me into a posture of extreme
recklessness. And you, Yulia, adopt a light-hearted
posture, but listen to me, all ears. And so, after
a certain time you'll find the Savant here con-
versing animatedly with the Official on Specially
Important Matters. And you, on some kind of
pretext, will lead the Savant away from here for

146

twenty minutes or so. That is all.

YULIA. Is that all?

MINISTER OF FINANCE. You see how simple it is? And these twenty minutes are just what will finally ruin him. Let's go to the jeweller's. I will buy you a ring of incalculable value. Come along! Flunkeys! Carry us away.

(They go away. Enter the ASSISTANT *and* CESAR BORGIA *with* PIETRO)

ASSISTANT. Good day, gentlemen!

PIETRO. But we've already met this morning.

ASSISTANT. I advise you to forget that we have already met this morning. I will not forget that at one point you found me, helped me to get a job at the palace and enabled me to get on in the world. But now, gentlemen, once and for all forget what I was and remember only what I've become.

C. BORGIA. And what are you now?

ASSISTANT. Now I'm an Official on Especially Important Matters at the office of his Excellency the Prime Minister.

C. BORGIA. How did you manage that? That's what I call success! Really, it's outrageous! The same old story, over and over again!

ASSISTANT. I achieved this success by my own efforts. For that reason I'm reminding you once again: forget what I was.

PIETRO. We can forget. Unless we have a quarrel why should we remember?

C. BORGIA. It's difficult to forget about it. But it's possible to keep silent meanwhile. Do you get my meaning?

ASSISTANT. I understand, gentlemen. We shall have no quarrel as long as you remain silent about what I have been. Now listen attentively. I'm in charge of the Case Number 8989. *(He shows them the file)* Here it is.

PIETRO. *(Reads)* The file on the Princess's marriage.

ASSISTANT. Yes. Here, in this file is everything: the Princess, and he, and you; the present and the future.

C. BORGIA. Who is earmarked as the bridegroom of that highly-placed person? It agitates me no more than anything else in this, so-called, terrestrial existence, but all the same. . .

ASSISTANT. As the Princess's prospective bridegrooms are designated both of you.

PIETRO. The hell of it! How — both?

C. BORGIA. I and he?

ASSISTANT. Yes. After all, it's necessary that the Princess has some choice.

C. BORGIA. But you must see yourself. . .

PIETRO. Who the devil else could she want if I exist?

ASSISTANT. Quiet! The decision is final. I make the offer — the Princess chooses. Pietro, take your daughter home. I must have a talk with the Savant, and she's protecting him like a whole regiment of Guards.

C. BORGIA. She's fallen in love with him. And Pietro's gone blind, as is the habit of fathers.

PIETRO. The devil! I'll kill them both!

C. BORGIA. High time you did.

PIETRO. Satan! You're tempting me on purpose. I'll be arrested for murder and then you'll be the only prospective husband. Is that what you want?

C. BORGIA. Yes, I do want it. And it's a perfectly natural wish. Au revoir.

PIETRO. Oh, no, you're not going! I know where you're about to go.

C. BORGIA. Where?

PIETRO. You want to gobble me up in some way or other. But that won't work! I shan't leave you even for a moment.

ASSISTANT. Quiet! He's coming here. Let's agree: whichever of you two becomes the king will pay

148

the other a good ransom. For instance: the one who
has no luck will be appointed First Royal
Secretary or Commander of the Guards. Look,
he's coming. He's very gay.

C. BORGIA.   But how will you talk to him?

ASSISTANT.   I talk to everyone in his own language.

(Enter the SAVANT *and* ANNUNZIATA)

SAVANT.   What a beautiful day, gentlemen!

PIETRO.   Yes, not a bad day, damn it! Annunziata!
Go home!

ANNUNZIATA.   Daddy!

PIETRO.   Home! Or else something bad is coming to
you and to someone else, as well. You didn't
even tell the cook what to prepare for supper
tonight.

ANNUNZIATA.   It makes no difference to me.

PIETRO.   What are you saying, you unnatural girl!
Mr Cesar Borgia, come home with us, my friend. . .
Or I swear on my honour, I'll finish you off
with my dagger on the quiet.

(They go out. The ASSISTANT, *who stood
aside during the preceding conversation, now
comes up to the* SAVANT)

ASSISTANT.   Don't you recognize me?

SAVANT.   Forgive me, I don't.

ASSISTANT.   Look more closely.

SAVANT.   What's that?. . . I feel as if I knew you. . .
as if I knew you very well, but. . .

ASSISTANT.   And we've lived so many years together. . .

SAVANT.   Can this really be true?

ASSISTANT.   Yes, I assure you. I followed you per-
sistently but you only occasionally and carelessly
glanced at me. And yet I was often taller than
you and rose to the roofs of the tallest houses.
Usually this happened on moonlit nights.

SAVANT.   Then you must be. . .?

ASSISTANT.   Speak quietly! Yes, I am your shadow.

149

Why do you look at me so mistrustfully? After
all, from the day of your birth, all your life I've
been attached to you.

SAVANT.   No, really. . . It's simply that I. . .

SHADOW.   You're angry with me because I deserted
you. But you yourself asked me to go in after
the Princess, and I immediately carried out your
wish. After all, we grew up together among the
same people. When you said 'Mother', I repeated
the same word without making a sound. I
loved those whom you loved and your enemies
were my enemies. When you were ill, I could not
raise my head from the pillow, just as you
couldn't. You got better and I got better. Is it
possible that after a whole life lived in such
friendship I could suddenly become your enemy?

SAVANT.   But no, of course not. Sit down, old friend.
I was ill while you were away, but I'm better now. . .
I'm feeling quite well. It's such a beautiful day
today. I am happy, my soul is wide open. . . I'm
telling you this, although, as you know, I don't
like words of this sort. But what you've said
touches me. That's why. . . But what about you?
What have you been doing all this time? Or no. . .
wait a moment, let's make friends again first!

SHADOW.   *(Putting out his hand to the* SAVANT)
Thank you. I've remained your shadow — that's
what I've been doing all these days.

SAVANT.   I don't understand you.

SHADOW.   You sent me to the Princess. First of all, I
got engaged as the assistant of the palace butler,
then I rose higher and higher, and from today
I am the Official on Specially Important Matters,
attached to the Prime Minister.

SAVANT.   Poor fellow! I can imagine how difficult
it is to associate with these people. But why did
you do it?

SHADOW.   For your sake.

SAVANT.   For my sake?

SHADOW.   You don't know what terrible hatred has
surrounded you from the moment you came to
love the Princess and the Princess came to love

you. They all want to gobble you up, and they would
have gobbled you up today but for me.

SAVANT. Really?

SHADOW. I'm among them in order to save you.
They trust me. They put me in charge of File
8989.

SAVANT. What file is that?

SHADOW. It's a file concerning the marriage of the
Princess.

SAVANT. It can't be!

SHADOW. And it's our luck that this file is now in
reliable hands. The Prime Minister himself
directed me to see you. I've been given the task of
buying you out.

SAVANT. Buying me out? *(Laughs)* For how much?

SHADOW. For a trifle. They promise you fame,
honours and riches if you give up the Princess.

SAVANT. And what if I don't sell myself?

SHADOW. You will be killed this very day.

SAVANT. Nothing in the world will make me believe
that I can die, especially today!

SHADOW. Christian, my friend, my brother, they will
kill you, believe me. You see, they don't know the
paths we used to run along when we were children,
the water-mill where we chatted with the water
spirit, the forest where we met the daughter of
the teacher and fell in love, you with her, and I
with her shadow. They can't even imagine you as
a living person. For them you're just an obstacle,
something like a tree stump or a log of wood.
Believe me, you'll be dead before the sun goes
down.

SAVANT. What then do you advise me to do?

SHADOW. *(Takes a paper from his brief-case)* Sign
this.

SAVANT. *(Reads)* 'I, the undersigned, decisively,
irreversibly and finally, refuse to enter into marriage
with the Princess, Heiress to the Kingdom, if in
exchange for this, I shall be assured of fame,

151

honours and wealth.' You're seriously suggesting that I should sign this?

SHADOW. Sign it if you're not just a boy, if you are a real man.

SAVANT. What is the matter with you?

SHADOW. Try to understand that you have no other way out. On one side there are us three. On the other side — the Ministers, Secret Counsellors, all the officials of the kingdom, the police and the Army. We can't win in a straight fight. Believe me, I was always more down to earth than you. Listen to me: this bit of paper will calm them. This very evening you will hire a coach — you're not going to be watched. And in the forest we'll get into your carriage — the Princess and I. And in a few hours we'll be free. Do understand this — free! Here's my pocket inkstand, here's a pen. Sign.

SAVANT. Well, all right. The Princess will come here presently. I'll consult her, and if there's no other way out, I'll sign.

SHADOW. It's impossible to wait. The Prime Minister gave me only twenty minutes. He doesn't believe that you can be bought. He regards our conversation as a mere formality. He already has murderers on duty and they're waiting his orders. Sign now!

SAVANT. I'm terribly reluctant to do it.

SHADOW. You, too, are a murderer! Refusing to sign this wretched piece of paper, you're killing me, your best friend, and the poor, helpless Princess. Do you imagine we'll survive your death?

SAVANT. Well, all right, all right. Let me have it, I'll sign... But one thing I'll never do again — come so close to palaces... *(Signs the paper)*

SHADOW. And here's the King's seal... *(Stamps the paper)*

(YULIA *runs in. The* SHADOW *steps aside, modestly)*

YULIA. Christian! I'm ruined!

SAVANT. What's happened?

152

YULIA. Help me!

SAVANT. I'm ready to, but how? You aren't joking?

YULIA. No. I'm not smiling, am I? It's a habit.
Come with me immediately! Come!

SAVANT. I give you my word — I can't leave here.
The Princess is coming to meet me any moment.

YULIA. This is a matter of life and death.

SAVANT. Ah! I can guess what's the matter. . .
You've found out from the Minister of Finance
what fate is threatening me, and you want to
warn me. Thank you, Yulia, but. . .

YULIA. Ah! You don't understand! Well, stay then. . .
No! I don't want to be a virtuous, sentimental
petty bourgeois! I don't want to warn you at all.
The matter concerns me. Christian, forgive me!
Come with me, or I'll be ruined. Well, I'll kneel
before you if you want me to!

SAVANT. All right, I'll just say a couple of words to my
friend here. *(Goes up to the* SHADOW) Listen,
the Princess will come here presently.

SHADOW. I know.

SAVANT. Tell her that I'll come running back in a
few moments. I can't refuse this woman. There's
been some sort of disaster. . .

SHADOW. Go in peace. I'll explain everything to the
Princess.

SAVANT. Thank you.

(The SAVANT *and* YULIA *go out)*

SHADOW. Damn this habit! My hands, my feet and my
neck are all aching. All the time I wanted to copy
his every movement. It's quite dangerous. . .
(Opens the file) So. . . Point four is completed.
(He concentrates on reading)

(Enter the PRINCESS *and the* SECRET COUN-
SELLOR. *The* SHADOW *draws himself up to his
full height and gazes fixedly at the* PRINCESS)

PRINCESS. Secret Counsellor, where is he? Why isn't
he here?

SECRET COUNSELLOR. *(Whispers)* He'll come

presently, Princess, and everything will be fine.

PRINCESS.   No, it's terribly upsetting. Be quiet, you
don't understand anything. You're not in love:
it's easy for you to say that everything's going
beautifully. Besides, I'm a Princess, I don't know
how to wait. What's this music?

SECRET COUNSELLOR.   That's the music in the
restaurant, Princess.

PRINCESS.   Why do they always have music in our
restaurant?

SECRET COUNSELLOR.   So that people don't hear
themselves chewing their food, Princess.

PRINCESS.   Leave me alone! Well, what's happening,
really? *(To the* SHADOW) Hey, you! Why are you
staring at me like that?

SHADOW.   I must speak to you but I daren't,
Princess.

PRINCESS.   Who are you?

SHADOW.   I'm his best friend.

PRINCESS.   Whose?

SHADOW.   I'm the best friend of the man for whom
you're waiting, Princess.

PRINCESS.   Is that true? Why are you silent?

SHADOW.   My answer will sound impertinent to you,
Princess.

PRINCESS.   That doesn't matter. Speak.

SHADOW.   I was silent because I was struck by your
beauty, Princess.

PRINCESS.   But that's not impertinent in the least. Has
he sent you to me?

SHADOW.   Yes. He asked me to tell you that he would
come presently, Princess. Something very
important has delayed him. Everything's all right,
Princess.

PRINCESS.   But will he come soon?

SHADOW.   Yes.

PRINCESS.   Well, I feel cheerful again. Will you amuse

154

me until he comes? Well? . . . *(The* SHADOW *is silent)*
Come on, now! It's embarrassing for me to remind
you — but I'm a Princess, after all. I'm accustomed
to being amused.

SHADOW. Very well. I will obey your orders. I will
tell you about some dreams, Princess.

PRINCESS. But are your dreams interesting?

SHADOW. I will tell you about your own dreams,
Princess.

PRINCESS. About *my* dreams?

SHADOW. Yes. Two days ago you dreamed in the night
that the walls of the palace suddenly became the
waves of the sea. You shouted: 'Christian!' and he
appeared in a boat and stretched out his hand to
you.

PRINCESS. But I haven't told anyone about this
dream!

SHADOW. And then you found yourself in a forest. . .
And suddenly a wolf sprang from the bushes, and
Christian said: 'Don't be afraid, it's a kind wolf,'
and he stroked it. And here's another dream: you
were galloping on horseback along a field. The
grass in your path was growing higher and higher,
and in the end it stood like a wall round you. You
thought it was beautiful, amazingly beautiful, so
beautiful that you began to weep and awoke in
tears.

PRINCESS. But how do you know this?

SHADOW. Love works miracles, Princess.

PRINCESS. Love?

SHADOW. Yes. You see, I'm a very unfortunate man,
Princess. I love you.

PRINCESS. Is that so? Counsellor!

SECRET COUNSELLOR. Yes, Princess?

PRINCESS. Call the. . . No, step aside five paces. . .
(The COUNSELLOR *counts five paces)* I. . .

SHADOW. You wanted him to call the Guards,

155

Princess. . . and then, not knowing yourself how it happened, ordered him to step aside five paces.

PRINCESS. You. . .

SHADOW. I love you, Princess. And you yourself feel this. I'm so full of you that your soul is as intelligible to me as my own. I told you only two of your dreams, but in fact I remember all of them. I know your frightening dreams as well as your funny dreams, and also the dreams you can only whisper into a friend's ear.

PRINCESS. No!

SHADOW. Would you like me to tell you the dream which startled you? Do you remember? In that dream it wasn't he who was with you, not Christian, but quite a different man, with a face you didn't know. . . and that was just what pleased you, Princess. And you and he. . .

PRINCESS. Counsellor! Call the Guards!

SECRET COUNSELLOR. I obey, Princess.

PRINCESS. But let the Guards stand over there, beyond those shrubs for the time being. Go on talking. I'm listening because. . . because I'm bored just waiting for him.

SHADOW. People don't know the shadow side of things. But it is just in the shadows, in the twilight, in the depths that something is hidden which gives a sharp edge to our feelings. In the depths of your soul you have — me.

PRINCESS. That's enough! I've suddenly come to my senses. Presently the Guards will arrest you, and tonight your head will be chopped off.

SHADOW. Read this! *(He takes the paper that the* SAVANT *had signed from his brief-case. The* PRINCESS *reads it)* He's a nice man, an attractive man, but he is shallow. He was trying to persuade you to run away with him because he was afraid of becoming a king — it's dangerous, you see. And so he sold you. He's a coward!

PRINCESS. I don't believe this paper.

SHADOW. But here's the King's seal. I bribed your

miserable suitor, and I've won you in a fight. Now order me to be decapitated.

PRINCESS. You don't give me time to collect myself. How can I know — perhaps you don't love me either! What an unfortunate girl I am!

SHADOW. But what about the dreams? You forgot the dreams, Princess! How could I know your dreams? Only love can work such miracles.

PRINCESS. Ah, yes, that's true. . .

SHADOW. Good-bye, Princess.

PRINCESS. You. . . you're going?. . . How dare you! Come here. . . give me your hand. . . This. . . all this. . . is so. . . so interesting. . . *(They kiss)* I. . . I don't even know what you're called. . .

SHADOW. Theodore-Christian.

PRINCESS. That's good! It's almost. . . almost the same thing. *(They kiss)*

(The SAVANT runs in and stops as if rooted to the spot)

SECRET COUNSELLOR. *(To the SAVANT)* I advise you to leave. The Princess is giving an audience to one of her subjects.

SAVANT. Louise!

PRINCESS. Go away, you shallow man!

SAVANT. What are you saying, Louise!

PRINCESS. You've signed a paper in which you renounce me.

SAVANT. Yes, but. . .

PRINCESS. That's enough. You are a nice person, but you're really a nonentity. Come on, Theodore-Christian, my dear!

SAVANT. Scoundrel! *(He rushes at the SHADOW)*

PRINCESS. Guards! *(The GUARDS run out of the bushes)* Accompany us to the palace!

(They go out. The SAVANT sits down on a garden seat. The DOCTOR comes quickly out of the pavilion)

157

DOCTOR. Wave all this aside! Wave your hand immediately, or you'll lose your reason.

SAVANT. But do you know what's happened?

DOCTOR. Yes. I have very acute hearing. I heard everything.

SAVANT. But how did he manage to get her to kiss him?

DOCTOR. He's stunned her. He told her all her dreams.

SAVANT. How did he know her dreams?

DOCTOR. Well, you see, dreams and shadows are closely related. I think they're sort of cousins.

SAVANT. You heard everything and you didn't interfere?

DOCTOR. What are you saying! After all, he's the Official on Specially Important Matters. Don't you know what terrible power that implies? I used to know a man of quite unusual courage. He used to go against bears armed with nothing but a knife. Once he decided to tackle a lion with his bare hands — true, he didn't come back from that particular hunt, his last. But this same man fainted when accidentally, on one occasion, he bumped into a Secret Counsellor. This is a special kind of fear. Is it surprising then that I'm afraid of him? No, I didn't interfere in that affair, and you ought to wave it all aside.

SAVANT. I don't want to.

DOCTOR. But what can you do?

SAVANT. I will destroy him.

DOCTOR. No. Listen to me, you don't know, and no one in the world knows that I once made a great discovery. I found a source of living hydrogenous water. Not far off. Quite close to this place, in fact. This water cures all the illnesses that exist on earth and even resurrects the dead if they are good people. And what came of it? The Minister of Finance ordered me to close that source. If we cured all the sick people, then who would come to visit us? I struggled against the Minister like one possessed — and then all the bureaucrats moved

158

against me. It's all the same to them. Life, and
death, and great discoveries. . . And just for that
reason they've won. And I waved my hand at
everything. And at once I found life in this
world ever so much easier. And you wave your
hand at everything, and live as I live.

SAVANT.   But what do you live by? What for?

DOCTOR.   Ah! there are things . . . For instance a
sick man gets better. Or my wife goes away for
a couple of days. Or they write in the papers that
I'm still showing promise.

SAVANT.   Is that all?

DOCTOR.   And you want to live so that you could
make as many people as possible happy? And you
expect the bureaucrats to allow you to live?
The very people whom you want to make happy
can't tolerate it. Wave them aside with your
hand — like this. Look through your fingers at
this mad unhappy world.

SAVANT.   I can't.

(The sounds of drums and trumpets backstage)

DOCTOR.   He's coming back. *(Hurriedly goes back
into the pavilion)*

*(A large detachment of GUARDS marches in,
preceded by trumpeters and drummers. At the
head of the detachment walks the SHADOW in
a black frock-coat and blindingly white linen. The
procession stops in the middle of the stage)*

SHADOW.   Christian! Just now I'm going to give a
few orders, and then I'll attend to you.

*(The PRIME MINISTER runs in, out of breath.
The FLUNKEYS come running after him, carrying
the MINISTER OF FINANCE. CESAR BORGIA
and PIETRO come in, arm-in-arm)*

PRIME MINISTER.   What does all this mean?
Haven't we decided?. . .

SHADOW.   But I have decided differently.

PRIME MINISTER.   But listen. . .

SHADOW.   No, you listen, my friend. Do you know who
you're speaking to?

159

PRIME MINISTER.   Yes.

SHADOW.   Then why don't you address me as 'Your Excellency'? Haven't you been to your office?

PRIME MINISTER.   No, I was having my dinner, your Excellency.

SHADOW.   If I were you, I should go there. The file number 8989 is completed. At the end of the file you'll find the will of the Princess and my order number 0001. That order confers on me the title of Excellency until we adopt a new, more suitable title.

PRIME MINISTER.   So everything's been formalized?

SHADOW.   Yes.

PRIME MINISTER.   Well, then there's nothing to be done. I congratulate you, your Excellency.

SHADOW.   Why are you frowning, Minister of Finance?

MINISTER OF FINANCE.   I don't know how the business circles will take it. You see, you come from the class of learned men. All kinds of changes will, no doubt, be introduced, and we abominate that.

SHADOW.   There will be no changes. Everything will remain as it was. No plans. No day-dreams. These are the latest conclusions of my science.

MINISTER OF FINANCE.   In that case I congratulate you, your Excellency.

SHADOW.   Pietro! The Princess has chosen her bridegroom, but it isn't you.

PIETRO.   The devil take him, your Excellency! I only want to be paid.

SHADOW.   Cesar Borgia! You're not going to be King either.

C. BORGIA.   All that's left to me is to write my memoirs, your Excellency.

SHADOW.   Don't get upset. I value old friends who knew me when I was a mere Official on Specially Important Matters. You are appointed as the King's Secretary, and you as the Commander of the Guards.

(PIETRO *and* C. BORGIA *bow)* Gentlemen, you
are free. *(Everyone goes out bowing. The*
SHADOW *comes up to the* SAVANT) Did you see?

SAVANT. Yes.

SHADOW. What do you say?

SAVANT. I say — renounce the Princess and the
throne immediately, or I'll make you do it.

SHADOW. Listen, miserable man! Tomorrow at the
latest I'll issue a number of orders and you'll
find yourself alone against the whole world.
Your friends will turn away from you in disgust.
Your enemies will laugh at you. And you will
crawl back to me and beg to be spared.

SAVANT. No!

SHADOW. We'll see. At midnight on Tuesday you'll
come to the palace and send me a note, saying:
'I surrender', and signed 'Christian-Theodore'.
And I will show condescension and agree to
employ you in my personal service. Guards!
Follow me.

(Drum beats and trumpets. The SHADOW *goes*
out with his suite)

SAVANT. Annunziata! Annunziata!

(ANNUNZIATA *runs in)*

ANNUNZIATA. I'm here. Sir! Maybe. . . maybe you'll
take the Doctor's advice? Maybe you'll wave your
hand at everything? Forgive me. . . Don't be
angry with me. I will help you. I'll be useful to
you. I'm a very faithful girl, Sir!

SAVANT. Annunziata, this is indeed a sad fairy-tale!

CURTAIN

ACT THREE

Scene One

*Night time. Torches are burning. On the cornices, pillars
and balconies of the palace lampions are alight. There is
a crowd, animated and noisy, in the streets.*

A VERY TALL MAN.   Who'd like me to tell them what
    I can see? For two farthings only! And who'd
    like me to tell him. . . Oh, it's most interesting!

A VERY SHORT MAN.   Don't listen to him. Listen to
    me — I can nip in anywhere, I know everything.
    And who'd like to hear the news — for a mere two
    farthings! I'll tell you how they met, how they
    became acquainted and how the first bridegroom
    was given his dismissal.

FIRST WOMAN.   Down our way, they're saying the
    first bridegroom was a very nice man.

SECOND WOMAN.   Rather! Very nice indeed! He
    gave her up for a million.

FIRST WOMAN.   Really? Is that so?

SECOND WOMAN.   Everybody knows it. She says to
    him: 'You're a strange man! If you'd become a
    King, you'd have earned no less than that!'
    And he said to her: 'Why should I work for it?'

FIRST WOMAN.   Men like that ought to be drowned.

SECOND WOMAN.   Yes, indeed! He thought it'd be
    hard to be a King. I wish he'd try being a house-
    wife.

THE TALL MAN.   And who'd like me to tell them what
    I can see through the window? The principal royal
    flunkey is walking along the passage and. . .
    well, who'd like to know what happens next? For
    two farthings only!

THE SHORT MAN.   And who'd like the portrait of the
    new King? Drawn up to his full height! With a
    crown on his head! With a kind smile on his lips.
    With benevolence in his eyes!

FIRST MAN IN THE CROWD.   Now we have a King,
    life will be much better.

SECOND MAN IN THE CROWD. Now tell my why.

FIRST MAN IN THE CROWD. I'll explain presently. Don't you see?

SECOND MAN IN THE CROWD. See what?

FIRST MAN IN THE CROWD. Don't you see who's standing there?

SECOND MAN. He looks like the Commander of the Guards.

FIRST MAN. Of course. It's him in disguise.

SECOND MAN. Ah, I see now. *(In a loud voice)* Now we have a King, we're going to have a fine life. *(In a quiet voice)* He's disguised himself but he's got on military boots with spurs. *(Loudly)* Oh, how delighted I am!

FIRST MAN. *(At the top of his voice)* Yes, of course, our life wasn't up to much without a King. We kept on longing for him.

THE CROWD. Long live our new King, Theodore the First! Hurrah!

(Little by little they all go their different ways, glancing cautiously at PIETRO. He is left alone. A figure of a man in a cloak separates itself from the wall)

PIETRO. Anything new, Corporal?

CORPORAL. No, nothing. Everything's quiet. We arrested two men.

PIETRO. What for?

CORPORAL. One shouted 'Long live the cow!' instead of shouting 'Long live the King!'

PIETRO. And the second?

CORPORAL. The second is my neighbour.

PIETRO. But what did he do?

CORPORAL. Well, nothing, in fact. He's got a nasty disposition. He nicknamed my wife 'a melon'. I've been wanting to get even with him for ages. And how are you getting on, Mr Commander?

163

PIETRO. Everything's quiet. The people are delighted.

CORPORAL. Allow me to make a personal remark, Mr Commander. Your boots.

PIETRO. What about my boots?

CORPORAL. You've again forgotton to change your boots. The spurs make a ringing noise.

PIETRO. Really? Fancy that!

CORPORAL. The people guess who you are. You see how empty the place has become.

PIETRO. Yes. However. . . you are our man, I can admit it to you. I came out wearing these boots quite deliberately.

CORPORAL. Impossible!

PIETRO. Yes. I'd rather they knew who I am, or I might overhear such stuff that I wouldn't be able to sleep for three nights.

CORPORAL. Yes, it does happen like that.

PIETRO. Wearing these boots makes it much less troublesome. You walk around jingling your spurs and hear only the right kind of talk around you.

CORPORAL. Yes, that's quite true.

PIETRO. It's very easy for them, up there in the office. They have to deal only with papers. But I've got to deal with people. Not so easy!

CORPORAL. Yes, I know. . . The people. . .

PIETRO. *(In whisper)* You know, I'll tell you something. . . The people go on living in their own way.

CORPORAL. You don't say!

PIETRO. You can believe me. Here the Sovereign celebrates his coronation, the solemn wedding of the highest persons in the land is about to take place, but do you know what the people permit themselves to do? Many youths and girls are embracing and kissing in dark corners only a few steps away from the palace. At the house number 8, a tailor's wife took it into her head to deliver herself of a baby. Such a great event is taking place in the kingdom, and she's screaming at the

164

top of her voice as if it was all nothing to her!
The old blacksmith in number 3 went and died. In
the palace they're celebrating, and he just lies in
his coffin and takes no notice of it at all. That's
not as it should be!

CORPORAL.   In which number is the woman giving
birth? I'll fine her.

PIETRO.   That isn't the point! What alarms me is the
thought that they dare behave like this! What sort
of stubborness is it, eh, Corporal? What if they
did in the same quiet, stubborn way, all together. . .
Hey! What's the matter with you?

CORPORAL   Nothing. . .

PIETRO.   Look out, brother! How are you standing?
(The CORPORAL *draws himself up)* I'll show
you! Old devil! Chattering away! Reasoning!
Fancying yourself perhaps as some Jean-Jacques
Rousseau? What's the time?

CORPORAL.   A quarter to midnight, Commander.

PIETRO.   D'you remember what it is you've got to
announce precisely at midnight?

CORPORAL.   Yes, Mr Commander.

PIETRO.   I'll go to the office now, rest a little, calm
myself, read various papers. . . and you here
announce what you must. Don't forget!

(Goes out.

Enter the SAVANT)

SAVANT.   It pleases me to see these little lampions.
It seems as if my head had never worked so
clearly in my life as at this moment. I can see all
the lampions simultaneously and every lampion
separately, as well. And I love all of them together
and each one separately. I know that in the morning
you will all be extinguished, my friends, but
don't you regret it! After all, you've been burning,
and you burnt gaily — this is something no one
can take away from you.

A MAN COVERED WITH A CLOAK FROM HEAD TO
FOOT.   Christian!

SAVANT.   Who's this? Ah! It's you, Doctor.

165

DOCTOR. You recognized me so easily?. . . *(Looks round)* Come over here. Turn away from me. No, it's the ringing in my ears — and I thought it was the spurs. . . Don't be angry. You see, I've got such a large family.

SAVANT. I'm not angry. *(They walk to the front of the stage)*

DOCTOR. Tell me as to your physician — have you decided to surrender?

SAVANT. No. I'm a conscientious man, I must go and tell them what I know.

DOCTOR. But this is suicide!

SAVANT. Possibly.

DOCTOR. I implore you — do surrender.

SAVANT. I can't.

DOCTOR. They'll cut your head off.

SAVANT. I don't believe it. On one side real life, on the other — a shadow. All I have ever learnt tells me that the shadow can conquer only for a time. You see, the world goes round only because of us, because of men who do the work! Good-bye!

DOCTOR. Listen, people are terrible when you fight against them. Only if you manage to live in peace with them do they seem not all that bad.

SAVANT. Is that all you wanted to tell me?

DOCTOR. No. Perhaps I've gone out of my mind, but I can't bear to see you go in there, unarmed. Listen! Memorize these words: 'Shadow! Know thy place!'

SAVANT. I don't understand you.

DOCTOR. All these days I've been digging into the ancient writings about people who've lost their shadows. In one study on this subject the author, a very reliable, solid professor, recommends this remedy: the owner of the shadow must shout at it: 'Shadow, know thy place!' And then it will again become the shadow for a time.

SAVANT. What are you saying! But this is remarkable! Then everyone would see that he's my shadow.

There! Haven't I been telling you that he'd fail?
Life is against him. We. . .

DOCTOR.   Not a word about me! Good-bye. . . *(Goes out quickly)*

SAVANT.   That's fine! I was preparing to perish with honour, but victory is very much better. They'll see that he's the shadow, and they'll understand. . . In a word, they'll understand everything. I. . .

(A crowd of people run in)

SAVANT.   What's happened?

FIRST MAN.   The Corporal's coming here with a trumpet.

SAVANT.   What for?

FIRST MAN.   He's going to announce something. Here he is. . . Quiet!

CORPORAL.   Christian-Theodore! Christian-Theodore!

SAVANT.   What is it? I feel afraid, it seems.

CORPORAL.   Christian-Theodore! Christian-Theodore!

SAVANT.   *(In a loud voice)* I'm here.

CORPORAL.   Have you got a letter for the King?

SAVANT.   Here it is.

CORPORAL.   Follow me!

(CURTAIN)

Scene Two

A hall in the royal palace. The COURTIERS *are sitting around in groups. Conversations in subdued voices are going on. The* MAJORDOMO *and his assistants carry around trays with food.*

FIRST COURTIER.   *(Grey-haired, with a beautiful, sad face)* Formerly, they used to serve ice-cream shaped into very charming lambs, or little rabbits, or kittens. My blood used to run cold in my veins when I was obliged to bite off the heads of such gentle, innocent creatures.

167

FIRST LADY.   Oh, yes, yes! My blood also ran cold in
my veins. Ice-cream is so cold, after all!

FIRST COURTIER.   Now they serve ice-cream shaped
like beautiful fruit. This is much more humane.

FIRST LADY.   You're right. How kind-hearted you
are! By the way, how are your dear little canary
birds?

FIRST COURTIER.   Ah! one of them, Golden Drop by
name, caught a cold and was coughing so badly,
that I nearly fell ill myself, because I was so sorry
for her. She's much better now. She even tries to
sing, but I don't permit her to.

(Enter PIETRO*))*

PIETRO.   How do you do? What are you eating there,
gentlemen?

SECOND COURTIER.   Ice-cream, Mr Commander of
the Guards.

PIETRO.   Hey, there! Bring me a portion. Quickly, you
devil! A bigger helping than that, curse you!

SECOND COURTIER.   Do you like ice-cream so much,
Mr Commander?

PIETRO.   I loathe it. But if they give it to you, you've
got to take it, blast it!

MAJORDOMO.   Pastries with pink cream! Who would
like some, gentlemen courtiers? *(Quietly to the*
FLUNKEYS) First you serve the dukes, then the
counts, then the barons. The dukes can have six
pastries, the counts four, the barons two each. All
the others can have what's left. Don't muddle it
up.

ONE OF THE FLUNKEYS.   And how many pastries
should we give to the new secretaries of the
King?

MAJORDOMO.   Six and a half each.

(Enter CESAR BORGIA)

C. BORGIA.   Good evening, gentlemen! Do look
at me! Well? What do you say? How do you like
my necktie? This necktie is more than fashionable.

It won't be fashionable for another two weeks
yet.

THIRD COURTIER.   But how did you manage to get
hold of this work of art?

C. BORGIA.   Oh, very simply. My supplier of neckties
is the Admiral of the King's fleet. He brings me my
ties from abroad, and he carries them ashore
hidden in his three-cornered hat.

THIRD COURTIER.   But this is as simple as a work of
genius!

C. BORGIA.   As the King's Secretary, I'm prepared to
arrange for you to get a dozen ties. Gentlemen, I
want to give you pleasure. Would you like me to?
Then come along with me, I'll show you my
apartments. Furnished in mahogany and full of
Chinese pottery. Would you like to have a look?

COURTIERS.   Of course! We're dying with impatience.
How amiable you are, Mr Royal Secretary!

(CESAR BORGIA *goes out, followed by the*
COURTIERS. *Enter* ANNUNZIATA *and after
her* YULIA DJULY)

YULIA.   Are you angry with me? Don't deny it. Now
you're the daughter of a highly placed person, I
can read quite clearly in your face that you're
angry with me. Isn't that so?

ANNUNZIATA.   Ah! Really, I have other things to
worry about, Madam!

YULIA.   You're still thinking of him? Of the Savant?

ANNUNZIATA.   Yes.

YULIA.   Do you really think he can win?

ANNUNZIATA.   It makes no difference to me.

YULIA.   You're wrong. You're still a very young girl.
You don't know that a real man is one who comes
out on top. The terrible thing is that you can never
know for certain who will win in the end.
Christian-Theodore is such a strange person. Do
you know anything about him?

ANNUNZIATA.   Ah, how unfortunate it all is! We

169

moved into the palace and Daddy's ordered the
flunkeys not to let me out. I can't even send a letter
to Mr Savant. And he must think, I'm sure, that
I've turned away from him. Cesar Borgia demolishes
him every day in his newspaper. Daddy reads it
and licks his chops, and I read and nearly burst
into tears. Just now in the passage I pushed that
Cesar Borgia and I didn't even apologize.

YULIA.   He didn't notice it, believe me.

ANNUNZIATA.   Maybe. Do you know anything about
Mr Savant, Madam?

YULIA.   Yes, I do know. My friends, the Ministers, tell
me everything. Christian-Theodore now finds
himself completely alone. And despite this, he goes
around smiling.

ANNUNZIATA.   How terrible!

YULIA.   Of course. Whoever would behave like this in
such difficult circumstances? It's quite incompre-
hensible. I've arranged my life to flow so easily, so
elegantly, and now suddenly I'm almost suffering.
To suffer — this is simply not done! *(She laughs
loudly and coquettishly)*

ANNUNZIATA.   What's the matter with you, Madam?

YULIA.   The courtiers are returning to this room.
Mr Minister, here you are at last! I've really missed
you! How are you?

(The FLUNKEYS *lead in the* MINISTER OF
FINANCE)

MINISTER OF FINANCE.   One, two, three, four. . .
All the diamonds are in place. One, two, three. . .
Pearls, too. And rubies. . . How are you, Yulia?
Where are you off to?

YULIA.   Ah, your proximity agitates me too much!. . .
People might notice it. . .

MINISTER OF FINANCE.   But our relationship has been
formalized by order. . .

YULIA.   All the same. . . I'll step aside. It'll be more
elegant.

(She goes aside)

MINISTER OF FINANCE. She's a real goddess...
Flunkeys, make me sit beside the wall. Put me
into a posture of complete satisfaction with the
present state of affairs. Hurry up! *(The* FLUNKEYS
fulfil his order) Now get out! *(The* FLUNKEYS
go out)

(The PRIME MINISTER, *as if he were taking a
stroll, approaches the* MINISTER OF FINANCE)

MINISTER OF FINANCE. *(Smiling, quietly)* How are
affairs, Mr Prime Minister?

PRIME MINISTER. *(Smiling)* It seems everything's in
order.

MINISTER OF FINANCE. Why — 'it seems'?

PRIME MINISTER. In the long years of my service I've
discovered one not very pleasant law. At the very
moment when we seem to achieve a complete
victory, Life suddenly raises it head.

MINISTER OF FINANCE. Raises its head?... Have you
called out the Royal Executioner?

PRIME MINISTER. Yes, he's here. Smile! We're being
watched.

MINISTER OF FINANCE. *(Smiles)* What about the
axe and the scaffold?

PRIME MINISTER. They've also been brought up. The
scaffold is erected in the King's drawing-room,
next to the statue of Cupid, and is masked with
forget-me-nots.

MINISTER OF FINANCE. What can the Savant do
now?

PRIME MINISTER. Nothing. He's alone and powerless.
But these honest, naive men sometimes do such
unexpected things.

MINISTER OF FINANCE. Why wasn't he executed at
once?

PRIME MINISTER. The King is against this. Smile! *(He
goes off, smiling)*

(Enter the SECRET COUNSELLOR)

SECRET COUNSELLOR. Gentlemen Courtiers, I

171

congratulate you! His Majesty and his august bride are directing their steps towards this hall. What a joy!

(Everyone stands up. The door is flung wide open. Enter the SHADOW *and the* PRINCESS *arm-in-arm)*

SHADOW. *(With an elegant and majestic gesture)* Sit down.

COURTIERS. *(All together)* We won't sit down.

SHADOW. Sit down.

COURTIERS. We daren't.

SHADOW. Sit down.

COURTIERS. Well, all right, if you wish. *(They sit down)*

SHADOW. Prime Minister!

PRIME MINISTER. I'm here, your Majesty.

SHADOW. What is the time?

PRIME MINISTER. It's a quarter to midnight, your Majesty.

SHADOW. You can go.

PRINCESS. What is this hall we're in?

SHADOW. In the small throne room, Princess. Don't you see?

PRINCESS. I see nothing but you. I don't recognize the rooms where I've grown up, the men among whom I've lived so many years. I feel like sending them all out and staying alone with you.

SHADOW. I, too.

PRINCESS. You're preoccupied with something?

SHADOW. Yes. I promised to forgive Christian if he would himself come here at midnight tonight. He's a failure but I've been friends with him for many years.

PRINCESS. How can you think of anybody but me? After all, our wedding is to be within an hour.

172

SHADOW. But we met one another through Christian.

PRINCESS. Ah, yes! What a good man you are,
    Theodore! Yes, we'll forgive him. He's a failure
    but you've been friends with him for many years.

SHADOW. Secret Counsellor!

SECRET COUNSELLOR. I'm here, your Majesty.

SHADOW. Presently a man will come here with whom I
    wish to speak alone.

SECRET COUNSELLOR. I obey, your Majesty.
    Gentlemen Courtiers! His Majesty has condescended
    to give an audience to one of his subjects in this
    hall. What a lucky man that fellow is!

(The COURTIERS *get up and go out bowing)*

PRINCESS. You think he'll come?

SHADOW. What else can he do? *(Kisses the*
    PRINCESS's *hand)* I'll call you as soon as I've
    consoled and comforted him.

PRINCESS. I'm going, my dear. What a remarkable
    person you are!

(Goes out after the COURTIERS.

The SHADOW *opens the window and listens. In
the neighbouring room the clock begins to strike)*

SHADOW. It's midnight. Presently he'll come.

(Very far below the CORPORAL *shouts)*

CORPORAL. Christian-Theodore! Christian-Theodore!

SHADOW. What's this? It seems I feel afraid.

CORPORAL. Christian-Theodore! Christian-Theodore!

SAVANT'S VOICE. I'm here.

CORPORAL. Have you a letter to the King?

SAVANT'S VOICE. Here it is.

CORPORAL. Follow me.

SHADOW. *(Slams the window to, walks over to the
    throne and sits down)* I can stretch along the floor,
    rise up the wall and fall through the window at one

173

and the same time. Is he capable of such flexibility?
I can lie on the pavement and the passers-by, the
wheels, the horses' hooves will not cause me the
slightest harm. . . Could he adapt himself in this
way to any conditions? In two weeks I've got to
know life a thousand times better than he.
Noiselessly, like a shadow, I penetrated everywhere
and peeped, and eavesdropped, and read other
people's letters. I know all the shadow side of
things. And now I'm sitting on a throne and he
lies at my feet.

*(The door opens wide and the Commander of the
Guards enters)*

PIETRO.   A letter for your Majesty.

SHADOW.   Give it me. *(Reads)* 'I have come. Christian-
Theodore.' Where is he?

PIETRO.   Just outside the door, your Majesty.

SHADOW.   Let him come in.

*(The Commander of the Guards goes out. The
SAVANT comes in. He stops in front of the
throne)*

SHADOW.   Well, how are your affairs, Christian-
Theodore?

SAVANT.   My affairs are bad, Theodore-Christian.

SHADOW.   In which way are they bad?

SAVANT.   I suddenly found myself completely alone.

SHADOW.   But what about your friends?

SAVANT.   They've been told lies about me.

SHADOW.   And where's the girl you loved?

SAVANT.   She's now your fiancée.

SHADOW.   But whose fault is all this, Christian-
Theodore?

SAVANT.   It's your fault, Theodore-Christian.

SHADOW.   That's what I call a real conversation
between a man and his shadow. Secret Counsellor!

(SECRET COUNSELLOR runs in)

174

SHADOW. Call everybody here. Be quick!

(Enter the PRINCESS *who sits down beside the* SHADOW. *The* COURTIERS *come in and stand around in a semi-circle. The* DOCTOR *is among them).*

SHADOW. Sit down!

COURTIERS. We won't sit down.

SHADOW. Sit down!

COURTIERS. We daren't.

SHADOW. Sit down!

COURTIERS. Well, we will if you so wish. *(They sit down).*

SHADOW. Gentlemen! Before you stands a man whom I wish to make happy. The whole of his life he's been a failure. At last he has had some luck in that I've ascended the throne. I appoint him to be my shadow. Congratulate him, gentlemen.

(The COURTIERS *stand up and bow).*

SHADOW. I make him equal in rank and honours to the Royal Secretary.

MAJORDOMO. *(In a loud whisper to the* FLUNKEYS). Prepare six-and-a-half pastries for him.

SHADOW. Don't feel embarrassed, Christian-Theodore. If in the beginning you find it rather difficult, I can give you several good lessons, similar to those you've received in the last few days. And very soon you'll be transformed into a real shadow, Christian-Theodore. Take your place at our feet!

PRIME MINISTER. Your Majesty, his appointment hasn't been formalized yet. Allow me to give orders to the Commander of the Guards to take him away until tomorrow.

SHADOW. No! Christian-Theodore! Take your place at our feet.

SAVANT. Not for anything in the world! Gentlemen! Listen as gravely as I'm going to speak. *There* stands the real shadow! My shadow! He has usurped the throne! D'you hear me?

175

PRIME MINISTER. I knew this was going to happen. Sire!

SHADOW. *(Calmly)* Prime Minister, be quiet. Go on, say what you wish, you failure! I'll enjoy watching the very last failure of your life.

SAVANT. Princess, I've never renounced you. He's deceived and confused both you and me.

PRINCESS. I'm not going to talk to you.

SAVANT. But don't you remember, you wrote me that you were ready to leave the palace and go away with me, wherever I go?

PRINCESS. I won't, I won't, I won't talk to you!

SAVANT. But I've come to take you away, Princess! Give me your hand, and let us run away. To be the wife of a Shadow — that means to be changed into a monstrously ugly and vicious frog.

PRINCESS. What you're saying is very unpleasant. Why should I listen to you!

SAVANT. Louise!

PRINCESS. I'll say nothing.

SAVANT. Gentlemen!

SECRET COUNSELLOR. I advise you not to listen to him. Really well brought-up people simply don't notice the behaviour of the ill-mannered.

SAVANT. Gentlemen! This cruel creature on the throne will ruin all of you. He's at the summit of power but he's empty. He's already losing strength and doesn't know what to do next. And he'll begin tormenting you all, out of sheer boredom and idleness.

FIRST COURTIER. My little lark eats out of my hand. And my little starling calls me 'papa'.

SAVANT. Yulia! We've made friends with you, haven't we? And you know who I am. Tell them!

MINISTER OF FINANCE. Yulia, I adore you, but if you allow yourself to say or do anything you shouldn't, I'll grind you into dust.

SAVANT. Yulia, do tell them!

YULIA. *(Pointing at the* SAVANT) The Shadow is
yourself.

SAVANT. Can it be possible that I'm a voice in a
wilderness?

ANNUNZIATA. No, no! My father threatened all the
time that he'd kill you, that's why I've kept silent.
Gentlemen, listen to me! *(Pointing at the*
SHADOW) There's the Shadow. I give you my
word! *(There is a slight movement among the*
COURTIERS) I myself saw how he left Mr Savant.
I'm not lying. The whole town knows that I'm a
truthful girl.

PIETRO. She can't be a witness.

SAVANT. Why not?

PIETRO. She's in love with you.

SAVANT. Is this true, Annunziata?

ANNUNZIATA. Yes, forgive me for this. And all the
same, gentlemen, listen to me!

SAVANT. That's enough, Annunziata. Thank you.
Hey, you! Even though you don't want to believe
me, you've got to believe your own eyes. Shadow!
Know thy place!

(The SHADOW *gets up with difficulty, struggling
with himself, and goes up to the* SAVANT)

PRIME MINISTER. Look! He copies all his movements!
Help!

SAVANT. Shadow! This man is merely a shadow.
You're only a shadow, Theodore-Christian!

SHADOW. Yes, I'm a shadow, Christian-Theodore!
No! Don't believe this! It's a lie! I'll give orders to
have you executed!

SAVANT. You will not dare, Theodore-Christian.

SHADOW. *(Falls down)* I will not dare, Christian-
Theodore.

PRIME MINISTER. That's enough. Everything's clear
to me. This Savant is a madman. And his illness is

177

infectious. Our Sovereign's fallen ill, but he'll get better! Flunkeys, carry the Sovereign away. *(The* FLUNKEYS *carry out his order. The* PRINCESS *runs after them)* Guards! *(Enter the* CORPORAL *with a detachment of soldiers)* Take him! Doctor! *(The* DOCTOR *comes out of the crowd of* COURTIERS. *The* PRIME MINISTER *points at the* SAVANT.) He's a madman, isn't he?

DOCTOR. *(Waves his hand)* I've been telling him a long time that this is madness.

PRIME MINISTER. Is his madness infectious?

DOCTOR. Yes. I've nearly caught his madness from him.

PRIME MINISTER. Is he curable?

DOCTOR. No.

PRIME MINISTER. Then it means we must cut his head off.

SECRET COUNSELLOR. Permit me, Mr Prime Minister! I'm the Master of Ceremonies, and the festivities are my responsibility.

PRIME MINISTER. Well. . . well. . .

SECRET COUNSELLOR. It would be brutal, it would be inhuman to cut off the head of a poor madman. I protest against execution, but it's clearly necessary to perform a slight medical operation on this poor fellow's head, and do it at once. A medical operation will not overcloud our festivities.

PRIME MINISTER. This is beautifully expressed.

SECRET COUNSELLOR. Our much respected doctor, as is well known, is a therapist, not a surgeon. For that reason, in order to amputate the diseased organ, I would advise making use of the services of Mr Royal Executioner.

PRIME MINISTER. Mr Royal Executioner!

FIRST COURTIER. Ready in a moment! *(He gets up and says to his lady neighbour as he pulls on white gloves)* Will you please excuse me? I'll be back soon, and I'll tell you then how I saved the life of my poor rabbits. *(To the* PRIME MINISTER*)* I'm ready.

ANNUNZIATA. Do let me say good-bye to him! Good-bye, Christian-Theodore!

SAVANT. Good-bye, Annunziata.

ANNUNZIATA. Are you afraid, Christian-Theodore?

SAVANT. Yes. But I'm not asking for mercy. I. . .

PRIME MINISTER. Drums!

(The DRUMMER *beats his drum)*

PRIME MINISTER. March!

PIETRO. March!

CORPORAL. March!

(The detachment of soldiers leads out the SAVANT. *The* EXECUTIONER *follows them)*

PRIME MINISTER. Gentlemen, I ask you to come out on to the balcony to watch the fireworks. And here meanwhile they can prepare cooling and calming beverages.

(Everyone gets up and moves towards the exit. Only ANNUNZIATA *and* YULIA *remain on the stage)*

YULIA. Annunziata, I couldn't act differently. Forgive me.

ANNUNZIATA. He's perfectly healthy — and yet, he's got to die so suddenly!

YULIA. I, too, find this terribly, terribly unpleasant, believe me. But what a scoundrel that doctor is! To betray so good a friend of his in that way!

ANNUNZIATA. But what about yourself?

YULIA. But how can you compare us? That miserable doctor wouldn't have lost anything by it. And I love the stage so much! Are you crying?

ANNUNZIATA. No. I will cry in my own room.

YULIA. One must learn to throw out of one's head everything that makes one suffer. You make a slight movement of your head — that's all. Just like that. Try it.

179

ANNUNZIATA. I don't want to.

YULIA. You're wrong there. Don't turn away from me.
I swear to you, I'm quite ready to kill myself—so sorry
do I feel for him. But this must remain between ourselves.

ANNUNZIATA. Is he still alive?

YULIA. Of course, of course! When everything's finished,
they'll beat the drum.

ANNUNZIATA. I don't believe that nothing can be done.
I implore you, Yulia, let us stop it! We must go there. . .
Hurry up!

YULIA. Quiet!

(The DOCTOR comes in quickly)

DOCTOR. Wine!

MAJORDOMO. Wine for the Doctor!

YULIA. Annunziata, if you give me your word that
you'll keep silent about it, I'll try to help you.

ANNUNZIATA. I won't tell anybody, I give you my
word of honour. But do it quickly.

YULIA. There's no need to hurry. My remedy can help
only when everything's finished. Be silent. Listen
attentively. *(Goes up to the DOCTOR)* Doctor!

DOCTOR. Yes, Yulia.

YULIA. I know what you're thinking about.

DOCTOR. Yes, about wine.

YULIA. No, about water.

DOCTOR. I'm not in the mood for joking just now,
Yulia.

YULIA. You know that I'm not joking.

DOCTOR. Do give me a moment just to calm down.

YULIA. I regret it, but it's impossible. Presently, our
common acquaintance is going to be. . . well, in a
word, you understand what I mean.

DOCTOR. But what can I do?

YULIA. What about the water?

DOCTOR. What water?

YULIA. Remember the time when you and I were such

180

friends? Once the moon was shining, the stars were
brilliant, and you told me that you'd discovered
living water which cured all illness and even
resurrected the dead if they were good people?

ANNUNZIATA.   Doctor, is this true? Is there such
water?

DOCTOR.   Yulia's joking, as always.

ANNUNZIATA.   You're lying, I can see that. I'll kill
you straight away!

DOCTOR.   I'll be very glad if you do.

ANNUNZIATA.   Doctor, you will wake up tomorrow
but he'll never wake up again! He used to call you
his friend, his comrade.

DOCTOR.   Silly, unfortunate little girl! What can I do?
All the water is in their hands, behind seven doors,
seven locks, and the keys are in the hands of the
Minister of Finance.

YULIA.   I don't believe you hadn't kept a bottle for
yourself, for a rainy day.

DOCTOR.   No, Yulia. I'm so honest that I didn't keep
a single drop for myself, as I couldn't cure
everybody.

YULIA.   Miserable man!

DOCTOR.   But the Minister of Finance loves you. Ask
him for the key, Yulia!

YULIA.   I? Egoist! You want to push the whole burden
on to my shoulders!

ANNUNZIATA.   Madam!

YULIA.   Not a word more! I've done all I can.

ANNUNZIATA.   Doctor!

DOCTOR.   What can I do?

MAJORDOMO.   His Majesty!

(The hall fills up with COURTIERS. *The*
SHADOW *and the* PRINCESS *come in slowly.
They sit down on the throne. The* PRIME
MINISTER *makes a sign to the* MAJORDOMO)

181

MAJORDOMO.   Presently, the soloist of his Majesty,
whose protector is his Excellency Mr the Minister
of Finance, Lady Yulia Djuly, will perform a
cooling and calming little song, entitled: 'It's
best not to lose your head'.

SHADOW.   'It's best not to lose your head'. . .
Excellent!

YULIA.   *(Makes a deep curtsey to the King, bows to
the* COURTIERS. *Sings)*

> Once there lived a dragon-fly,
> She was a dreadful flirt,
> Her pretty face and shining eyes
> Worked the ruin of many flies —
> And to her victims she often said:
> 'You shouldn't ever lose your head'. . .

*(Loud beating of the drums interrupts the
song.)*

SHADOW.   *(Jumps up, reeling)* Water!

(The MAJORDOMO *rushes up to the* SHADOW
and stops, struck with amazement. The
SHADOW's *head suddenly flies off his
shoulders. The headless* SHADOW *is sitting,
motionless on the throne)*

ANNUNZIATA.   Look!

MINISTER OF FINANCE.   Why has that. . .?

PRIME MINISTER.   Oh, my God! We haven't
foreseen this! After all, it's his own shadow.
Gentlemen, you're present at a reception in the
Royal Palace. You must feel gay, gay, whatever
happens!

PRINCESS.   *(Runs up to the* MINISTERS*)*
Immediately! Immediately! At once!

PRIME MINISTER.   What, your Highness?

PRINCESS.   Put him right at once! I don't want this!
I don't want this! I don't want it!

PRIME MINISTER.   Princess, I implore you, stop it!

PRINCESS.   And what would you say if your fiancé
lost his head?

SECRET COUNSELLOR. That's from love, Princess.

PRINCESS. If you don't put him right, I'll order all of you to be beheaded! All the Princesses in the world have husbands that are complete, and look what I've got? What a dirty trick!

PRIME MINISTER. Living water! Quickly! Quickly! Hurry up!

MINISTER OF FINANCE. For whom? For this man? But it resurrects only good people.

PRIME MINISTER. Well, we'll have to ressurect the good one. Ah! I don't feel at all like doing it!

MINISTER OF FINANCE. There's no other way out. Doctor! Follow me! Flunkeys, lead me! *(Goes out)*

PRIME MINISTER. Calm yourself, Princess. Everything will be done.

(FIRST COURTIER enters, taking off his gloves. Noticing the headless King, he stops dead in his tracks.)

FIRST COURTIER. Excuse me, but who's done that? It's enough for me to absent myself from a room for half-an-hour, and my job is pinched from me. These intriguers!

(The door is flung open and an entire procession marches through. In front the FLUNKEYS lead the MINISTER OF FINANCE. Behind him four soldiers carry a large barrel. The barrel is emitting its own light. Tongues of flame break through the crevices. Shining drops fall on to the parquet floor. Behind the barrel walks the DOCTOR. The procession crosses the stage and goes out. The PRINCESS and the COURTIERS follow)

YULIA. Annunziata, you were right!

ANNUNZIATA. What about?

YULIA. He will conquer! This very moment he'll conquer! They brought the living water. It'll resurrect him.

ANNUNZIATA. Why would they want to resurrect a good man?

YULIA. So that the bad man could live. You're a fortunate girl, Annunziata.

ANNUNZIATA. I don't believe it. Something else will happen. Remember, we're in the palace.

YULIA. Ah, I'm afraid nothing else will happen. Will it really become fashionable — to be a good man? It's so troublesome.

C. BORGIA. Mr Commander of the Royal Guards!

PIETRO. What do you want?

C. BORGIA. The Courtiers are looking askance at us. Shall we show them a clean pair of heels?

PIETRO. The hell I know! They might catch us.

C. BORGIA. We got linked up with a failure.

PIETRO. I'll be damned if I ever forgive him!

C. BORGIA. To lose his head at such an important moment!

PIETRO. Blockhead! And in everyone's presence, too! Couldn't he go to his study and lose there anything he chose, the brute!

C. BORGIA. A tactless creature!

PIETRO. An ass!

C. BORGIA. You're right. We'll have to gobble him up. We'll have to.

PIETRO. Yes, we'll have to.

(Drums thunder. The head suddenly appears on the shoulders of the SHADOW)

C. BORGIA. Congratulations, your Majesty!

PIETRO. Hurrah, your Majesty!

MAJORDOMO. Would you like a drink of water, your Majesty?

SHADOW. Why is the hall so empty? Where's everyone? Louise!

(The PRINCESS *runs in, followed by the* COURTIERS)

PRINCESS. How your head becomes you, darling!

SHADOW. Louise, where is he?

184

PRINCESS. I don't know. How are you feeling, darling?

SHADOW. I find it rather painful to swallow.

PRINCESS. I'll make a compress for you to wear in the night.

SHADOW. Thank you. But where is he? Call him here!

(The PRIME MINISTER *and the* MINISTER OF FINANCE *run in)*

PRIME MINISTER. That's fine. Everything's in place.

MINISTER OF FINANCE. No changes!

PRIME MINISTER. Your Majesty, do us the favour of nodding your head.

SHADOW. Where is he?

PRIME MINISTER. Good! His head's working. Hurrah! Everything's in order.

SHADOW. I'm asking you, where is he?

PRIME MINISTER. And I'm replying — everything's in order, your Majesty. Presently he'll be thrown into jail.

SHADOW. Have you lost your reason? How dare you even think of it? Guard of honour!

PIETRO. Guard of honour!

SHADOW. Go, ask him, implore him to come here.

PIETRO. Ask and implore him — march!

(He goes out with the GUARDS*)*

PRINCESS. Why are you calling him here, Theodore-Christian?

SHADOW. I want to live.

PRINCESS. But you've told me that he's a failure.

SHADOW. All that's true, but I can't live without him!

(The DOCTOR *runs in)*

DOCTOR. He's recovered! Listen, all of you! He behaved like a madman, went straight ahead, taking no turnings. . . he was executed — and here he is, alive, alive more than any of us!

185

MAJORDOMO. His Serene Highness Mr Savant.

(Enter the SAVANT. *The* SHADOW *jumps up and stretches his arms towards him. The* SAVANT *takes no notice of him)*

SAVANT. Annunziata!

ANNUNZIATA. I'm here.

SAVANT. Annunziata! They didn't give me time to finish what I was telling you. Yes, Annunziata, I was afraid of dying. You see, I'm still so young.

SHADOW. Christian!

SAVANT. Be quiet! But I went to meet my death, Annunziata. You see, if you want to conquer, you must be prepared to die. And now I've conquered. Come away from here, Annunziata!

SHADOW. No! Stay with me, Christian! Live in the palace. Not a single hair would fall from your head! If you wish, I'll appoint you my Prime Minister.

PRIME MINISTER. But why precisely Prime Minister? Here's the Minister of Finance who's ailing. . .

MINISTER OF FINANCE. I – ailing? Look! *(He skips lightly around the hall)*

PRIME MINISTER. He's recovered!

MINISTER OF FINANCE. In moments of real danger we businessmen grow wings on our feet.

SHADOW. If you wish, I'll drive them all out, Christian. I'll let you govern — within reasonable limits, of course. I'll help you to make a certain number of people happy. You don't want to answer me? Louise! Order him to.

PRINCESS. Be quiet, you coward! What have you done, gentlemen! For once in my life I met a good man, and all of you attacked him like a pack of wolves. Away! Get out of here, Shadow!

(The SHADOW *slowly descends from the throne and presses himself against the wall, wrapping his cloak around him)*

PRINCESS. You may assume any pitiful posture you like! You won't make me feel pity for you! Gentlemen! He's no longer my fiancé. I'll find a new fiancé for myself.

SECRET COUNSELLOR. Oh, what joyous news!

PRINCESS. Now I've understood everything, Christian, dear. Hey! Commander of the Guards. Arrest him! *(She points at the* SHADOW*)*

PIETRO. With pleasure. *(To* GUARDS*)* Take him. *(Goes to the* SHADOW.*)*

PRIME MINISTER. I'll help you!

MINISTER OF FINANCE. I, too, I, too!

C. BORGIA. Down, Shadow!

(They seize the SHADOW *but there is no one there. An empty cloak hangs over their arms)*

PRINCESS. He's run away!

SAVANT. He's vanished, so that he can stand in my way again and again. But I'll recognize him, I'll recognize him anywhere! Annunziata, give my your hand and let's go away from here.

ANNUNZIATA. How are you feeling now, Christian-Theodore, my dear?

SAVANT. I find it rather painful to swallow. Good-bye, gentlemen.

PRINCESS. Christian-Theodore, forgive me! I've made only one mistake, after all! Well, I've been punished, and that's enough. Stay here, or take me with you. I'll behave very well. You'll see.

SAVANT. No, Princess.

PRINCESS. Don't go! What an unfortunate girl I am! Gentlemen, you ask him.

COURTIERS. Where are you off to? Do stay! Sit down, please. . . Why are you in such a hurry? The night is young yet. . .

SAVANT. Forgive me, gentlemen, but I'm far too busy. *(He takes* ANNUNZIATA'*s hand and walks along with her)*

PRINCESS. Christian-Theodore! It's raining outside. It's dark. And in the palace, it's warm and cosy. I'll give orders to heat up all the stoves. Do stay!

SAVANT. No. We'll put on more warm clothes and
drive away. Don't delay us, gentlemen.

C. BORGIA. Give way, give way to him! Here are
your goloshes, Mr Professor.

PIETRO. Here's a cloak. *(To* ANNUNZIATA) Put a
word in for your father, you unnatural girl!

CORPORAL. The carriage is at the gates.

SAVANT. Annunziata, we begin our journey.

C U R T A I N

1940

THE DRAGON

CHARACTERS

Lancelot
Cat
Charlemagne
Elsa
Dragon
Mayor
Henrik
Sentry. Girl-Friends of Elsa. Servants. Donkey.
Crowd. Gaoler. Hatter. Weavers. Musical Instruments'
Maker. Gardener. Smith.

ACT ONE

A spacious kitchen, comfortable and very clean. A large hearth in the background. Floor of shiny stone flags. In front of the hearth an armchair, on which CAT *is dozing.*

LANCELOT. *(Enters, looks round and calls)* Mister! Mistress! Answer me! Is there anyone alive here? No one. . . The house is empty, the gate wide open and the door unlocked. . . The windows are wide open, too. . . What a good thing I'm an honest man, or else I'd be all of a tremble now, looking over my shoulder, choosing the most expensive things and taking to my heels as fast as I could — when I really feel I'd like to have a good rest. *(Sits down)* I can wait, though. Mr Cat! Will your masters be back soon? Eh? Won't you answer?

CAT. No, I'd rather keep silent.

LANCELOT. And why, may I ask?

CAT. When you're warm and you've got a soft cushion to lie on, it's wiser just to doze and hold your tongue, my friend.

LANCELOT. All the same, where are your masters?

CAT. They've gone out, and I'm very pleased about it.

LANCELOT. Don't you like them?

CAT. I love them with every hair of my fur and with my paws and whiskers, too, but a terrible sorrow is in store for them. My mind is only at rest when they're out of the house.

LANCELOT. Is that how it is? So a terrible sorrow's in store for them? What is it? Won't you answer me?

CAT. No, I'd rather keep silent.

LANCELOT. Why?

CAT. When you're warm and resting comfortably, it's wiser to doze and keep mum, than talk about unpleasant future events. Mi-ou!

LANCELOT. Cat, you frighten me! It's so cosy in this

191

kitchen, the fire in the hearth is so well laid. I
simply don't want to believe that a disaster is
threatening this charming, spacious house.
Cat! What's been happening here? Answer me!
Come on!

CAT. Let me sleep, Stranger.

LANCELOT. Just listen, Cat! You don't know me. I'm
a person of such light weight that I'm carried all
over the world like a bit of down. And I find it
very easy to meddle in other people's affairs. For
that reason I've been wounded — slightly,
nineteen times, badly, five times and almost
fatally, three times. But I'm still alive because I'm
not only as light as a feather but also as stubborn
as a donkey. Come on, speak up, Cat! Tell me
what's been happening here! Suppose I could
save your masters? That sort of thing does happen
to me on occasions. Well? Come on! What's your
name?

CAT. Máshenka.

LANCELOT. I thought you were a tom-cat.

CAT. Yes, I am a tom, but people are sometimes so
unobservant. My masters are still surprised even at
this late stage that I haven't had kittens at least
once. They keep asking me: 'What's the matter
with you, Máshenka?' The poor, dear people! I'm
not going to say another word!

LANCELOT. At least tell me who your masters are?

CAT. Mr Charlemagne, the Archivist, and his only
daughter — she's got such lovely, soft hands.
Sweet, charming, quiet Elsa.

LANCELOT. But which of the two is threatened with
disaster?

CAT. Oh, she is — but that means all of us.

LANCELOT. But what is it that's threatening her?
Come on now!

CAT. Mi-ou! It's nearly four hundred years ago that the
Dragon took up his abode above our town.

LANCELOT. A dragon? How charming!

CAT. He imposed a tribute on our town. Every year he

192

chooses a girl and we surrender her up to him without so much as a mi-ou. And he leads her away to his cave and we never see her again. I've been told that the girls die in the cave out of sheer disgust. Hss! Get out! Go away! Hss!

LANCELOT. Who are you saying this to?

CAT. To the Dragon. He's chosen our Elsa, the accursed lizard!

LANCELOT. How many heads has he got?

CAT. Three.

LANCELOT. That's a fair number. And how many paws?

CAT. Four.

LANCELOT. Well, that's not too bad. With claws?

CAT. Yes. Five claws on each paw. And every claw is as big as a stag's horn.

LANCELOT. Really? And are the claws sharp?

CAT. As sharp as knives.

LANCELOT. H-mm. So that's the way it is! . . . And does he breathe out fire?

CAT. Yes.

LANCELOT. Real fire?

CAT. He sets the forests alight.

LANCELOT. Aha! Has he got scales?

CAT. Yes, he has.

LANCELOT. And I dare say his scales are pretty tough?

CAT. They're substantial.

LANCELOT. Well, how, for instance?

CAT. You couldn't cut them with a diamond.

LANCELOT. I see. I've got the idea. What about his size?

CAT. He's about as big as a church.

LANCELOT. Aha! That's all clear now. Well, thank you, Cat.

CAT. Will you fight him?

LANCELOT. I'll see. . .

CAT. I implore you — do challenge him to a fight. He'll kill you, of course — but while it's all going on, I'll still have time to day-dream, stretched out in front of the hearth. I'll picture to myself that by some accident or miracle, you've somehow managed, unexpectedly, against all the probabilities, to kill him.

LANCELOT. Thank you, Cat.

CAT. Get up.

LANCELOT. What's the matter?

CAT. They're coming.

LANCELOT. I do hope I find her attractive. Oh, how I do hope I like her! It would be such a help. . . *(Looks through the window)* I do like her. Cat, she's a very charming girl. But what does this mean? Cat! She's smiling! She's perfectly calm! And her father's smiling and cheerful, too. Have you been deceiving me?

CAT. No. That's the saddest part of it all — they keep smiling. Be quiet now! Good evening, my dear friends. Shall we have supper now?

(Enter ELSA *and* CHARLEMAGNE)

LANCELOT. Good evening to you, Sir — and to you, lovely young lady!

CHARLEMAGNE. Good evening, young man.

LANCELOT. Your house looked so inviting, the gate was open and the fire was burning in the kitchen, so I came in without being invited. Forgive me.

CHARLEMAGNE. There's no need to ask forgiveness. Our doors are open to everybody.

ELSA. Sit down, please. Let me take your hat. I'll hang it behind the door. I'll lay the table in a minute. But is there anything the matter?

LANCELOT. No, nothing.

ELSA. I had the impression for a moment that I. . .
frightened you.

LANCELOT. Oh, no. . . There's nothing the matter.

CHARLEMAGNE. Sit down, my friend. I like strangers.
Maybe that's because I've lived all my life in this
town and I've never been anywhere else. Where do
you come from?

LANCELOT. From the South.

CHARLEMAGNE. And did you have many adventures
on the way?

LANCELOT. Oh, yes! More than I really wanted.

ELSA. I'm sure you must be tired. Do sit down. Why
are you standing?

LANCELOT. Thank you.

CHARLEMAGNE. You can have a good rest here. Our
town's a very quiet place. Nothing ever happens
here.

LANCELOT. Never?

CHARLEMAGNE. Never. It's true that last week we
had a very strong wind. It nearly blew the roof off
one of the houses. But that's not such a great event,
after all.

ELSA. Here's the supper. Please have something. Well,
why don't you sit down?

LANCELOT. Excuse me, but. . . You say your town is
a very quiet place?

ELSA. Certainly.

LANCELOT. But. . . what about the Dragon?

CHARLEMAGNE. Oh, that. . . But we've got so
accustomed to him. He's been living with us for
the last four hundred years.

LANCELOT. But I've been told. . . that. . . your daughter. . .

ELSA. Mr Stranger. . .

LANCELOT. My name's Lancelot.

195

ELSA. Mr Lancelot, excuse me, I don't want to be discourteous. . . but I beg you all the same — not a word about this.

LANCELOT. Why not?

ELSA. Because nothing can be done about it.

LANCELOT. Is this really true?

CHARLEMAGNE. Yes, there's nothing to be done. Just now we took a walk in the woods and we talked everything over so well and thoroughly. Tomorrow, as soon as the Dragon takes her away, I shall die, too.

ELSA. Father, there's no need to talk about this.

CHARLEMAGNE. That's all then. I won't say any more.

LANCELOT. Excuse me, may I ask you just one more question? Has no one ever tried to fight him?

CHARLEMAGNE. Not in the last two hundred years. Before that, people often had fights with him, but he killed all his opponents. He's a superb tactician. He attacks his enemy suddenly, showers stones on him from above, then he swoops down straight at the head of his opponent's horse, and breathes fire on it, so that the poor animal is completely demoralized. And then he tears the rider to pieces with his claws. So, in the end people stopped challenging him to a fight.

LANCELOT. Hasn't the town ever risen up against him?

CHARLEMAGNE. Yes, it has.

LANCELOT. Well, what happened?

CHARLEMAGNE. He burnt down all the suburbs and drove half the inhabitants out of their minds with his poisonous smoke. He's a great fighter.

ELSA. Please help yourself to some more butter. Do!

LANCELOT. Yes, yes, I will take some more. I must build up my strength. And so — forgive my asking you so many questions — no one makes any attempt

196

to stand up to the Dragon? He's completely shameless now?

CHARLEMAGNE.   Oh, no! What an idea! He's a very kind dragon.

LANCELOT.   Kind?

CHARLEMAGNE.   I assure you he is. When our town was threatened with a cholera epidemic, the town doctor requested him to breathe fire on to the lake to make it boil. Then the whole town drank boiled water and was spared the epidemic.

LANCELOT.   Was that long ago?

CHARLEMAGNE.   Oh, no. Only eighty-two years ago. But good deeds are never forgotten.

LANCELOT.   And what other good deeds has he done?

CHARLEMAGNE.   He freed us from the Gipsies.

LANCELOT.   But the Gipsies are very charming people.

CHARLEMAGNE.   Whatever are you saying! How dreadful! It's true I've never seen a Gipsy in my life but even at school I've learned that they're dreadful people.

LANCELOT.   But why?

CHARLEMAGNE.   They are vagabonds by nature, it's in their blood. They're enemies of any kind of State system, otherwise they'd have settled down somewhere and wouldn't have wandered all over the place. Their songs lack in virility and their ideas are destructive. They steal children. They sneak in everywhere. Now we're completely clear of them, but only a hundred years ago any man with black hair was under an obligation to prove that he had no Gipsy blood in him.

LANCELOT.   Who's told you all that about the Gipsies?

CHARLEMAGNE.   Our Dragon. The Gipsies had the impertinence to rise against him in the early years of his reign.

LANCELOT.   They had? Fine, impatient people!

197

CHARLEMAGNE. Don't! Don't talk like that, please!

LANCELOT. And what does he eat, your Dragon?

CHARLEMAGNE. Every month our town gives him a thousand cows, two thousand sheep, five thousand hens and eighty pounds of salt. In the summer and autumn we add the produce of ten kitchen gardens — lettuce, asparagus and cauliflower.

LANCELOT. He's eating you out of house and home.

CHARLEMAGNE. Oh, no, what an idea! We're not complaining. How could it be done in any other way? While he's here no other dragon will dare touch us.

LANCELOT. Surely all other dragons have been exterminated long ago!

CHARLEMAGNE. But what if they haven't been? I assure you — the only certain way of keeping free from dragons is to have one of your own. That's enough about him, I beg you. You'd better tell us something interesting about your own experiences.

LANCELOT. Very well. Do you know what a book of complaints is?

ELSA. No.

LANCELOT. Well, I'll tell you. About five years' walk from here, in the Black Mountains, there's an enormous cave. And in that cave there lies a book which is half filled with writing. No one touches it, yet page after page gets added to those that have already been filled in. Every day something is added. Who writes these pages? The world! The mountains, the grasses, the stones, the trees, the rivers, they all see what men are doing. They know about all the misdeeds of criminals, about the miseries of everyone who suffers through no fault of his own. From branch to branch, from raindrop to raindrop, from cloud to cloud, the complaints of humanity reach the book in the Black Mountains, and the book is growing. If there were no book like that in the world, the trees would wither away out of anguish and the waters would turn bitter. And for whom is that book written? For me.

ELSA. For you?

LANCELOT. For us. For me and for a few others. We are observant people, quick on the uptake. We found out that there was such a book, and we weren't too lazy to find our way to it. And he who glances inside that book, even once, will never rest for centuries. Ah, what a book it is, that book of complaints! It's impossible not to respond to those complaints. And we do respond.

ELSA. How do you respond?

LANCELOT. We involve ourselves in other people's affairs. We help those whom it's necessary to help, and we destroy those whom it's necessary to destroy. Do you want me to help you?

ELSA. How?

CHARLEMAGNE. In what way can you help us?

CAT. Mi-aou!

LANCELOT. I've been almost mortally wounded three times, and it was always just by the very people I was trying to save against their will. But all the same — though you're not asking me to do it — I will challenge the Dragon to a fight. Elsa, do you hear?

ELSA. Oh, no! He'll surely kill you and that will poison the last hours of my life.

CAT. Mi-aou!

LANCELOT. I shall challenge the Dragon to a fight!

(A noise of whistling, howling and roaring is heard. It increases until the window panes rattle. A great glow of light flares up outside the windows)

CAT. Talk of the devil!. . .

(The howling and whistling suddenly break off. There is a loud knocking on the door)

199

CHARLEMAGNE.   Come in!

(Enter a richly dressed FOOTMAN)

FOOTMAN.   Mr Dragon's come to visit you.

CHARLEMAGNE.   He's welcome.

(The FOOTMAN *flings the door wide open. A pause. Then a* MAN *enters, middle-aged but strong and youthful-looking. He has a soldier's bearing. His fair hair is cut* en brosse. *He smiles broadly. In general, his manner, despite a slight roughness, has something agreeable about it. He is slightly deaf)*

MAN.   Hullo, you people! How are you, Elsa, my little one? I see you have a visitor. Who is he?

CHARLEMAGNE.   He's a stranger, he happened to be passing by.

MAN.   What's that? Report in a clear, loud voice, like a soldier.

CHARLEMAGNE.   He's a stranger.

MAN.   Not a Gipsy?

CHARLEMAGNE.   Good gracious, no! He's a very nice man.

MAN.   Eh?

CHARLEMAGNE.   A nice man.

MAN.   Very good. Stranger! Why don't you look at me? Why are you staring at the door?

LANCELOT.   I'm waiting for the Dragon to come in.

MAN.   Ha-ha! *I* am the Dragon.

LANCELOT.   You! But I was told that you've got three heads, huge claws and are enormously tall.

DRAGON.   Today I am visiting privately, without insisting on my rank.

CHARLEMAGNE.   Mr Dragon's been living among people for such a long time that sometimes he turns into a man himself and comes to visit us like a friend.

DRAGON.   Yes, we truly are friends, my dear Charlemagne. In fact, I'm even more than just a friend to you all. I'm your childhood friend.

200

More than that, indeed. I was the childhood friend of your father, your grand-father and your great-grandfather. I remember your great-grandfather when he was still in short breeches. What the hell?. . . An involuntary tear! I see the visitor's staring at me. You didn't expect me to show such feeling? Well, answer me! He's quite taken aback, the son of a bitch! Well, well. . . No matter. Ha-ha! Elsa!

ELSA. Yes, Mr Dragon.

DRAGON. Give me your little paw.

(ELSA *puts her hand out to the* DRAGON)

DRAGON. You little mischief! What a warm little paw! Raise your little muzzle higher! Now smile! That's it. What's up, Stranger? Eh?

LANCELOT. I'm admiring the spectacle.

DRAGON. Smart fellow! You give your answers smartly. Go on admiring then! Our manners are simple, Stranger. Soldiers' manners. One, two, buckle my shoe! Get on with your eating.

LANCELOT. Thanks, I'm not hungry any more.

DRAGON. No matter. Go on eating. Why have you come here?

LANCELOT. On business.

DRAGON. What kind of business? Come on now, tell me. Eh? Maybe I can help you. Why have you come here?

LANCELOT. I've come to kill you.

DRAGON. Speak louder!

ELSA. No, no! He's joking. Would you like to hold my hand again, Mr Dragon?

DRAGON. What's it you're saying?

LANCELOT. I'm challenging you to a fight. Do you hear me, you Dragon?

(The DRAGON *remains silent but turns purple)*

LANCELOT. For the third time I challenge you to a fight! D'you hear?

(A terrifying, deafening, triple roar is heard. Despite its great volume, which makes the walls shake, this roar is not without certain musical quality. There is nothing human about it — it is the DRAGON roaring, as he clenches his fists and stamps his feet)

DRAGON. *(Suddenly stops roaring. Calmly)* Well, you fool? Why don't you say anything? Aren't you frightened?

LANCELOT. No.

DRAGON. No?

LANCELOT. No.

DRAGON. Very well then. *(He makes a slight movement with his shoulders and suddenly undergoes a most striking change. A new head appears on his shoulders and the previous head vanishes without a trace. In front of LANCELOT stands a man, serious, restrained, with fair, greying hair, a high forehead and a narrow face)*

CAT. Don't be surprised, dear Lancelot. He's got three heads. He changes them when he feels like it.

DRAGON. *(His voice is changed like his face. He speaks quietly and rather flatly)* Your name is Lancelot?

LANCELOT. Yes, it is.

DRAGON. Are you a descendant of the well-known knight-errant, named Lancelot?

LANCELOT. He was a distant relative of mine.

DRAGON. I accept your challenge. Knights-errant are the same as Gipsies. You'll have to be annihilated.

LANCELOT. I won't let you annihilate me.

DRAGON. I've annihilated 809 knights, 905 men of unknown origin, one drunken old man, two madmen, two women, the mother and aunt of the girls chosen by me, and one little boy of 12, the brother of one of the girls. In addition to those,

202

I've destroyed six armies and five lots of rebels.
Please sit down.

LANCELOT. *(Sits down)* Thank you.

DRAGON. Do you smoke? Carry on — don't mind me!

LANCELOT. Thank you. *(Takes out a pipe and slowly fills it with tobacco)*

DRAGON. You know what day I was born on?

LANCELOT. On a very unhappy day.

DRAGON. It was the day of a terrible battle. On that day Atilla himself was defeated — can you imagine how many warriors had to be slaughtered for that? The ground was soaked with blood. The leaves on the trees turned brown by midnight. By dawn huge black mushrooms — they're called coffin mushrooms — sprang up under the trees. And after the mushrooms I crawled out of the ground. I am the son of war. War is me! The blood of the dead Huns flows through my veins. It is cold blood — in battle I am cold, calm and precise.

(As he says the word 'precise', the DRAGON makes a slight movement with his hand. A dry click is heard and a ribbon of flame unfolds from the DRAGON's second finger. It lights the tobacco in LANCELOT's pipe which he has just finished filling)

LANCELOT. Thank you. *(He inhales the smoke of his pipe with evident pleasure)*

DRAGON. You're against me — so it follows that you're against war, doesn't it?

LANCELOT. Why, no! I've been fighting all my life.

DRAGON. You're a stranger here, while we have learned to understand one another over the years. The whole town will look on you with horror and will rejoice in your death. Death without glory, that's going to be your fate! Do you understand that?

LANCELOT. No.

DRAGON. I see you're as determined as ever.

LANCELOT. Even more than I was before.

DRAGON. You're a worthy antagonist.

LANCELOT. Thank you.

DRAGON. I shall fight you in earnest.

LANCELOT. That's fine.

DRAGON. That means that I shall kill you at once. Now. Here.

LANCELOT. But I'm unarmed.

DRAGON. Do you want me to give you time to get armed? Oh, no! Didn't I tell you just now that I'm going to fight you in earnest? I'm going to attack you suddenly, now! . . . Elsa, bring the broom.

ELSA. What for?

DRAGON. In a moment I'm going to burn this man to ashes and you'll have to sweep it up.

LANCELOT. You're afraid of me!

DRAGON. I don't know what fear is.

LANCELOT. Why are you in such a hurry then? Give me until tomorrow. I'll find weapons for myself and we'll meet out on a battle field.

DRAGON. Why should we do that?

LANCELOT. So that the people won't think you're a coward.

DRAGON. The people won't know anything. These two here will keep quiet. You're going to die now — bravely, quietly and without glory.

(He raises his hand)

CHARLEMAGNE. Stop!

DRAGON. What is it?

CHARLEMAGNE. You mustn't kill him!

DRAGON. What!

CHARLEMAGNE. I beg you — don't be angry — I'm devoted to you with all my heart. But do remember, I'm an archivist.

DRAGON. What has your job to do with it?

CHARLEMAGNE. I have a document signed by you 382 years ago. This document has never been annulled. Now, I'm not objecting, I'm only reminding you. It has your signature on it — 'Dragon'.

DRAGON. Well, what of it?

CHARLEMAGNE. After all, she is my daughter. I'd like her to live a little longer. It's only natural.

DRAGON. Be brief!

CHARLEMAGNE. Whatever happens, I do object. You can't kill him. Anyone who challenges you has to remain in safety until the day of the battle — that's what you've written and confirmed by oath. And the day of the battle has to be fixed not by you but by whoever challenges you. That's what's written in the document and confirmed by oath. Also, the whole town has to help the challenger, and no one is to be punished — that's also confirmed by oath.

DRAGON. When was this document written?

CHARLEMAGNE. 382 years ago.

DRAGON. I was a naive, sentimental, inexperienced youth then.

CHARLEMAGNE. But the document hasn't been cancelled.

DRAGON. Whatever does it matter?

CHARLEMAGNE. But the document...

DRAGON. Oh, enough about the document! We are grown men now.

CHARLEMAGNE. But you yourself signed it... I can run and fetch it.

DRAGON. I forbid you to budge from here.

CHARLEMAGNE. Here's a man trying to save my daughter. It is permitted, isn't it, to love your own child — and besides, hospitality's permitted, too. Why are you looking at me with such a terrible expression? *(Covers his face with his hands)*

ELSA. Father, father!

205

CHARLEMAGNE. I protest!

DRAGON. Very well. Then I'll wipe out the whole
nest straight away!

LANCELOT. And the whole world will know that
you're a coward!

DRAGON. How will they know?

*(The CAT, with one giant leap, flies out through
the window. Outside, he hisses from a distance)*

CAT. I'll tell everybody, everything, you old lizard!
Everybody!

*(The DRAGON again bursts into a roar. This
roar is just as powerful as before, but this time the
sounds clearly distinguishable in it are moans,
coughs and a whizzing noise. It is the roar of a
huge, ancient, malevolent monster)*

DRAGON. *(Suddenly stopping his roar)* All right,
then! We'll fight tomorrow, as you asked.

*(He walks out quickly. And at once a whistling,
humming noise is heard outside. The walls
shake, the lamp flickers. Then the whistling
and humming gradually recede and die away)*

CHARLEMAGNE. He's flown away. What have I
done? Oh, what have I done! I could curse
myself — a selfish old man! But I couldn't act
any other way. Elsa, are you angry with me?

ELSA. No, certainly not!

CHARLEMAGNE. I feel terribly weak all of a sudden.
Forgive me. I'll lie down. No, no, don't accompany me. Stay with our guest. Amuse him with a
bit of conversation — after all, he's been so nice
to us. Excuse me, I'll go and lie down. *(Goes out)*

(A pause)

ELSA. Why did you start all this? I'm not reproaching
you — but everything was so straightforward and
dignified. It's not all that frightening to die
young — you don't grow old like everybody else.

LANCELOT. What a thing to say! Just think a little!
Even the trees sigh when they're cut down.

ELSA. But I'm not complaining.

LANCELOT.   Aren't you sorry for your father?

ELSA.   But he'll die just when he wishes to die.
Surely that's a great good fortune.

LANCELOT.   And you're not sorry to part with your
girl friends?

ELSA.   No. If it were not for me, the Dragon would
have chosen one of them.

LANCELOT.   And what about your fiancé?

ELSA.   How do you know that I have a fiancé?

LANCELOT.   I just felt it. Aren't you sorry to part
with your fiancé?

ELSA.   But you see, in order to console Henrik, the
Dragon has appointed him his private secretary.

LANCELOT.   Ah! that's how it is! Well then, of
course, you won't be so sorry to part with him.
But what about your native town? Aren't you
sorry to leave that?

ELSA.   But I'm being destroyed for the sake of my
native town.

LANCELOT.   And does the town accept your sacrifice
with indifference?

ELSA.   No, no. I shall disappear on Sunday, and until
the following Tuesday the town will be plunged
into deep mourning. For three whole days no
one will eat meat. And at tea they'll be served
with special buns called 'poor maids' in my
memory.

LANCELOT.   And is that all?

ELSA.   But what else can they do?

LANCELOT.   They can kill the Dragon.

ELSA.   That's impossible.

LANCELOT.   The Dragon has warped your soul,
poisoned your blood and dimmed your eyesight.
We shall have to put all this right.

ELSA.   You mustn't. If what you say about me is true,
it's better for me to die.

(The CAT *runs in)*

207

CAT. Eight of my cat friends and 48 of my own kittens ran around to all the houses and told everybody about the coming fight. Mi-aou! The Mayor is coming over here; he's running.

LANCELOT. The Mayor? Splendid!

(The MAYOR *runs in)*

MAYOR. Good day, Elsa. Where's this stranger?

LANCELOT. Here I am.

MAYOR. First of all, I must ask you to speak quietly and preferably without gestures. Move gently and don't look me straight in the face.

LANCELOT. Why?

MAYOR. Because my nerves are in a terrible state. I suffer from every nervous and psychological illness in existence. And in addition, I also suffer from three other diseases, hitherto unknown. Do you imagine it's easy to be Mayor under the Dragon?

LANCELOT. Well, when I kill the Dragon it'll be easier for you.

MAYOR. Easier! Ha-ha! Easier? Ha-ha! Easier! *(He becomes hysterical. Takes a drink of water. Calms down)* Your daring to challenge Mr Dragon to a fight is a calamity. All our affairs were in order. Mr Dragon was able, through his influence, completely to control my assistant, who's a rare scoundrel, as well as all his gang of men, merchants and flour-millers. Now everything will get mixed up. Mr Dragon will be preparing for the battle and he'll neglect the matters concerning the town administration to which he'd only recently begun to give attention.

LANCELOT. But can't you understand, you miserable man, that I'm going to save your town?

MAYOR. The town? Ha-ha! The town, the town! Ha-ha! *(Drinks water and calms down)* My assistant is such a scoundrel that I'd sacrifice two towns if I could only destroy him. I'd much rather have five dragons than a viper like him as my assistant. Do go away, I beg you!

LANCELOT. I won't go away.

MAYOR. Congratulations! Now you've brought on a
          cataleptic fit. *(He grows rigid, with a bitter smile
          on his lips)*

LANCELOT. Won't you understand that I'm going to
             save everybody?

   (The MAYOR *is silent)*

   Don't you understand?

   (The MAYOR *remains silent.* LANCELOT *throws
   water at him)*

MAYOR. No, I don't understand you. Who asked
          you to fight him?

LANCELOT. The whole town wants me to.

MAYOR. Really? Just you look out of the window!
          The leading men of the town have come running
          here to beg you to take yourself off.

LANCELOT. Where are they?

MAYOR. There, pressing themselves against the wall.
          Come nearer, friends!

LANCELOT. Why do they walk on tip-toe?

MAYOR. So that they won't upset my nerves.
          Friends, tell Mr Lancelot what you want from him.
          Well? One, two, three!

A CHORUS OF VOICES. *(Off)* Go away from us!
             Quickly, this very day!

   *(*LANCELOT *goes away from the window)*

MAYOR. You see! If you are a humane and cultured
          man, you'll submit to the will of the people.

LANCELOT. Not for anything.

MAYOR. Congratulations! Now you've driven me
          slightly off my head. *(He puts one arm akimbo
          and delicately curves up the other arm)* I'm a
          tea-pot. Use me for making tea.

LANCELOT. I understand why these little men
             came running here on tip-toe.

MAYOR. Why, then?

LANCELOT. So that they won't wake up the real men.
             I'm going to talk to *them* straight away! *(Runs out)*

209

MAYOR. *(Still pretending to be a tea-pot)* Boil me up!
(Dropping the pretence) However, what can he
do, in fact? The Dragon will issue an order and
we'll put him in goal. Now, Elsa dear, don't get
agitated. Precisely at the appointed time, to the
very second, our dear old Dragon will clasp you
in his arms. Be assured of that.

ELSA. All right.

(A knock on the door)

ELSA. Come in!

(Enter the FLUNKEY *who previously announced
the arrival of the* DRAGON)

MAYOR. Good day, Sonny.

FLUNKEY. Good-day, Father.

MAYOR. Have you come from him? There won't be
any battle, of course? Have you brought the
order to lock Lancelot up?

FLUNKEY. Mr Dragon orders as follows: first, fix the
battle for tomorrow; second, provide Lancelot
with weapons; and third, sharpen your wits.

MAYOR. Congratulations! You've driven me completely
out of my wits. Wits! Hey! Answer me! Show
yourselves!

FLUNKEY. I've been ordered to have a talk with
Elsa alone.

MAYOR. I'm going, I'm going, I'm going. *(Hurriedly
goes out)*

FLUNKEY. Good day, Elsa.

ELSA. Good day, Henrik.

HENRIK. Are you hoping that Lancelot will save you?

ELSA. No. Are you?

HENRIK. No, I'm not.

ELSA. What did the Dragon order you to tell me?

HENRIK. He ordered me to tell you that he wants
you to kill Lancelot if it becomes necessary.

ELSA. *(Horrified)* But how?

210

HENRIK.   With a knife. Here it is. It's poisoned.

ELSA.   I don't want to!

HENRIK.   On that point Mr Dragon ordered me to say: if you don't do it, he'll kill all your girl friends.

ELSA.   All right. Tell him that I'll do my best.

HENRIK.   And on that point Mr Dragon ordered me to tell you: any sign of hesitation will be punished as if it were disobedience.

ELSA.   I hate you!

HENRIK.   And on that point Mr Dragon ordered me to say: he knows how to reward faithful servants.

ELSA.   Lancelot will kill your Dragon!

HENRIK.   And on that point Mr Dragon ordered me to say: we shall see!

CURTAIN

ACT TWO

*The square in the centre of the town. On the right, the
town hall with a small tower, on the top of which stands
a sentry. In the middle background a huge, gloomy,
brown building without windows, having an enormous
cast-iron door which occupies the whole of the wall from
the ground to the roof. On the door an inscription in
Gothic lettering: 'Entry is absolutely forbidden to
humans.' On the left, a wide, ancient fortress wall. In the
centre of the square, a well with wrought iron railings and
a roof. HENRIK, without his livery and wearing an apron,
is cleaning the brass ornaments on the cast-iron door.*

HENRIK. *(Sings quietly to himself)* 'We'll see, we'll see,'
   declared the Dragon. 'We'll see, we'll see!' roared
   the old Drag-Drag. The old Dragonman roared:
   'We'll see, the Devil take it!' Well, we really will
   look and see! We'll look and see, tra-la-la!

   *(The MAYOR runs out of the Town Hall. He is
   wearing a strait jacket)*

MAYOR.   Good morning, Sonny! Did you send for me?

HENRIK.   Good morning, Father. I just wanted to find
   out how things are going in there. Has the meeting
   of the town council finished?

MAYOR.   Nowhere near it! It took us the whole night
   to agree on the agenda for today.

HENRIK.   So you're worn out, are you?

MAYOR.   What do you think? In the last half-hour
   they've changed my strait jacket three times.
   (Yawns) I don't know whether it foretells rain or
   something, but today my schizophrenia's been
   playing me up terribly. I keep on raving, raving. . .
   hallucinations, obsessions, and so on. *(Yawns)*
   Have you got any tobacco?

HENRIK.   Yes, I have.

MAYOR.   Untie me. Let's have a smoke.

   *(HENRIK unties his father's strait jacket. They
   sit down side by side on the steps of the palace
   and light their cigarettes)*

212

HENRIK. When will you come to a decision about
weapons then?

MAYOR. What weapons?

HENRIK. For Lancelot.

MAYOR. What Lancelot?

HENRIK. Have you really gone out of your mind?

MAYOR. Of course I have. What a wonderful son
you are! You've completely forgotten how seriously
ill your father is. *(Shouts)* Oh, men, men, love
one another! *(Quietly)* You see the way I'm
raving?

HENRIK. Never mind, Dad, it'll pass off.

MAYOR. I know myself it'll pass off, but it's
unpleasant all the same.

HENRIK. You'd better listen to me. I've got some
important news for you. The dear old Dragon is
nervous.

MAYOR. That's not true!

HENRIK. I assure you he is. All night long the dear
old man's been fluttering around, no one knows
where, not sparing his poor wings. Only at dawn
he got back. He stank of fish something awful!
That always happens to him when he's worried.
D'you understand?

MAYOR. Yes, yes.

HENRIK. Well, I succeeded in establishing the following
facts. Our kind-hearted old lizard was fluttering
about all night for the exclusive purpose of finding
out all he could about the famous Mr Lancelot.

MAYOR. Well now, really? Is that so?

HENRIK. I don't know in what disreputable dens he
found it out — in the Himalayas, on Mount Ararat,
in Scotland or in the Caucasus — but our old man's
discovered that Lancelot is a professional hero.
Personally, I despise little men of that breed. But
Drag-Drag, as a professional malefactor, obviously
considers them to be of some importance. He
swore, and he growled, and he moaned. Then he
felt like a little drink of beer. Having lapped up a

213

whole barrel of his favourite beverage and without
even giving any orders to anyone, the Dragon
stretched his webbed wings once again and even at
this moment is swooping around in the sky like a
little bird. Tell me, doesn't this worry you?

MAYOR. Not in the least.

HENRIK. Daddy, dear! Tell me — you're older than
me. . . more experienced. . . Tell me, what do
you think about this forthcoming battle? Please,
do answer me. Could Lancelot really. . . Only do
answer me straight, without lapsing into official
expressions of admiration — could Lancelot really
win? Eh? Daddy! Do answer me!

MAYOR. Of course, Sonny, I'll answer you straight —
straight from the heart. You know, my dear boy,
how sincerely I'm attached to our dear Dragon.
I give you my word of honour, I feel as if I were
a relation of his. Sometimes, do you know, I
even feel as if I'd be ready to lay down my life
for him. I swear by God that's true; may I fall
through the ground if it's a lie. No, no, no! He,
our dear one, will conquer. He'll conquer, our
miraculous being, our glorious flyer! Oh, how I
love him! I'll love him till I die! That's my
complete answer!

HENRIK. I see, Daddy, you don't wish to have a simple,
heart-to-heart talk with your only son!

MAYOR. No, I don't want to, Sonny. I haven't lost my
senses yet. That is, of course, I have lost my
senses, but not quite to that extent. Was it the
Dragon who ordered you to question me?

HENRIK. What a thing to say, Dad!

MAYOR. You're a fine fellow, Sonny! You've conducted
this conversation very ably. I'm proud of you.
Not because I'm your father, that I swear. I'm
proud of you as a connoisseur in these matters,
as an old hand. Did you memorize my answers?

HENRIK. That goes without saying.

MAYOR. And my exact words: 'the miraculous
being', 'the glorious flyer', and so on?

HENRIK. I've memorized all of it.

214

MAYOR. Well, report it just as I told you, then.

HENRIK. All right, Dad.

MAYOR. Oh, you — my only son! Oh, my dear little
spy! You're making progress in your little
career, my little one! Do you need any money?

HENRIK. No, I don't need any just yet, thank you,
Daddy.

MAYOR. Do take some, don't be embarrassed. I've
got money. It just happens that yesterday I had
an attack of cleptomania. Here, take it.

HENRIK. Thanks, I don't want it. And now tell me
the truth. . .

MAYOR. Really, Sonny, you're being childish —
the truth, the truth. . . I'm not just any man-in-
the-street, after all, I'm the Mayor. . . I haven't
been telling myself the truth for so many years
now that I've quite forgotten what it's like — the
truth! I can't even help being repelled by it. You
know what the truth smells of — the beastly
thing? That's enough of this, son. Glory be to
the Dragon! Glory be to the Dragon! Glory be to
the Dragon!

*(The SENTRY on the tower strikes the floor
with his halberd. Shouts)*

SENTRY. Quiet! Atten-shun! Eyes to the sky! His
Excellency's appeared above the Grey
Mountains!

*(HENRIK and the MAYOR jump up and stand
to attention, raising their heads towards the sky.
A distant roar is heard which gradually dies away)*

SENTRY. Stand at ease! His Excellency has turned
back and vanished in smoke and flames.

HENRIK. He's out on patrol.

MAYOR. Yes, yes. Listen! Now you answer just one
little question. The Dragon hasn't really given you
any orders? Eh, Sonny?

HENRIK. No, he hasn't Dad.

MAYOR. Aren't we going to kill him, then?

215

HENRIK. Kill whom?

MAYOR. Our saviour.

HENRIK. Oh, Dad, Dad!

MAYOR. Tell me, Sonny. Hasn't he ordered us to bump off Mr Lancelot on the quiet? Don't be shy, tell me. . . Why beat about the bush? There's nothing out of the common in it, after all. Eh, Sonny? You're not saying anything?

HENRIK. No, Dad.

MAYOR. Well, stay silent then. I understand — nothing doing — that's service.

HENRIK. May I remind you, Mr Mayor, that any minute now a solemn ceremony is due to take place, the ceremony of handing over the weapons to Mr Hero? It's possible that Drag-Drag himself will wish to honour the ceremony with his presence, and you've got nothing ready yet.

MAYOR. *(Yawns and stretches himself)* Well, I'd better be going then. We'll find some weapons for him in half a jiffy. He'll be quite pleased with them. Come, tie up my sleeves now. Here he comes himself. Lancelot's coming.

HENRIK. Take him away from here. Elsa will be here in a moment. I must have a talk with her.

(Enter LANCELOT*)*

MAYOR. *(Acting like a man in a fit of religious hysteria)* Glory be to you, glory, hosannah, Saint George, the Conqueror! Ah! forgive me, I made a mistake, I didn't recognize you in my delirium. I imagined suddenly that you looked just like Saint George.

LANCELOT. That's quite possible. He's a distant relative of mine.

MAYOR. How did you spend the night?

LANCELOT. I wandered around.

MAYOR. Made friends with anybody?

LANCELOT. Of course.

MAYOR. With whom?

LANCELOT. The timid inhabitants of your town set their dogs on me. But your dogs are a very sensible lot. It was with them that I made friends. They understood me because they love their masters and wish them well. We chatted away almost till dawn.

MAYOR. You haven't caught any fleas from them?

LANCELOT. No. They were very nice, clean dogs.

MAYOR. You don't recollect, by any chance, what they were called?

LANCELOT. They asked me not to mention their names.

MAYOR. I can't stand dogs.

LANCELOT. You make a mistake on that.

MAYOR. They're far too simple-minded.

LANCELOT. You think it's so simple to love men? After all, dogs know perfectly well what kind of people their masters are. They weep for them but they still love them. They are real workers. Did you send for me?

MAYOR. Follow me, exclaimed the stork, and he pecked at the snake with his sharp bill. Follow me, said the King, and he looked round at the Queen. Beautiful girls, astride elegant broomsticks, were flying along behind me. Well, to put it briefly, yes, I did send for you, Mr Lancelot.

LANCELOT. What can I do for you?

MAYOR. A fresh consignment of cheese has been received at Muller's shop. Modesty and a transparent little frock is the best adornment for a young girl. At sunset wild ducks flew over the little cradle. You're expected at the town council's meeting, Mr Lancelot.

LANCELOT. What for?

MAYOR. Why do lime trees grow in the Street of the Dragon Paws? What is dancing for when people feel like kissing? What is kissing for when you hear the sound of hooves?. . . The members of the town council must see you personally in order to decide exactly what kind of weapons would suit you best, Mr Lancelot. Come along, let's show ourselves to them!

(They go in to the Town Hall)

HENRIK.   'We'll see, we'll see,' declared the Dragon. 'We'll see, we'll see!' roared the old Drag-Drag. 'We'll see, the devil take it!' the old dear Dragon thundered. And we will indeed see!

(Enter ELSA)

HENRIK. Elsa!

ELSA.   Yes, it's me. Did you send for me?

HENRIK.   Yes, I did. What a pity there's a sentry standing on the tower! But for this very annoying impediment, I'd have embraced and kissed you.

ELSA.   And I'd have hit you.

HENRIK.   Ah, Elsa, Elsa! You always have been a little too virtuous. But it becomes you. Behind that modesty of yours something deep is hidden. Drag-Drag has a feeling for girls. He's always chosen the most promising ones, the old bounder! And what about Lancelot? Has he tried to pay court to you yet?

ELSA.   Be quiet!

HENRIK.   No, of course not. Even if some old fool of a woman were in your place, he'd still be spoiling for a fight. He'd pick a quarrel. That's the way he's been trained. He hasn't even noticed what you look like.

ELSA.   We've only just met.

HENRIK.   That's no excuse.

ELSA.   Did you call me here just to tell me this?

HENRIK.   Oh, no. I sent for you in order to ask you if you'd like to marry me.

ELSA.   Stop it.

HENRIK.   I'm not joking. I've been instructed to tell you this: if you'll be obedient and will kill Lancelot when it becomes necessary, then to reward you Drag-Drag will let you go.

ELSA.   I don't want to be let go.

HENRIK.   Just let me finish. Instead of you, a girl
completely unknown to you, a girl of the common
people, will become the chosen one. In any case,
she's marked out for next year. You can choose
which you prefer — a stupid death or a life of
such joys as you've only dreamed of up to now,
and that so rarely it's a real shame!

ELSA.   He's funking it!

HENRIK.   Who? Drag-Drag? I know all his weaknesses.
He's a martinet, a capricious brute, a parasite —
anything you like, but certainly not a coward.

ELSA.   Yesterday he was threatening, yet today he's
bargaining, isn't he?

HENRIK.   It's I who brought this about.

ELSA.   You?

HENRIK.   I'm the real conqueror of the Dragon, if
you want to know. I waited for the right moment,
and I didn't wait in vain. I'm not so stupid as
to give you up to anyone, whoever he is.

ELSA.   I don't believe you.

HENRIK.   Yes, you do.

ELSA.   It makes no difference: I can't kill a man!

HENRIK.   All the same, you've brought the knife with
you — there it is, hanging on your belt. I must be
off, my dear. I must put on my very best livery.
But I go, feeling completely at ease. You're going to
carry out his order for your sake and for mine.
Just think of it! Life, the whole of life is before us
if you only wish it to be. Think it over, my charmer.
(Goes out).

ELSA.   Merciful Heavens! My cheeks are burning as if
we'd been kissing. How shameful! He's almost
persuaded me. . . That's what I'm like then!. . .
Oh, well, let it be so. All right then! I've had enough
of that, anyway. I've always been the most
obedient girl in our town. I've believed everything
I was told. And how did it all end? Oh, yes, everybody respects me, but the happiness has gone to
others. Just now they're sitting in their homes,

219

choosing the most attractive dresses and ironing
their flounces. Curling their hair, too. Getting
ready to go out and watch me in my unhappiness.
Ah! I can almost see them powdering their faces
in front of their looking-glasses and saying:
'Poor Elsa! Poor girl! She was such a good girl!'
I am the only person in the town who's standing
in this square and tormenting myself. . . And
that fool of a sentry is staring his eyes out at me,
thinking what the Dragon will do with me today.
And tomorrow the soldier will be alive and he'll be
resting after his spell of duty. He'll go for a walk
to the waterfall — the place where the river looks
so happy that even the most melancholy people
have to smile as they watch it leaping about so
gaily. Or he'll go to the park where the gardener
has made such wonderful pansies grow — pansies
with eyes which can half-close and wink, and
even seem to be able to read, if only the letters
are large enough and the story has a happy
ending. Or he'll go for a boat trip on the lake,
the lake where the Dragon made the water boil
such ages ago and where the water nymphs have
been so tame ever since. Far from trying to
drown anyone, they actually sell safety belts
as they sit around in the shallow water. But they
are as beautiful as ever, and the soldiers like
chatting to them. And this stupid soldier will tell
the nymphs how the gay music started to play,
how everyone began to weep and how the Dragon
led me to his lair. And the water nymphs will
say: 'Ah, poor Elsa! Ah, poor girl! It's such a
fine day today and she's no longer in this world!'
I don't want it to be like this! I don't want to
die! I want to see everything, hear everything,
feel everything! So there! I want to be happy! So
there! I brought this knife in order to kill
myself! But I'm not going to kill myself! So
there!

(LANCELOT *comes out of the Town Hall)*

LANCELOT.   Elsa! How happy I am to see you!

ELSA.   Why?

LANCELOT.   Ah, my dear young lady! I have such a
difficult day in front of me that my soul needs
rest, if only for a moment. And now — suddenly —

as if by design you come here to meet me!

ELSA. Were you at the meeting of the Council?

LANCELOT. Yes.

ELSA. Why did they ask you in?

LANCELOT. They offered me some money if I'd give
up the idea of the fight.

ELSA. And what answer did you give them?

LANCELOT. I just said: 'Oh, you poor, poor fools!'
But don't let's talk about them. Elsa, today you
look even more beautiful than yesterday. That's
a sure sign that I really like you. Do you believe
that I'm going to set you free?

ELSA. No, I don't.

LANCELOT. You see, I don't take offence at your
saying so. That shows how much I like you.

(GIRL-FRIENDS *of Elsa run in)*

FIRST GIRL-FRIEND. Here we come!

SECOND GIRL-FRIEND. We are Elsa's best friends.

THIRD GIRL-FRIEND. We've been her boon
companions for so many years — since we were
children, really.

FIRST GIRL-FRIEND. She's always been the
cleverest of us.

SECOND GIRL-FRIEND. She was the nicest one
among us.

THIRD GIRL-FRIEND. And yet despite that, she
loved us more than anybody. And she'd mend
anything you asked her, and she'd help you
solve problems and comfort you when you felt
you were the most unfortunate of people.

FIRST GIRL-FRIEND. We aren't late, are we?

SECOND GIRL-FRIEND. You are really going to
fight him, aren't you?

THIRD GIRL-FRIEND. Mr Lancelot, could you
arrange for us to have places on the roof of the
Town Hall? They won't refuse you if you ask
them. We would so much like to have the best

221

view of the fight.

FIRST GIRL-FRIEND.   But now you seem to be
   annoyed!

SECOND GIRL-FRIEND.   Don't you want to talk to us?

THIRD GIRL-FRIEND.   We're not such bad girls, when
   all's said and done!

FIRST GIRL-FRIEND.   Do you think we interrupted
   your saying good-bye to Elsa on purpose?

SECOND GIRL-FRIEND.   We didn't do it on purpose.

THIRD GIRL-FRIEND.   It was Henrik — he ordered us
   not to leave you alone with her until Mr Dragon
   permits it.

FIRST GIRL-FRIEND.   It was he who ordered us to
   come and prattle. . .

SECOND GIRL-FRIEND.   And so, here we are,
   prattling like a lot of little fools.

THIRD GIRL-FRIEND.   Because otherwise we'd
   have had to start weeping. . . And you, being a
   visitor, can't imagine how shameful that is —
   weeping before strangers.

   (CHARLEMAGNE *comes out of the Town Hall)*

CHARLEMAGNE.   The meeting's over, Mr Lancelot.
   The decision about the weapons has been taken.
   Forgive us. . . pity us, poor murderers, Mr
   Lancelot.

   *(A thunderous noise of trumpets. SERVANTS
   run out of the Town Hall, spread carpets and set
   up armchairs. A large and luxuriously decorated
   armchair is placed in the centre, while to the right
   and left of it the servants place more ordinary
   chairs. The MAYOR comes out, surrounded by the
   members of the town administration. He is very
   cheerful. HENRIK, in parade livery, comes out
   with the others)*

MAYOR.   That was a very funny anecdote. . . How
   did she put it? 'I thought that all boys knew how
   to do it!' Ha-ha-ha! And do you know that other
   anecdote? Very funny! Well, they chopped off a
   gipsy's head, and. . .

(Trumpets blare)

MAYOR. Ah! everything's ready . . . All right, I'll
tell you the story after the ceremony. Come on,
come on, gentlemen! We'll finish this off very
quickly. Members of the Town Council, take
your places to the right and left of the chair in
the middle.

(HENRIK *places himself behind the big chair. The*
MAYOR *bows to the empty chair)*.

MAYOR. *(Speaking very fast)* Overwhelmed and
deeply moved by the confidence your Excellency
has placed in us by permitting us to make such
important decisions, we beg you to take the
place of the Honorary Chairman. We beg you
once, we beg you twice, we beg you three times.
We're distressed at your absence but we can do
no more. We're going to begin on our own. Sit
down, gentlemen. I declare the meeting. . .
(Pause) Bring me some water. *(A* SERVANT *gets*
water out of the well. The MAYOR *drinks)* I
declare the meeting. . . More water! *(Drinks,*
clears his throat, and continues in a squeaky
voice) I declare. . . *(in a deep bass)* the
meeting. . . Water! *(Drinks. In a high-pitched*
voice) Thank you, my dear! *(In a bass voice)*
Get out, you scoundrel! *(In his own voice)*
Congratulations, gentlemen! I've developed a
split personality. *(In a bass voice)* What are you
doing, you old fool? *(In a high-pitched voice)*
Don't you see, I'm taking the chair. *(In a bass*
voice) But is this a woman's business? *(In a*
squeaky voice) But I'm not happy about it
myself, darling. Don't impale me on this chair,
poor little me, but permit me to read the
minutes. *(In his own voice)* We have heard the
case concerning a certain Lancelot whom we
are to supply with weapons. We have resolved to
supply him with weapons though it goes against
the grain. Hey, you there! Bring out the weapons!

(Trumpets blare. Enter SERVANTS. *The* FIRST
SERVANT *hands* LANCELOT *a small brass bowl*
with leather straps on either side)

LANCELOT. That's a barber's bowl.

MAYOR. Yes, but we've appointed it to stand in as a
helmet. A small brass tray will serve as a shield.
Don't worry about it. In our town even inani-
mate objects are disciplined and obedient. They'll
do their duty with complete reliability. We regret
that there wasn't any knightly armour in our
store. But there's a spear. . . *(He hands
LANCELOT a piece of paper)* This certificate
is issued to you to inform you that the spear is,
in fact, being repaired — it's confirmed by this
signature and seal. You'll show it to Mr Dragon
in the course of the battle and everything will
end in the best possible way. That's all. *(In a bass
voice)* Now then, you old bitch, you can close
the meeting! *(In a high-pitched voice)* All right,
I'm closing it, I'm closing it, damn it! Why do
people keep on being cross, and don't even know
themselves why they're cross? *(Sings)* One, two,
three, four, five. . . a knight goes out for a
drive. . . *(In a bass voice)* Damn you, woman,
close the meeting! *(In a high-pitched voice)*
But what do you think I'm doing? *(Sings)* The
Dragon he flies out and gives the knight a
clout. . . Hi-ty-ti-ty. Oi-oi-oi, I declare our little
meeting closed!

SENTRY. Attention! All eyes to the sky! His
Excellency's appeared above the Grey Mountains
and is flying towards us at a terrific speed.

*(Everyone jumps up and stands stock still, their
heads raised to the sky. A distant hum is heard,
growing louder with terrifying speed. The stage
darkens. Complete darkness ensues. The noise
ceases)*

SENTRY. Attention! His Excellency is hovering
over us like a storm cloud, cutting off the sun.
Hold your breath!

(Two small green lights suddenly appear)

CAT. *(In a whisper)* Lancelot, it's me, the Cat.

LANCELOT. *(In a whisper)* I recognized you at
once by your eyes.

CAT. I'll be dozing on the fortress wall. Choose a
good moment and steal up to me, and I'll purr
something extremely pleasant to you.

224

SENTRY. Attention! His Excellency is now diving head first down to the square.

(A deafening roar and whistling. Light flares up. A tiny manikin, middle-aged and deathly pale is seen sitting in the large chair with his legs folded under him).

CAT. *(From the fortress wall)* Don't be alarmed, dear Lancelot. This is his third silly head. He changes them when the fancy takes him.

MAYOR. Your Excellency! In the town with whose administration I'm entrusted no events of significance have taken place. In district Number One there are. . .

DRAGON. *(In a small, rather high, cracked voice, quite calmly)* Get out. All of you get out, except the Stranger.

(Everyone goes out except for LANCELOT, the DRAGON and the CAT who is dozing, curled up, on the fortress wall)

DRAGON. How are you?

LANCELOT. Very well, thank you.

DRAGON. And what are these small bowls on the ground?

LANCELOT. The weapons.

DRAGON. Did my chaps think this up?

LANCELOT. Yes, it's their idea.

DRAGON. The scoundrels! I suppose you feel offended?

LANCELOT. No.

DRAGON. That's a lie. My blood is cold, but even I would have taken offence at this. Are you scared?

LANCELOT. No.

DRAGON. That's another lie. My people are a terrifying lot. You won't find any other people like them anywhere. That's my work. That's how I fashioned them.

LANCELOT. But they're men all the same.

DRAGON. Only on the outside.

225

LANCELOT. That's not so.

DRAGON. If only you could see inside their souls. . .
Oh! it would make you shudder.

LANCELOT. No.

DRAGON. You'd be turned to flight. You wouldn't
volunteer to die for cripples like these. You see,
my dear fellow, I crippled them myself. Oh, I
crippled them good and proper! Human souls, my
friend, are very tough. You can chop a man's body
in half and he'll die, but if you tear a soul to pieces,
it just becomes more compliant, that's all. No, no,
you won't find souls like these anywhere. Only in
my town. Souls without arms, souls without legs,
souls deaf and dumb, souls like chained-up dogs,
servile, damned souls. Do you know why the
Mayor pretends to be out of his mind? Just to
conceal the fact that he hasn't got a soul at all.
Souls full of holes, mercenary souls, souls that are
burnt right up — dead souls. Really, it's a pity
that souls are invisible — that you can't see them
with your own eyes!

LANCELOT. Fortunately for you.

DRAGON. How do you mean?

LANCELOT. People would get scared if they saw with
their own eyes what their souls had turned into.
They wouldn't go on submitting, they would rather
die. Who would feed you then?

DRAGON. The devil alone knows — maybe you're right.
Well, shall we begin?

LANCELOT. Let's.

DRAGON. First you'd better say good-bye to the girl
for whose sake you're going to your death. Hey,
boy!

(HENRIK *runs in*)

Bring Elsa here!

(HENRIK *runs out*)

Do you like the girl I chose for myself?

LANCELOT. I like her very much indeed.

226

DRAGON.   I'm pleased to hear it. I also like her very
        much indeed. She's an excellent girl. An obedient
        girl.

    (Enter ELSA *and* HENRIK)

    Come here, my dear. Look me in the eye — yes,
    like that. That's fine. Your eyes are clear. You may
    kiss my hand. Yes, like that. Very good! Your lips
    are warm. That means you're calm in spirit. Would
    you like to say good-bye to Mr Lancelot?

ELSA.   If you order it, Mr Dragon.

DRAGON.   That's what I do order. Go along. Talk to
        him in a friendly, affectionate way. *(Quietly)* Be
        affectionate, be kind to him. Kiss him good-bye. It
        doesn't matter — I'll be here, you see. You may do
        it in my presence. And then kill him. Don't worry,
        don't worry — I'll be here, you see. You'll do it in
        my presence. Go along! You may go a little
        farther away with him. I have an excellent eyesight,
        you know. I'll see everything. Go.

    (ELSA *comes up to* LANCELOT)

ELSA.   Mr Lancelot, I'm ordered to say good-bye to
        you.

LANCELOT.   Very well, Elsa. Let's say good-bye to
        each other, just in case. It's going to be a serious
        fight. One never knows what might happen. I want
        to tell you, now we're saying good-bye, that I love
        you, Elsa.

ELSA.   You *love* me?

LANCELOT.   Yes, Elsa. Even yesterday, when I saw you
        through the window, walking home so slowly and
        quietly with your father, I felt I liked you very
        much indeed. And then I found that when we met
        again you looked more and more beautiful every
        time. Oh, I thought, this is it! And when you kissed
        the Dragon's paw, I didn't feel angry with you,
        only terribly upset. . . So then everything became clear
        to me. I love you, Elsa. Don't be angry. I wanted
        you to know this so much.

ELSA.   But I thought that you would have challenged
        the Dragon anyway. I mean, even if there were
        another girl in my place.

227

LANCELOT. Of course I would have challenged him.
I can't stand these dragons. But for your sake I'd
be ready to strangle him with my bare hands —
though it would certainly be a very disgusting thing
to do.

ELSA. So you really do love me?

LANCELOT. Very much. It frightens me to think of
what would have happened if, as I came along
yesterday, I'd turned left at the crossroads,
instead of right! We'd never have come to know one
another! That's a dreadful thought, isn't it?

ELSA. It is.

LANCELOT. It's terrible to think of it. It seems to me
now that there's no one in the whole world closer
to me than you, and I regard your town as mine
because you live here. If I am. . . well, in a word, if
we don't get another chance of talking to one
another, please don't forget me.

ELSA. No, I never will.

LANCELOT. Don't forget! Just now you looked
straight at me for the first time today. And I felt
warmed all through as if you'd given me a caress.
I'm a wanderer, a light-weight sort of man, but all
my life's been spent in heavy-weight battles. In one
place — dragons, in another — ogres, in another —
giants. A man keeps getting involved. It's unreward-
ing, wearisome kind of work. But all the same, I've
always been happy. I've never felt tired. And I've
often been in love.

ELSA. Often?

LANCELOT. Of course. You go everywhere, you wander
about, you meet girls. You see, they're always
getting captured by brigands, or stuffed into sacks
by giants, or locked in kitchens by ogres. And
these villains always choose some of the best
girls, especially the ogres. So, well, you can't
help falling in love sometimes. But have I ever
been in love the way I am now? With those other
girls I was always joking, I used to make them
laugh. But as for you, Elsa, if we were on our own,
I'd be kissing you all the time! It's true. And I'd
have taken you away from here. We'd have

marched through the forests and trudged up the
mountains — it wouldn't be at all difficult! No,
I'd have got you a horse with such a saddle that
you'd never have felt tired. And I'd have walked at
your side, by your stirrup, and admired you.
And not a man in the world would have dared to
hurt you.

(ELSA *takes* LANCELOT's *hand)*

DRAGON. Good girl! She's taming him.

HENRIK. Yes. She's no fool, your Excellency.

LANCELOT. Elsa, you look as if you were going to cry.

ELSA. Yes, I am.

LANCELOT. Why?

ELSA. I'm sorry.

LANCELOT. Who for?

ELSA. For myself and for you. We're never going to
have our happiness, Mr Lancelot. Oh, why was I
born into this world under the Dragon!

LANCELOT. Elsa, I always tell the truth. We shall
have our happiness. Believe me!

ELSA. Oh! Don't, don't!

LANCELOT. You and I will walk along a forest path
and we'll be gay and happy. Just you and I.

ELSA. No, no, don't say that!

LANCELOT. And above us there'll be a clear sky.
No one will dare to swoop down on us.

ELSA Is this really true?

LANCELOT. It's true. Ah, do they know, your poor folk
here, how people can love each other? All the fear,
fatigue and mistrust will be burnt up inside you—
they'll vanish for ever. That's how I'll love you. And
you'll smile as you fall asleep, and when you wake
up, you'll smile again and call me. That's how you'll
love me. And you'll come to love yourself, too.
You'll walk about calmly and proudly. You'll
understand that if I kiss you, it means that you're
a very good person. And the trees in the forest will
talk to us caressingly, and the birds and beasts will
too, because people who are truly in love understand

229

everything and are at one with the whole world.
And everyone'll be glad to welcome us because
people who are truly in love bring happiness.

DRAGON. What is he cooing to her about?

HENRIK. He's preaching to her. Knowledge is light,
ignorance is darkness. He's telling her to wash her
hands before meals — and such like stuff. He's
certainly a dry stick.

DRAGON. Aha! Aha! She's put her hand on his
shoulder. Good girl!

ELSA. Well, even if we don't live to have such
happiness, it's no matter! I'm happy already.
Those monsters are watching us. But we managed
to get a long, long way from them. Nobody has
ever spoken to me like this, my dear. I didn't
know men like you existed on this earth. Only
yesterday I was as obedient as a little dog, and I
dared not think of you. And yet in the night I
came downstairs very quietly and drank the
wine you'd left in your glass. Only now I
realize that it was a kiss I gave you last night —
very secretly, in my own way — because you
defended me. You can hardly imagine how all our
feelings are mixed up, the feelings of us poor,
downtrodden girls. Only a little while ago it
seemed to me that I hated you. But in fact, in
my own way, very secretly, I was falling in love
with you. My dear one! I love you — how happy I
am that I can say this to your face! And what
happiness it is!... *(She kisses* LANCELOT)

DRAGON. *(Stamping his little feet impatiently)* In a
moment she'll do it, in just a moment, now —
she'll do it!

ELSA. And now let me go, my dear. *(She frees
herself from* LANCELOT's *embrace and
snatches the knife from its sheath)* Do you see
this knife? The Dragon has ordered me to kill you
with it. Look!

DRAGON. Come on, come on, come on!

HENRIK. Do it! Be quick, do it!

(ELSA *flings the knife into the well)*

The miserable girl!

DRAGON. *(Thunders)* How dare you!

ELSA. Not a word more from you! Do you imagine that I'll allow you to abuse me now, after he's kissed me? I love him. And he's going to kill you.

LANCELOT. That's perfectly true, Mr Dragon.

DRAGON. Oh, well! Nothing doing then. We'll have to fight. *(Yawns)* To speak frankly, I don't regret this. Not so long ago I thought up a very interesting blow with my paw X in Y direction. Now I can try it out on a living body. Boy, call the guards.

(HENRIK *runs out*)

(To ELSA*)* Go home, you little fool. And after the fight we'll have a heart-to-heart talk, you and I.

(HENRIK *enters with the* GUARDS)

Listen, guards, I meant to tell you something. . . Ah, yes!. . . See this young lady home and keep an eye on her.

(LANCELOT *takes a step forward*)

ELSA. Don't now. Save your strength. When you've killed him, come for me. I'll wait for you and in my mind I'll go through every word you said to me today. I believe you.

LANCELOT. I'll come for you.

DRAGON. Well, that's fine. Go now.

(The GUARDS *lead* ELSA *away)*

(To HENRIK) Boy, get the sentry off the tower and send him to jail. His head will have to be chopped off tonight. He's heard how that silly girl shouted at me and he might blurt it out in the barracks. Give orders accordingly. Then come back and annoint my claws with poison.

(HENRIK *runs off*)

(To LANCELOT) And you stay here, do you hear? Just wait — I shan't tell you when I'm going to start. Real war starts suddenly. You understand?

(He climbs off the armchair and goes into the palace. LANCELOT *goes up to the* CAT*)*

LANCELOT.   Well, Cat? What was this pleasant news you were going to purr to me?

CAT.   Take a glance to the right, dear Lancelot. There's a little donkey standing there in a cloud of dust. He's kicking up his hind legs and there are five men trying to talk him into being reasonable, the obstinate beast. I'm just going to sing them a little song. *(Mi-oos)* Now you see how the obstinate beast is bounding straight towards us? But when he gets to this wall he'll turn stubborn again, and you'll have a chance to talk to his drovers. Here they are.

(Behind the wall appears the head of a donkey which comes to a halt in a cloud of dust. Five DROVERS *shout at it.* HENRIK *runs across the square)*

HENRIK.   *(To the first and second* DROVERS) What are you doing here?

DROVERS.   *(Together)* We're taking our wares to the market, your Honour!

HENRIK.   What wares?

DROVERS.   Carpets, your Honour.

HENRIK.   Move on then, move on. You mustn't hang about near the palace.

DROVERS.   The donkey's turned stubborn, your Honour!

DRAGON'S VOICE.   Boy!

HENRIK.   Move on, move on! *(Runs rapidly into the palace).*

DROVERS.   *(Together)* Good day, Mr Lancelot. We're your friends, Mr Lancelot. *(They both clear their throats at the same time).* Khe-khe. Don't take offence at our talking together like this — we've been working together since we were children and we've got so close that we think and speak as one man. We even fell in love on the same day, at the same moment, and we married two sisters who are twins. We've woven many, many carpets,

232

but last night we got our best one ready. It's for you. *(They take the carpet off the back of the donkey and spread it on the ground)*

LANCELOT. What a beautiful carpet!

DROVERS. Yes, it's a carpet of the best sort, double-weave, wool mixed with silk and dyed with dyes prepared to our own secret recipe. But the secret of the carpet isn't in the wool, or the silk, or the colours it's made with *(Quietly)* It's a flying carpet.

LANCELOT. How delightful! Tell me quickly, how do I steer it?

DROVERS. It's quite simple, Mr Lancelot. Here's the corner for ascent where the sun's woven into it. And that's the corner for descent where the earth's woven into it in colour. That's the corner for flight direction. There are swallows woven into it. And this is the corner for the Dragon. If you pull it up and fly down steeply, you'll land straight on the enemy's head. And you see there's a goblet of wine and some marvellous hors-d'oeuvres woven in here. Conquer and feast!. . . No, no! Don't thank us. Our great-grandfathers used to look at the road, waiting for you, and our grandfathers used to wait for you too, and now we here have met you at last!

(They go away quickly, and immediately the THIRD DROVER runs up to Lancelot, carrying a cardboard box in his hand)

THIRD DROVER. Good day, Sir! Excuse me. Just turn your head this way. And now that way. That's excellent. I'm a master hatter, Sir. I make the best hats and caps in the world — I'm very famous in this town. Every dog knows me here.

CAT. And every cat, too.

THIRD DROVER. You see! Without a single fitting, just by taking one glance at my customer, I can make hats that improve people's looks wonderfully, and I find such joy in that! There's one lady, for instance, who's only loved by her husband when she wears the hat I made for her. She even sleeps in it, and tells everyone that she owes her life's happiness to me. Last night I worked all night for you, Sir, but I was so sad I wept like a child.

233

LANCELOT.   But why?

THIRD DROVER.   This is such a strange, sad sort of
fashion. It's an invisible cap.

LANCELOT.   How delightful!

THIRD DROVER.   As soon as you put it on you'll
vanish, and the poor maker will never know whether
it suits you or not. Take it, only don't try it on in
front of me. I shouldn't be able to bear it. No, I
know I wouldn't.

(He runs away and immediately the FOURTH
DROVER *approaches* LANCELOT. *He is a
bearded, morose-looking man who carries a long
object, wrapped up in a parcel, on his shoulder.
He unwraps it. It contains a sword and a spear)*

FOURTH DROVER.   Here now! We've been forging
them all night. Good hunting to you!

(Goes away. The FIFTH DROVER *runs up to*
LANCELOT. *He is a small grey-haired man with a
stringed instrument in his hands)*

FIFTH DROVER.   I'm a musical instrument maker, Mr
Lancelot. It was my great-great-grandfather who
began making this little instrument. Then from
generation to generation our family worked on it,
and now in our human hands it has become quite
human itself. It will be your faithful companion in
battle. Your hands will be occupied with the spear
and the sword, but it will take care of itself. It
produces a tuning note by itself and it tunes itself.
It changes a string if it snaps and it starts playing
on its own. When required, it will do an encore, or
if necessary it will keep silent. That's true, isn't
it?

*(The musical instrument replies by a musical
phrase)*

You see? We heard — we all heard — how you
were wandering about the town alone, and we all
made haste, such haste, to arm you from head to
foot. We've been waiting, waiting for centuries —
the Dragon made us keep quiet, so we just waited
quietly, quietly. And at last our waiting has been
answered. Kill him and give us our freedom. Have

I said the right thing?

(The musical instrument replies with a musical phrase. The FIFTH DROVER *goes off, bowing)*

CAT. When the fight begins, we — the donkey and I — will hide in the shed behind the palace, so that the flames don't burn my fur by accident. If you need us, call us. Here in the pack on the donkey's back we've got fortifying drinks and cherry pies, a sharpening stone for the sword, spare points for the spear and needles and thread.

LANCELOT. Thank you. *(Steps on the carpet, takes the weapons and puts the musical instrument at his feet. Takes out the invisible cap, puts it on and vanishes)*

CAT. A very good job! Excellent craftsmen! Are you still there, dear Lancelot?

LANCELOT'S VOICE. No, I'm slowly going up in the air. Au revoir!

CAT. Au revoir, dear friend. Oh, what a lot of troubles, what a lot of cares! No, it's really more pleasant to give up in despair. You just go on dozing and don't expect anything. Is it right what I'm saying, little donkey?

(The DONKEY *moves his ears)*

I don't know how to talk with my ears. Let's talk in words, little donkey. We don't know each other very well, but as we're working together now, we might just as well exchange a friendly mi-aou. It's such a torment to wait. Let's mi-aou for a bit.

DONKEY. I won't mi-aou.

CAT. Well anyway, at least let's talk. The Dragon thinks that Lancelot is here, but he's vanished without a trace. It's funny, isn't it?

DONKEY. *(Glumly)* Very funny.

CAT. Why don't you laugh then?

DONKEY. They hit me if I do. As soon as I laugh out loud, people say 'This damned donkey's shouting again!' And they hit me.

CAT.   Oh! That's the way it is. You must have very penetrating laughter.

DONKEY.   Aha!

CAT.   And what does make you laugh?

DONKEY.   It depends. I keep on thinking and thinking, and suddenly I remember something funny. Horses make me laugh.

CAT.   Why horses?

DONKEY.   Just because. . . They're stupid.

CAT.   Please forgive me if I'm impertinent. I've been wanting to ask you something. . . for a long time. . .

DONKEY.   Well?

CAT.   How can you eat all kinds of prickly things?

DONKEY.   And why shouldn't I?

CAT.   It's true that in among the grass one sometimes comes upon little stems of plants that are edible. But prickles. . . they're so dry!

DONKEY.   That's nothing. I like piquant foods.

CAT.   And what about meat?

DONKEY.   What about it?

CAT.   Have you ever tasted it?

DONKEY.   Meat isn't food. Meat is a load to be moved. They put it into a cart, you little fool.

CAT.   What about milk?

DONKEY.   Ah! I used to drink that when I was a baby.

CAT.   Well, thank goodness for that! Now we may be able to chat about a few pleasant, comforting things.

DONKEY.   That's true. That's a pleasant memory. Comforting. . . Mother was kind, her milk was warm. You sucked and sucked. . . It was paradise. It tasted so good.

CAT.   It's even pleasanter to lap milk up.

DONKEY.   I don't want to lap it up.

236

CAT. *(Jumps up)* D'you hear that?

DONKEY. The horrible reptile is stamping his hooves.

(A triple roar from the DRAGON*)*

DRAGON. *(Off)* Lancelot! *(A pause)* Lancelot!

DONKEY. Coo-coo! *(Breaks into donkey laughter)* Ee-ah! Ee-ah! Ee-ah!

(The doors of the palace fly open. Through smoke and flames are faintly visible now the three gigantic heads, now the huge paws and now the glowing eyes of the DRAGON*)*

DRAGON. Lancelot! Do look and admire me before we fight. Where are you?

*(*HENRIK *runs out into the square. He dashes around looking for* LANCELOT*, then peeps down into the well)*

DRAGON. Where is he?

HENRIK. He's hidden himself, your Excellency!

DRAGON. Hey, Lancelot! Where are you?

(The clang of a sword is heard)

DRAGON. Who dared to strike me?

LANCELOT'S VOICE. I did, Lancelot.

(Complete darkness ensues. A threatening roar, then light again. HENRIK *runs headlong into the Town Hall. Noise of battle)*

CAT. Come, let's run to shelter.

DONKEY. High time, too!

(They run away. The square fills with people. They are unusually quiet. They whisper to one another, looking up at the sky)

FIRST TOWNSMAN. How painfully the fight drags on!

SECOND TOWNSMAN. Yes, two minutes gone already — and still no result.

FIRST TOWNSMAN. I hope everything will be finished at one go.

SECOND TOWNSMAN.   Ah! we've had such a quiet
     life! And now it's lunch time, and I don't feel
     like eating anything. It's terrible! Good day, Mr
     Gardener. Why are you looking so sad?

GARDENER.   My tea roses came out today; my
     bread roses and wine roses, too. You know, you
     just have to look at them and your hunger and
     thirst are satisfied. Well, Mr Dragon promised to
     call and have a look at them, and give me money
     for further experiments. And now he's fighting.
     Because of this horrible event the fruits of many
     years' work may be ruined.

A HAWKER.   *(In an urgent whisper)* Who'd like to
     buy smoked glass? You just look through it —
     and you see Mr Dragon being smoked.

     (Everyone laughs quietly)

FIRST TOWNSMAN.   What a scurrilous thing to say!
     Ha-ha-ha!

SECOND TOWNSMAN.   See him being smoked!
     Indeed!

     (They buy smoked glass)

A BOY.   Mamma! Who's chasing the Dragon all over
     the sky?

EVERYBODY.   Sh-sh!

FIRST TOWNSMAN.   No one's chasing him, boy.
     He's manoeuvring.

BOY.   And why has he got his tail between his legs?

EVERYBODY.   Sh-sh!

FIRST TOWNSMAN.   His tail's between his legs,
     according to plan, Boy.

FIRST TOWNSWOMAN.   Just think of it! The
     fight's been going on for a full six minutes, and
     there's no end in view. Everyone's so worked up
     about it that even the common tradeswomen
     have raised the price of milk already three times
     over.

SECOND TOWNSWOMAN.   Oh, why talk about the
     tradeswomen. We saw a sight on the way here to
     make our hearts freeze. Sugar and butter, pale as

238

death, were rushing from the shops back to the warehouses. They're terribly nervous commodities — as soon as they hear the noise of battle, they immediately go into hiding.

(Screams of horror. The crowd shies to one side. CHARLEMAGNE *appears)*

CHARLEMAGNE. Good day, gentlemen!

(Silence)

Don't you recognize me?

FIRST TOWNSMAN. Of course we don't Since last night you've become absolutely unrecognizable.

CHARLEMAGNE. Why is that?

GARDENER. Some people are quite dreadful! They admit strangers to their homes. They upset the Dragon. That's worse than trampling on a newly sown lawn. And he's asking why!

SECOND TOWNSMAN. Personally, I haven't been able to recognize you at all since the moment the guards surrounded your house.

CHARLEMAGNE. Yes, it's terrible, isn't it? Those stupid guards won't let me see my own daughter. They say that the Dragon's forbidden anyone to enter Elsa's room.

FIRST TOWNSMAN. Well, what of it? From his point of view, he's perfectly right.

CHARLEMAGNE. Elsa is there all by herself. True, she nodded to me through the window quite cheerfully, but that must be just to comfort me. Oh! I don't know where to turn! There's no place where I can go to!

FIRST TOWNSMAN. How do you mean? Have you lost your place as archivist then?

CHARLEMAGNE. No.

SECOND TOWNSMAN. Then what place are you talking about?

CHARLEMAGNE. Don't you really understand what I mean?

FIRST TOWNSMAN. No. From the moment you became

239

friends with that stranger, you and I speak different languages.

(Noise of battle and clanging of swords)

BOY. *(Pointing to the sky)* Mamma, Mamma, look! He's turned upside down. Someone's hitting him so hard that sparks are coming out of him!

EVERYBODY. Sh-sh!

(Trumpets blare. HENRIK *and the* MAYOR *come out of the Town Hall)*

MAYOR. Listen everyone! Here's an order. To prevent epidemics of eye disease and only for that reason — people are forbidden to look at the sky. You will learn what's happening up in the sky from a communiqué which will be issued by Mr Dragon's personal secretary when required.

FIRST TOWNSMAN. That's the right way to do it!

SECOND TOWNSMAN. High time, too!

BOY. Mamma, why is it harmful to look at him being walloped?

EVERYBODY. Sh-sh!

(Enter Elsa's GIRL-FRIENDS)

FIRST GIRL-FRIEND. The battle's been going on for ten minutes. Why doesn't this Lancelot surrender?

SECOND GIRL-FRIEND. He must know that the Dragon can't be beaten.

THIRD GIRL-FRIEND. He's tormenting us on purpose!

FIRST GIRL-FRIEND. I left my gloves in Elsa's house. But it's all the same to me now. I'm so tired of this battle that I don't regret anything.

SECOND GIRL-FRIEND. I can't feel anything anymore either. Elsa wanted to give me her new court shoes to be remembered by, but I've almost forgotten that, too.

THIRD GIRL-FRIEND. Just fancy! If it were not for this stranger, the Dragon would have taken

Elsa away a long time ago, and we'd all be sitting at home, quietly weeping.

HAWKER. *(Urgently, in a whisper)* Who'd like to buy an interesting scientific instrument, a looking-glass as it's called — you look down into it and see the sky above. For a small cost anyone can see the Dragon at his feet.

(Everyone laughs quietly)

FIRST TOWNSMAN. What impertinence! Ha-ha-ha!

SECOND TOWNSMAN. See him at your feet! You just wait!

(All the looking-glasses are bought up. Everyone looks into them, as they break up into groups. The noise of the battle becomes fiercer all the time)

FIRST TOWNSWOMAN. But this is simply dreadful!

SECOND TOWNSWOMAN. Poor Dragon!

FIRST TOWNSWOMAN. He's stopped breathing out flames!

SECOND TOWNSWOMAN. He's just giving off smoke.

FIRST TOWNSMAN. What complicated manoeuvres!

SECOND TOWNSMAN. In my opinion. . . No, I won't say anything.

FIRST TOWNSMAN. I don't understand anything.

HENRIK. Listen everyone! Here's a communiqué of the Town Council. The battle is approaching its end. The enemy has lost his sword and his spear is broken. Moths have been discovered in his flying carpet and are destroying the flying capability of the enemy with incredible speed. Deprived of his base, the enemy is unable to get moth-balls and is trying to catch the moths by clapping his hands together, thus depriving himself of necessary manoeuvrability. Mr Dragon is not annihilating the enemy for the sole reason that he loves battle. He's not yet had his fill of exploits and hasn't had sufficient time to admire his own miraculous courage.

FIRST TOWNSMAN. I understand everything now.

BOY. I say. Mummy, do look! On my word of honour, someone's giving him a hard biff on the neck.

FIRST TOWNSMAN. He's got three necks, Boy.

BOY. Well, look, now you can see he's being bashed on all his three necks!

FIRST TOWNSMAN. That's an optical illusion, Boy. A deception of the eye. . .

BOY. That's just what I'm saying. A deception. . . I often have fights myself, and I can tell who's being beaten. Ouch! What's this now?

FIRST TOWNSMAN. Take the child away!

SECOND TOWNSMAN. I don't believe it! I can't believe my own eyes. Get me a doctor, an oculist!

FIRST TOWNSMAN. It's falling down here! I can't bear to see it! Don't get in the way! Let me have a look!

(The DRAGON's *head drops into the square with a crashing noise)*

MAYOR. Oh, for a communiqué! I'd give half my life for a communiqué!

HENRIK. Listen everyone! Here's the communiqué of the Town Council. Lancelot, deprived of all his strength, has lost everything and is partially captured.

BOY. How do you mean — 'partially' captured?

HENRIK. Never you mind. That's a military secret. The parts of him that are left are still resisting in some disorder. Incidentally Mr Dragon has released one of his heads from military service on account of indisposition. It's put on the reserve list, first rank.

BOY. I still don't understand. . .

FIRST TOWNSMAN. There's nothing special to understand! Have you ever lost any teeth?

BOY. Yes, I have.

FIRST TOWNSMAN. Well then — you go on living, don't you?

BOY. But I've never lost my head.

FIRST TOWNSMAN. That doesn't prove anything.

HENRIK. Listen everyone! Here's the commentary on current events. It's entitled: why is two in essence more than three? Two heads are fixed on two necks: that makes four. So there you are! Moreover, they're permanently fixed to the necks.

(The second head of the DRAGON *crashes into the square)*

HENRIK. The commentary is postponed for technical reasons. Here is a communiqué. The battle action is developing in accordance with the plans prepared by Mr Dragon.

BOY. Is that all?

HENRIK. For the moment, it's all.

FIRST TOWNSMAN. I've lost two thirds of my respect for the Dragon. Mr Charlemagne, my dear friend, why are you standing there all by yourself?

SECOND TOWNSMAN. Come nearer to us, do!

FIRST TOWNSMAN. Is it really conceivable that the guards won't permit you to enter your only daughter's room? How outrageous!

SECOND TOWNSMAN. Why don't you say anything?

FIRST TOWNSMAN. Have we offended you?

CHARLEMAGNE. No, I'm just bewildered. At first, apparently genuinely, you couldn't recognize me. I knew *you*, of course. And now, apparently just as genuinely, you're glad to see me.

GARDENER. Ah, Mr Charlemagne! You shouldn't be giving it too much thought. It's too frightening. It's terrifying to think how much time I've wasted running along to lick the paw of that one-headed monster! Think what a lot of flowers I could have grown!

HENRIK. Here's the commentary on current events!

GARDENER. Leave us alone! You bore us!

HENRIK. Never mind! There's a war on — you must be

243

patient. Well, then, I'll begin. There's one God, one sun and one moon, and there's one head on the shoulders of our Lord and Master. To have only one head is human, and it is also humane in the highest meaning of the term. Besides, it's extremely convenient from the purely military point of view. It reduces the front line. To defend one head is three times easier than to defend three.

(The DRAGON's third head crashes into the square. A burst of shouting. Now everybody starts talking very loudly)

FIRST TOWNSMAN. Down with the Dragon!

SECOND TOWNSMAN. We've been told nothing but lies from infancy.

FIRST TOWNSWOMAN. That's good! There's no longer anyone we have to obey!

SECOND TOWNSWOMAN. I feel quite drunk. On my word of honour I do!

BOY. Mamma, I bet there won't be any lessons at school today. Hurrah!

HAWKER. Who would like to buy a toy — a little dragon shaped like a potato? One stroke — and the head's gone!

(Everyone roars with laughter)

GARDENER. Very witty! What did he say? The dragon's a root vegetable? Only fit to be stuck in the park? All his life stuck there for good? Hurrah!

EVERYONE. Hurrah! Down with him! Potato-dragon! Come! Wallop everybody!

HENRIK. Listen to the communiqué!

EVERYONE. We're not going to listen! We'll shout as much as we like. We'll snarl just how we want to. What a joy! Smash up everybody!

MAYOR. Hey, guards!

(The GUARDS run out into the square)

(To HENRIK) Go on speaking. Softly at first, then hit them hard. Attention, there!

244

(Everyone grows quiet)

HENRIK. *(Very softly)* Please listen to the communiqué. On all fronts, nothing, literally nothing worthy of notice has occurred. Everything is absolutely all right. We are declaring a mild state of siege. As punishment for spreading rumours *(threateningly)* we'll chop heads off without the alternative of fines. You understand that? All of you go to your homes! Guards, clear the square!

(The square empties)

(To the MAYOR*)* Well, how did you like that spectacle?

MAYOR. Just be quiet a moment, Sonny.

HENRIK. What are you smiling for?

MAYOR. Be quiet, my dear boy.

(A hollow-sounding, heavy thump which makes the ground shake)

MAYOR. That's the Dragon's body crashing to the ground behind the mill.

FIRST DRAGON'S HEAD. Boy!

HENRIK. *(To* MAYOR*)* Why are you rubbing your hands together, Papa?

MAYOR. Ah, my dear son! Power's dropped into my hands all by itself!

SECOND DRAGON'S HEAD. Mayor, come here! Give me some water. Mayor!

MAYOR. Everything's going splendidly, Henrik. Our late Master brought them up so well that anyone who gets the reins will be able to drive them.

HENRIK. However, just now in the square. . .

MAYOR. Oh, all that is nothing. . . Every dog jumps about like mad when you let him off the chain, but then afterwards he runs to his kennel of his own free will.

THIRD DRAGON'S HEAD. Boy! Come over to me! I'm dying.

HENRIK. *(To* MAYOR*)* But aren't you afraid of Lancelot, Papa?

MAYOR. No, my dear son. Do you really think that it
was easy to kill the Dragon? I'm pretty sure that
Mr Lancelot is lying exhausted on his flying
carpet, and that the wind is carrying him away
from our town.

HENRIK. But what if he suddenly swoops down on us?

MAYOR. Then we'll dispose of him quite easily.
I assure you, he must be quite exhausted. Our
dear late Master did know how to fight, after all.
Let's go. Let's write out our first orders. The main
thing is to behave as if nothing had happened.

FIRST DRAGON'S HEAD. Boy! Mayor!

MAYOR. Let's go! Come along! No time to spare!

(They go out)

FIRST DRAGON'S HEAD. Why, oh why did I strike
him with my second left paw? I should have
struck out with my second right!

SECOND DRAGON'S HEAD. Hey, someone! You,
Miller! You used to kiss my tail whenever we met.
Hey, Friedricksen! You presented me with a
pipe with three mouth-pieces and an inscription
saying 'Yours for ever'. Where are you, Anna-
Maria-Frederica Weber? You used to tell me you
were in love with me and you wore a bit of my
claw in a little velvet bag on your breast. We
learned to understand one another over the years.
Where are you all? Give me some water! Don't
you see, the well's just here, beside me. A mouthful
would do! Half a mouthful! Give me just enough
to moisten my lips!

FIRST DRAGON'S HEAD. Let me — do let me begin
again from the beginning! I'll strangle the lot of
you!

SECOND DRAGON'S HEAD. Just a drop. . . someone. . .
please!. . .

THIRD DRAGON'S HEAD. I should at least have
moulded one loyal soul. But the material just
wouldn't respond.

SECOND DRAGON'S HEAD. Be quiet! I can sense
there's someone alive just beside me. Come
closer! Give me some water!

246

LANCELOT'S VOICE. I can't.

> (LANCELOT *appears in the square. He is standing on the flying carpet, leaning on his bent sword. 'He holds the invisible cap in his hand and the musical instrument lies at his feet*)

FIRST DRAGON'S HEAD. You won by accident. If I'd struck you with my second right paw. . .

SECOND DRAGON'S HEAD. Well, anyway. . . Good-bye!. . .

THIRD DRAGON'S HEAD. It's a consolation to me that I'm leaving you burnt out souls — souls full of holes, dead souls. . . But anyway. . . good-bye!

SECOND DRAGON'S HEAD. Just one man at my side! And he's the one who killed me! That's the way my life ends!

ALL THREE HEADS. *(Together)* My life's over. Good-bye! *(They die)*

LANCELOT. They are dead — but I feel somewhat unwell too. My arms won't obey me. I can't see too well. And I'm all the time hearing a voice calling my name: 'Lancelot! Lancelot!' A familiar voice! A mournful voice. I don't feel like going, but it seems I'll have to this time. What do you think — am I dying?

> *(The musical instrument replies)*

> Yes, listening to you, my deed looks like a high-minded, noble act, but I am feeling terribly unwell all the same. I must be mortally wounded. But wait — wait just a little . . . After all, the Dragon's been killed and I can breathe more easily. Elsa! I've vanquished him. But it's true I'll never see you again, Elsa. You'll never smile at me, or kiss me, or ask: 'Lancelot, what's the matter with you? Why are you so sad? Why do you feel giddy? Why do your shoulders ache? And who is it calling you so insistently — Lancelot, Lancelot?' It's Death who's calling me, Elsa. I'm dying. It is very sad, isn't it?

> *(The musical instrument replies)*

> This is very distressing. They've all hidden

themselves. As if a victory were some kind of calamity. . . But do wait a little, Death. I've looked you in the eyes more than once, and I've never tried to hide myself. I won't move from here. I can hear you. Just let me think a few more moments. They've all hidden themselves — that's true. But now in their own homes they're very quietly coming to their senses. Their souls are getting straightened out. Why have we fed and pampered that monster? they are whispering. Because of us, a man is dying in the square now, all alone. Well, from now on we'll be wiser. What a battle took place in the sky for our sake! And now, how painfully poor Lancelot is struggling for breath! No, we've had enough of this! Because we were weak, the strongest, the kindest, the most eager of men has perished. This could make the very stones wiser, and we are men, after all. . . That's what they're whispering now in every house, in every room. Do you hear them?

(The musical instrument replies)

Yes, yes, that's just it. It means I'm not dying in vain. Good-bye, Elsa. I knew I'd love you all my life. But I didn't believe that my life would end so soon. Good-bye town, good-bye, morning, day, evening! Now the night has come. Hey, you people! Death is calling me, hurrying me along. . . My thoughts are getting mixed up. . . Something. . . I've left something unsaid. . . Hey, you people! Don't be afraid! It's permissible not to hurt widows and orphans. It's permissible to be compassionate to one another! Don't be afraid to pity one another! Be compassionate — and you'll be happy. I give you my word, that's the truth, the pure truth, the purest truth that exists on earth. . . That's all. Now I'm going. Good-bye!

(The musical instrument replies)

CURTAIN

ACT THREE

A luxuriously furnished hall in the MAYOR's *palace. In the background on both sides of the main door oval tables laid for supper. In front of them in the centre a smaller table on which lies a thick book in gold binding. As the curtain goes up, an orchestra is playing loudly. A group of* TOWNSPEOPLE *shout as they look towards the door.*

TOWNSPEOPLE. *(Quietly)* One, two, three. . . *(Loudly)* Long live the Conqueror of the Dragon! *(Quietly)* One, two, three. . . *(Loudly)* Long live our Master! *(Quietly)* One, two, three. . . *(Loudly)* Oh, how contented we are! No brain can encompass it! *(Quietly)* One, two, three. . . *(Loudly)* We can hear his steps!

(Enter HENRIK)

TOWNSPEOPLE. *(Loudly, but harmoniously)* Hurrah! Hurrah! Hurrah!

FIRST TOWNSMAN. Oh, our glorious liberator! It was exactly a year ago that that accursed, hateful, cruel, repulsive monster, the Dragon, was annihilated by you!

TOWNSPEOPLE. Hurrah, hurrah, hurrah!

FIRST TOWNSMAN. Since that time we've had a very good life. . . We. . .

HENRIK. Stop, stop, my dear fellows! Put the stress on 'very'.

FIRST TOWNSMAN. As you order. From that time on we've had a *ve-ery*. . .

HENRIK. No, no, my dear man. Not like that! You mustn't draw out the 'e-e'. It makes a sort of ambiguous sounding noise — *'ve-ery'* — something like a wail. Emphasize the second syllable.

FIRST TOWNSMAN. Since that time we've had a *very-y*. . .

HENRIK. Yes, that's it! I agree to this version. Surely you must know by now what the Conqueror of the Dragon is like! He's a simple man, simple almost to the point of naiveté. He loves people who're cordial

249

and sincere. Carry on!

FIRST TOWNSMAN.   We simply don't know what to do or say — we're so happy!

HENRIK.   That's excellent. Now wait a moment. Let's insert something just here. . . Something virtuous and humane. You know the Conqueror of the Dragon likes that sort of thing. *(Snaps his fingers)* Wait, wait, wait! It's coming, it's coming! I've got it — here it is! Even the birds are chirping gaily. . . The Evil's departed, the Good has arrived. Chik-chiric! Chik-hurrah!. . . Let's repeat that.

FIRST TOWNSMAN.   Even the little birds are chirping gaily. The Evil's departed, the Good has arrived. Chik-chiric! Chik-hurrah!

HENRIK.   You're chirping rather gloomily, my dear fellow. Take care — if you don't want to get a chiric-chiric yourself!

FIRST TOWNSMAN.   *(Cheerfully)* Chik-chiric! Chik-hurrah!

HENRIK.   That's better. Well, that'll do. We've rehearsed the other bits already.

TOWNSPEOPLE.   Exactly so, Mr Mayor.

HENRIK.   That's all right then. Presently the Conqueror of the Dragon, the President of the liberated city will come out to you. Remember, you must all speak in unison, and at the same time sound cordial, humane and democratic. It was the Dragon who used to insist on ceremonial proceedings, whereas we. . .

SENTRY.   *(From the middle door)* Attention! Eyes on the door! His Excellency, the President of the liberated city is proceeding along the passage. *(Woodenly, in a bass voice)* Oh, you, our dear one! Oh, you, our benefactor! The killer of the Dragon! Just think of it!

(Music thunders. Enter PRESIDENT, *formerly Mayor).*

HENRIK.   Your Excellency, Mr President of the Liberated City! During my spell of duty nothing special has happened. Ten men are present here. Everyone of them is madly happy. In the district. . .

250

PRESIDENT. Stand at ease, stand at ease, gentlemen. Good day, Mayor. *(Shakes hands with* HENRIK) Oh! And who are these people? Eh, Mayor?

HENRIK. These are fellow citizens of ours. They remembered that it was exactly a year ago that you killed the Dragon. So they've come here to congratulate you.

PRESIDENT. Is that really so? What a pleasant surprise!... Well, well, get on with it!

TOWNSPEOPLE. *(Quietly)* One, two, three... *(Loudly)* Long live the Conqueror of the Dragon! *(Quietly)* One, two, three... *(Loudly)* Long live our Master!

(Enter the GAOLER)

PRESIDENT. Stop, quiet now! Good day, Goaler.

GAOLER. Good day, your Excellency.

PRESIDENT. *(To the* TOWNSPEOPLE) Thank you, gentlemen, thank you! Anyway, I already know all you want to say to me. Damn this involuntary tear! *(Flicks off a tear)* But you must understand that here in this house we're about to have a wedding, and I still have some business to attend to. Go home now, and then come back to the wedding. We'll have a gay time. The nightmare is over, and now we're really living. Isn't that so?

TOWNSPEOPLE. Hurrah, hurrah, hurrah!

PRESIDENT. That's it! That's fine! Slavery has receded into the sphere of legend and we are all regenerated. Remember what I was like under the accursed Dragon? I was sick, I was a madman — but now I'm as fit as a fiddle. As for you, there's no question about it... Under my care you're always as gay and happy as little birds. Very well, fly away then! Be quick! Henrik, see them out.

(The TOWNSPEOPLE *go out)*

PRESIDENT. *(To the* GAOLER) Well, how are things in your gaol?

GAOLER. The fellows are safe inside all right!

PRESIDENT. What about my ex-assistant? How is he?

251

GAOLER. He's in a real torment, he is.

PRESIDENT. Ha-ha! I bet that's a lie!

GAOLER. I swear to it, he's in a real torment.

PRESIDENT. More precisely?

GAOLER. Well, he's trying to climb up the wall with pain.

PRESIDENT. Ha-ha! That's just what he deserves. A disgusting individual! When I used to tell a joke everyone would laugh except him. . . He'd point at his beard. . . to show that it was an old joke, you see — so old that it had grown a beard. Well, let him rot in gaol now. Did you show him my portrait?

GAOLER. Not half!

PRESIDENT. Which one? The one where I'm happily smiling?

GAOLER. That's the one.

PRESIDENT. And what did he do?

GAOLER. He wept.

PRESIDENT. I bet that's a lie.

GAOLER. I swear to it, he wept.

PRESIDENT. Ha-ha! That's what I like to hear! And what about the weavers who supplied the flying carpet to that. . .?

GAOLER. I'm sick of them, damn them! They're locked up on different floors but they're all behaving the same, like peas in a pod. What one says, the other repeats exactly.

PRESIDENT. But I suppose they've got thinner?

GAOLER. How could they help it under my care?

PRESIDENT. And the smith?

GAOLER. He's sawn through the bars again. I had to put diamond bars in his cell window.

PRESIDENT. Fine, fine! Don't spare expense. And how did he take it?

GAOLER. He can't quite make it out.

PRESIDENT. Ha-ha! I'm mighty pleased about that.

GAOLER. The hatter's been making such peculiar caps for the mice that the cats don't go for them any more.

PRESIDENT. Really? Why not?

GAOLER. They can't help admiring them. And the way the musician sings — it makes you awful sad. Whenever I go into his cell, I stop up my ears with wax.

PRESIDENT. That's very good. And what's happening in town?

GAOLER. It's quiet there. But they will keep on writing.

PRESIDENT. What do they write?

GAOLER. The letter 'L' — on the walls. That means 'Lancelot'.

PRESIDENT. Nonsense! The letter 'L' means 'love' for the President.

GAOLER. Aha! So I needn't put the fellows who keep writing it under lock and key?

PRESIDENT. Well, yes, why not? Do put them under lock and key. What else do they write?

GAOLER. I'm ashamed to say it. They write: 'The President is a brute. His son's a crook. The President is. . .' *(He giggles in a bass voice.)* I daren't repeat the words they use. . . However, mostly they just write the letter 'L'.

PRESIDENT. Aren't they queer, these people! What do they want with that Lancelot? There's still no news of him, I suppose?

GAOLER. He's vanished.

PRESIDENT. Have you questioned the birds about it?

GAOLER. Aha!

PRESIDENT. All of them?

GAOLER. Aha! Here's the mark the eagle left on me. He gave me a peck on the ear.

PRESIDENT. Well, what do they say?

GAOLER. They say that they haven't seen Lancelot. . . Only the parrot always agrees with you. You say: 'Have you seen him?' and he replies: 'Seen him.' You ask: 'Lancelot?' and he answers: 'Lancelot!' Well, you know yourself what sort of bird the parrot is!

PRESIDENT. What about the snakes?

GAOLER. Well, they'd have come crawling to me of their own accord if they'd found out anything. They're on our side. Besides, they're relatives of the deceased. However, they haven't come crawling to me.

PRESIDENT. And the fish?

GAOLER. They keep silent.

PRESIDENT. Perhaps they know something?

GAOLER. No. Experts on fish breeding have been looking into their eyes — and they confirm that the fish don't know anything. In a word, Lancelot or St George, or Perseus the Wanderer — every country knows him by a special name of its own — hasn't been discovered up to now.

PRESIDENT. Well, he can go to the devil!

(Enter HENRIK).

HENRIK. The father of the happy bride, Mr Archivist Charlemagne, has arrived.

PRESIDENT. Aha! Aha! He's just the man I want. Ask him in.

(Enter CHARLEMAGNE)

PRESIDENT. You can go, Gaoler. Carry on with your work. I'm quite pleased with you.

GAOLER. I'm doing my best.

PRESIDENT. Yes, do your best. Charlemagne, you're acquainted with the Gaoler?

CHARLEMAGNE. Very slightly, Mr President.

PRESIDENT. Well, well. No matter. Perhaps you'll
get to know him more intimately.

GAOLER. Shall I take him?

PRESIDENT. There you go! 'Take him!' What's the
hurry? Off with you — for the time being! I'll
see you again.

(The GAOLER *goes out)*

PRESIDENT. Well, Charlemagne, you no doubt
guess why we've asked you here. All sorts of
worries and preoccupations concerned with State
matters prevented me from dropping in to see you.
But anyway you and Elsa know from the orders
posted around the town that today is her wedding
day.

CHARLEMAGNE. Yes, we know that, Mr President.

PRESIDENT. We statesmen have no time to make
proposals of marriage with flowers and gasps
of passion, and so on. . . We don't propose, we
just give orders, very simply. . . Ha-ha! It's
extremely convenient, really. Elsa is happy about it,
of course?

CHARLEMAGNE. No.

PRESIDENT. There you go! Of course she's happy!
What about you?

CHARLEMAGNE. I'm in despair about it, Mr
President. . .

PRESIDENT. What ingratitude! After I've killed the
Dragon. . .

CHARLEMAGNE. Excuse me, Mr President, but I
really can't believe that.

PRESIDENT. Oh, yes, you can!

CHARLEMAGNE. On my word of honour, I just
can't.

PRESIDENT. Of course you can. If even I believe it,
you certainly can.

CHARLEMAGNE. No.

HENRIK. He simply doesn't want to believe it.

PRESIDENT. But why not?

HENRIK. He wants to get a better price.

PRESIDENT. Very well. I offer you the post of being my first assistant.

CHARLEMAGNE. I don't want it.

PRESIDENT. Rubbish. Of course you do.

CHARLEMAGNE. No.

PRESIDENT. Now do stop bargaining: we're too busy for that. You'll get a rent-free flat near the park, not far from the market. A flat of 153 rooms with all the windows facing south. A fabulous salary, and besides, every time you go to your office you'll be paid your expenses, and every time you go home, you'll be paid holiday money. When you decide to go visiting people, you'll be paid your travelling expenses, and when you stay at home you'll be paid your rent. You'll be almost as rich as I am. That's it then. Do you agree?

CHARLEMAGNE. No.

PRESIDENT. What do you want then?

CHARLEMAGNE. We want only one thing — to be left alone, Mr President.

PRESIDENT. That's very fine — to be left alone! But what if I feel like doing just the opposite? Besides, from the point of view of the State this is a very appropriate thing to do. The Conqueror of the Dragon weds the girl he has rescued. It proves the point. Why won't you understand this?

CHARLEMAGNE. Why are you tormenting us? I've learnt how to think for myself, Mr President. That, in itself, is very painful. And now this wedding! It's enough to drive the man out of his mind.

PRESIDENT. That's not allowed! Not allowed at all! All these psychic illnesses are nonsense: it's all just imagination.

CHARLEMAGNE. Oh, good God! How helpless we are! The fact that our town is quite as calm and obedient as before — that alone is so terrifying.

PRESIDENT. What are these ravings? Why should it be

256

terrifying? Are you and your daughter determined
to start a rebellion?

CHARLEMAGNE. No, I just took a walk with her in
the forest and we discussed everything in so much
detail and so thoroughly. Tomorrow, when she
ceases to exist, I'll die too.

PRESIDENT. What do you mean — ceases to exist?
What rubbish you talk!

CHARLEMAGNE. But do you imagine she'll survive
this wedding?

PRESIDENT. But of course! It will be a fine, gay
celebration and a holiday. Anyone in your place
would be delighted to marry his daughter off to
a rich man.

HENRIK. I'm sure he is delighted, too.

CHARLEMAGNE. No. I'm not a young man and I've
always been courteous. It's hard for me to tell
you this straight to your face. But all the same,
I have to say it. This wedding is a great misfortune
for us.

HENRIK. What a tiresome way of bargaining this is!

PRESIDENT. Listen, my dear fellow! You won't
get more than I've already offered you. Obviously
you're wanting a share in all our business under-
takings. Well, this won't come off. Everything
that the Dragon used to grab shamelessly for
himself is now in the hands of the best men of
the town. To put it more simply, in my own hands
and partly in Henrik's. It's all perfectly legitimate.
I won't give you a farthing of the money!

CHARLEMAGNE. Permit me to leave, Mr President.

PRESIDENT. You may go. But remember this. First,
at the wedding you'll please be gay, full of *joie
de vivre* and wit. Second: no deaths of any kind.
Please endeavour to live as long as I wish you to.
You'd better tell that to your daughter. Third:
in future you are to call me your Excellency. . .
Do you see this list of names? There are fifty
names on it. If you rebel against me, all fifty
hostages will vanish without a trace. Now go. No,
wait! Presently a carriage will be sent to fetch you.

You'll bring your daughter here — and you will not make a sound! You understand? Now go!

(CHARLEMAGNE *goes*)

Well, everything's going swimmingly.

HENRIK.   What did the gaoler report?

PRESIDENT.   Not a cloud in the sky!

HENRIK.   What about the letter 'L'?

PRESIDENT.   Oh, that! Didn't they write a lot of letters on walls under the Dragon's regime? Let them write. Anything that comforts them and does no harm to us. Have a look, though — is that chair empty?

HENRIK.   Ah, Daddy, Daddy! *(Feels over it)* There's no one in it. Sit down.

PRESIDENT.   Don't smile, please. In his invisible cap he can penetrate anywhere.

HENRIK.   Dad, you don't know that man. He's full of old-fashioned prejudices up to his neck. Out of sheer knightly courtesy he'd take his cap off as he entered the house, and then the guards would seize him.

PRESIDENT.   His character might have deteriorated in the course of a year. *(Sits down)* Well, Sonny, my little pet, now let's talk over our own little affairs. You're in my debt, light of my life.

HENRIK.   What debt, Daddy?

PRESIDENT.   You bribed three of my footmen to watch me and read my papers, etc. Is that so?

HENRIK.   What are you talking about, Daddy!

PRESIDENT.   Wait, Sonny, don't interrupt! I gave them a rise of 500 Thalers of my own money and told them only to report to you what I permit them to report. Consequently, you owe me 500 Thalers, dear boy.

HENRIK.   No, Dad. I found out about that and I gave them a rise of 100 more.

PRESIDENT.   I guessed you would, so I gave them a thousand, my dear little piggy. Consequently, the

balance is in my favour. And don't give them any
more, dear boy. These huge salaries make them
gross, perverse and wild — before long they'll
start attacking their own side. . . But to continue. . .
It's necessary to get my personal secretary out of a
muddle. I've had to send the poor man to a psy-
chiatric hospital.

HENRIK. Really? Why?

PRESIDENT. Because you and I have bribed and bought
him over so many times, day after day, that he
can no longer figure out who it is he's supposed to
serve. He actually denounces me to myself. He
intrigues against himself in order to get back
his own job. He's an honest, industrious lad and
it hurts me to see how he's tormenting himself.
Let's go and see him tomorrow at the hospital
and settle who he's really working for. . . Ah, my
darling boy! My little pet! You do want to get
into your Dad's boots, don't you?

HENRIK. Really, Dad, really!

PRESIDENT. Never mind, little man! No matter!
That's what life is like. You know what I'd
like to suggest to you? Let's just spy on one
another simply, the way you do in a family — as
a father and son would — without making use of
any strangers. Think how much money we'd
save!

HENRIK. Oh, money's of no importance, Dad!

PRESIDENT. You're quite right. You can't take it
with you when you die. . .

*(Sound of horses hooves and jingling of harness
bells.)*

PRESIDENT. *(Rushing to the window)* She's come!
Our beauty's arrived! What a carriage! How
marvellous! It's decorated with the Dragon's
scales. And Elsa herself, she's a marvellous sight.
Dressed all in velvet. No, whatever you say,
power is a thing worth having! *(In a whisper)*
Go and question her!

HENRIK. Whom?

PRESIDENT. Elsa. She's been so silent these last few

259

days. Maybe she knows where that . . . *(Looks round)* where that Lancelot is. Question her cautiously. And I'll listen here behind the door curtain. *(Hides)*

(Enter ELSA *and* CHARLEMAGNE)

HENRIK.   Greetings, Elsa! You're getting prettier every day — how nice of you to do it!. . . The President is changing his clothes. He asked me to make his apologies. Sit down in this chair, Elsa. *(Helps her to sit down with her back to the curtain behind which the* PRESIDENT *is hiding)* Charlemagne, will you wait in the hall?

(CHARLEMAGNE *goes out with a bow)*

HENRIK.   Elsa, I'm glad that the President had to go and change into his state dress. For a long time I've wanted to have a talk with you alone, to talk to you as a friend, with an open heart. Why are you so silent all the time? Eh? Don't you want to answer me? You know, I'm fond of you in my own way. . . Do talk to me!

ELSA.   What about?

HENRIK.   Anything you want.

ELSA.   I don't know. . . I don't want anything.

HENRIK.   That's impossible. It's you wedding day, after all. . . Ah, Elsa. . . I've got to give you up for the second time. . . But the fact is that he is the conqueror of the Dragon! I'm a cynic, I'm always scoffing, but I have to bow my head before him. You're not listening to me.

ELSA.   No.

HENRIK.   Oh, Elsa. . . Have I really become quite a stranger to you? Remember, we used to be such friends when we were children. Do you remember when you had measles, I used to keep running to your window until I fell ill myself? And you used to come to see me and you used to cry because I was so quiet and gentle? Do you remember.

ELSA.   Yes.

HENRIK.   Is it possible that those children, who were

such good friends, have suddenly ceased to exist? Is it possible that nothing of them is left in either of us? Let's talk as we used to in the olden days, as a brother and sister would.

ELSA. Very well then, let's talk.

(The PRESIDENT *peeps out from behind the curtain and noiselessly applauds* HENRIK)

ELSA. You want to know why I'm silent all the time?

(The PRESIDENT *nods his head)*

ELSA. Because I am afraid.

HENRIK. Of whom?

ELSA. Of people.

HENRIK. Really? Name the people you're afraid of. We'll throw them into gaol and you'll feel easier in your mind immediately.

(The PRESIDENT *takes out his note-book)*

HENRIK. Come on, name them.

ELSA. No, Henrik, this isn't going to help.

HENRIK. It will help, I assure you. I've experienced it myself. You'll sleep better, and your appetite and general mood will improve.

ELSA. You see. . . I don't know how to explain it to you. . . I feel afraid of everybody. . .

HENRIK. Ah, that's how it is! I understand. . . I understand very well. Everyone, including me, seems cruel to you. . . Isn't that so? You may not believe me but I am afraid of them myself. I'm afraid of my father.

(The PRESIDENT *spreads his hands in be- wilderment)*

HENRIK. I'm afraid of our loyal servants. And so I pretend to be cruel to make them afraid of me. Ah, we've all got so entangled in our own web! Go on talking, go on! I'm listening.

(The PRESIDENT *nods his head with a knowing air)*

ELSA. Well, what else can I tell you?. . . At first I was

angry, then I grieved, and in the end everything
became indifferent to me. Now I'm obedient
as I've never been before. You can do anything
you wish with me.

(The PRESIDENT *giggles loudly, then, alarmed,
hides behind the curtain.* ELSA *looks round)*

ELSA. Who was that?

HENRIK. Don't take any notice. They're preparing
for the wedding feast over there. My poor, dear
little sister! What a pity that Lancelot's vanished
without a trace. It's only now I've really understood him. He's a wonderful man. We are all
guilty about him. Is there no hope at all that
he'll come back?

(The PRESIDENT *peeps out again from behind
the curtain. He is all* attention)

ELSA. He. . . He won't come back.

HENRIK. You mustn't think that. For some reason
or other it seems to me that we're going to see
him again.

ELSA. No.

HENRIK. Believe me, we are.

ELSA. It's pleasant to hear you say that, but. . .
Is there no one listening to us?

(The PRESIDENT *crouches behind the back of
the chair)*

HENRIK. Of course, no one's listening, my dear.
Today is a holiday. All the spies are having a
rest.

ELSA. You see, I know what happened to Lancelot.

HENRIK. There's no need to — don't tell me if it
hurts you so much.

(The PRESIDENT *shows him his fist)*

ELSA. No, I've been silent so long that now I want
to tell you everything. It's always seemed to me
that no one here but myself could understand
how sad it was — because that's the kind of
place I was born into! But you're listening to me
so attentively today that. . . Well, exactly a year

ago, when the fight was just going to end, the Cat ran along to the town square. And he saw Lancelot there, pale as death, standing beside the lifeless heads of the Dragon. He was leaning on his sword and he was smiling so as not to upset the Cat. The Cat came rushing back to me to call for help. But the guards were guarding me so carefully that even a fly couldn't get inside the house. They drove the Cat away.

HENRIK.   Those rude soldiers!

ELSA.   Then the Cat called the donkey he knew. He put the wounded man on the donkey's back and led them out of our town by some secret paths he knew of.

HENRIK.   But why did he do that?

ELSA.   Oh, Lancelot was so weak that people might have killed him. They started off along a little path into the mountains. The Cat sat beside the wounded man and kept listening to his heart, to see whether it was beating.

HENRIK.   It was beating, I hope?

ELSA.   Yes, but fainter and fainter every time. Suddenly the Cat shouted: 'Stop!' and the donkey stopped. It was already night time. They had climbed up very high into the mountains and it was so cold there, so quiet all around. 'Turn back home,' the Cat said. 'Now people won't be able to hurt him any more. Just let Elsa say good-bye to him, and then we'll bury him.'

HENRIK.   Did he die then, poor man?

ELSA.   Yes, Henrik, he died. The donkey was obstinate though and said: 'I don't consent to turn round', and he went on with Lancelot still on his back. But the Cat came back because he's so attached to the house. He returned home and told me everything, and now I'm not waiting for anybody. Everything's finished.

PRESIDENT.   Hurrah! Everything's finished! *(He dances and rushes round the room)* Everything's finished! I'm absolute master of everybody! Now there's no one to be afraid of! Thank you, Elsa! It's going to be a real holiday now! Who'll

263

dare to say now that it wasn't me who'd killed the Dragon? Well, who?

ELSA.   So he was eavesdropping on us?

HENRIK.   Of course.

ELSA.   And you knew that?

HENRIK.   Ah, Elsa, don't act the naive little girl! After all, you're getting married today. Heaven be praised!

ELSA.   Father, Father!

(CHARLEMAGNE *runs in*)

CHARLEMAGNE.   What's the matter, my little one? *(He is about to embrace her)*

PRESIDENT.   Attention! Stand to attention in front of my fiancée!

CHARLEMAGNE.   *(Standing to attention. To* ELSA) Oh, don't! Do calm yourself! Don't cry! There's nothing we can do. . . What can we do?

(Music thunders)

PRESIDENT.   *(Runs up to the window)* How lovely! How elegant! The guests are arriving for the wedding. The horses are decked out with ribbons. There are fairy-lights on the shafts. What a good life this is! How good to know that no fool of any kind can spoil it! Come on, Elsa, smile! Precisely to the second, at the appointed time the President of the Liberated City himself will take you in his arms!

(The doors are flung wide open)

Welcome, welcome, dear guests!

(Enter the guests. They walk in pairs past ELSA *and the* PRESIDENT. *They speak sedately, almost in a whisper)*

FIRST TOWNSMAN.   Congratulations to the bride and bridegroom! Everyone is so glad.

SECOND TOWNSMAN.   All the houses are decorated with lampions.

FIRST TOWNSMAN.   In the streets it's as bright as daylight.

SECOND TOWNSMAN.   All the wine bars are full of
people.

BOY.   And all are fighting and swearing.

GUESTS.   Sh-sh-sh!

GARDENER.   Permit me to make you a present of
these campanillas. It's true their little bells ring a
little sadly but that doesn't matter. In the morning
they'll wither and grow silent anyway.

FIRST GIRL-FRIEND.   Elsa, my dear, do try and
cheer up! Otherwise I'll start crying and spoil
my eyelashes, and I managed to make them up so
well today.

SECOND GIRL-FRIEND.   After all, he is a little better
than the Dragon. He's got hands and feet and no
scales. And although he's a President, he's still a
man. Tomorrow you'll tell us everything. That
will be so interesting.

THIRD GIRL-FRIEND.   You'll be able to do so much
good for people. For instance, you might ask
your fiancé to dismiss my Dad's boss. Then my
Dad would get his job and he'd get a salary twice
what he has now, and we'd be so happy.

PRESIDENT.   *(Counting the guests under his breath)*
One, two, three, four. . . *(Then he counts the
plates set out on the table)* One, two, three. . .
So! It seems there's one extra guest. . . Ah, that's
you, boy! Well, well, don't start snivelling. You
can eat from the same plate as your Mamma.
Everybody's here now. Gentlemen, I beg you
to sit down to table. We'll perform the marriage
ceremony quickly and without fuss and then
we'll start on the wedding feast. I've managed to
get hold of a fish which was specially created to
be eaten. It actually laughs for joy when it's
being cooked, and it even tells the cook when it's
done. And here's a turkey stuffed with its own
chicks. A cosy family group, so to speak. And
there are some sucking pigs that have not merely
been fed but also properly trained for our table.
They know how to sit up and put out their paws
despite the fact that they're roasted already. Now
don't squeal, boy, that's not at all frightening,

it's just amusing. And here we've got some wines,
so old that they're in their second childhood —
they're jumping up and down in the bottle as
if they were small. And here's some vodka, so
pure that the bottle looks quite empty. Excuse
me, as a matter of fact I see it *is* empty. Those
scoundrels must have drunk it up, those flunkeys!
Well, never mind, there are plenty of bottles on
the sideboard. How pleasant it is to be rich,
gentlemen! Are you all seated now? Excellent!
Wait, wait! Don't start eating yet! We're going to
have the wedding first. Just a minute! Elsa,
give me your little paw!

(ELSA *puts her hand out to the* PRESIDENT)

Ah, you little scamp! What a warm little paw!
Lift your little muzzle up! Smile! Is everything
ready, Henrik?

HENRIK.   It is, Mr President.

PRESIDENT.   Go on, then.

HENRIK.   I'm a poor speech-maker, gentlemen, and
   I'm afraid I'm going to talk in a rather inconse-
   quential way. Well, a year ago a certain over-
   confident wanderer challenged the accursed
   Dragon to a fight. A special commission, appointed
   by the Town Council, confirmed the following
   facts: the impertinent challenger, who's now
   dead, did nothing but make the late monster
   annoyed, and only wounded him slightly. Then
   our former Mayor, who is now the President of
   the Liberated City, rushed at the Dragon like a
   true hero and killed him once and for all, after
   performing miracles of bravery.

(The guests applaud)

Thus were the poisonous weeds of abominable
subjection pulled out, root and branch, from
the soil of our communal field.

(The guests applaud)

The grateful City then made the following
decision: if we formerly had to give our best
maidens to the accursed monster, we certainly
could not refuse this same privilege, this simple

266

and natural right, to our dear liberator!

(The guests applaud)

And so, in order to underline on the one hand
the greatness of the President, and on the other the
obedience and devotion of the City, I, as Mayor,
am now going to perform the ceremony of
marriage. Organist! Let's have the wedding march!

(The organ thunders)

Scribes! Open the book that contains the register
of happy events.

(Enter SCRIBES *with huge fountain-pens in
their hands)*

For four hundred years all the names of the poor
girls condemned to be given to the Dragon were
entered in this book. Four hundred pages had
been filled. Now for the first time, on page 401,
we're going to enter the name of the happy girl
who'll be taken to wife by the valiant man who
destroyed the monster.

(The guests applaud)

Bridegroom! Answer me with a clear conscience.
Do you agree to take this girl as your wife?

PRESIDENT.   For the good of my native city I'm
prepared to do anything.

(The guests applaud)

HENRIK.   Scribes! Write this down. Be careful now.
If you make a blot, I'll force you to lick it off!
Well, that's all. Ah! Forgive me! There's only
one empty formality that remains. You, bride! I
take it that, of course, you consent to become the
wife of the President of the Liberated City?

(A pause)

HENRIK.   Well, answer me, girl! You do consent?

ELSA.   No.

HENRIK.   Well, that's fine. Scribes, write down — she
consents.

ELSA.   Don't you dare write it!

(The SCRIBES *shy away from her)*

HENRIK. Elsa, don't interfere with our work.

PRESIDENT. But, my dear boy, she's not inter-
fering at all. When a girl says 'no', she means
'yes'. Write it down, scribes!

ELSA. No! I'll tear the page out of the book and
trample on it!

PRESIDENT. Charming girlish hesitations, tears,
day-dreams, and all that! Every girl weeps in her
own way before her wedding, but afterwards
she's quite contented. Now we're going to hold
her little hands for a bit and do the necessary!
Scribes!. . .

ELSA. Let me say at least one word. Please!

HENRIK. Elsa!

PRESIDENT. Don't shout, Sonny! Everything's
going just as it should. The bride is asking to
say a word. Let her have her say, and we'll
finish the official part with that. Never mind,
never mind, let her! Everyone here is in the
family, so to speak.

ELSA. Friends, my friends! Why do you want to kill
me? This is all like some terrifying dream!
When a bandit holds his knife over your head,
you still have a chance to survive. The bandit
might be killed, or you might escape from him. . .
But what if the knife itself attacks you? What if
a rope creeps up to you like a snake and ties you
hand and foot? What if even a curtain on the
window, a still, lifeless curtain, suddenly throws
itself at you and stops up your mouth? What
would you say then, all of you? I thought you
were only obedient to the Dragon, as the knife is
obedient to the bandit. But you yourselves, my
friends, have turned out to be bandits! I'm not
blaming you — you yourselves don't realize it.
But I implore you — do come to your senses!
Is it possible that the Dragon isn't really dead but
has just turned himself into a man, as he often
used to do? Only this time he's turned into many,
many men, and here they are, all killing me!
Don't kill me! Come to your senses! Oh, my God!

How dreadfully sad this is! Tear the web in which you're all entangled! Is it possible that no one's going to defend me?

BOY. I would defend you but my mother's holding my hands.

PRESIDENT. Well, that's over now. The bride's finished her little piece. Life's continuing as if nothing had happened.

BOY. Mamma!

PRESIDENT. Keep quiet, little one. We're all going to enjoy ourselves as if nothing had happened. Enough of these formalities! Henrik! Write down now: 'The marriage is considered to have been solemnized' — and let's start eating! I'm terribly hungry.

HENRIK. Scribes, write down: 'The marriage is considered to have been solemnized'. . . Hurry up! What are you thinking about?

(The SCRIBES *pick up their pens. A loud knocking on the door. The* SCRIBES *shy away from it)*

PRESIDENT. Who's there?

(Silence)

Hey, you there! Whoever you are, come back tomorrow! Tomorrow, during office hours. Report to the secretary. I'm busy now. I'm getting married.

(Knocking is repeated)

Don't open the door! Write it down, scribes!

(The door flies open of its own accord — there is no one behind it)

Henrik, come here! What does that mean?

HENRIK. Oh, it's the usual story, Dad. The childish complaints of our young woman here have disturbed all the simple-minded denizens of the rivers and woods and lakes. The house spirit's come running down from the loft, the water spirit's climbed out of the well. Well, let them! What can they do to us? They're just as

269

invisible and powerless as what they call conscience and such like things. We might have a few frightening dreams in the night, and that'll be the end of the matter.

PRESIDENT.   No, it's him!

HENRIK.   Who?

PRESIDENT.   Lancelot. He's wearing his invisible cap. He's standing beside us here. He's listening to what we're saying. And his sword is poised over my head.

HENRIK.   My dear Papa! If you don't come to your senses, I'll have to take over power myself.

PRESIDENT.   Hey, musicians! Play something! Dear guests! Forgive this unintended interruption, but I'm so afraid of draughts. A draught opened the door — that was all. Elsa, calm yourself, little girl! I declare the marriage solemnized, to be confirmed later. What's that? Who's that running?

(A terrified FOOTMAN *runs in)*

FOOTMAN.   Take it back! Take it back!

PRESIDENT.   Take back what?

FOOTMAN.   Take your accursed money back! I'm not going to work for you any more.

PRESIDENT.   Why not?

FOOTMAN.   He's going to kill me for all the vile deeds I've done! *(Runs away)*

PRESIDENT.   Who's going to kill him? Eh? Henrik!

(The SECOND FOOTMAN *runs in)*

SECOND FOOTMAN.   He's coming up the corridor already! I bowed deeply to him but he didn't respond. He doesn't look at people any more. Oh, we'll have to answer for everything! Oh, yes, we will! *(Runs away)*

PRESIDENT.   Henrik!

HENRIK.   Just behave as if nothing were the matter. Whatever happens! That'll see us through.

270

(A THIRD FOOTMAN *comes in, walking backwards. He shouts into the distance)*

THIRD FOOTMAN.   I'll prove it! My wife can confirm it! I've always condemned their behaviour. I only took money from them because I was a nervous wreck. I'll bring you a certificate! *(Vanishes)*

PRESIDENT.   Look!

HENRIK.   Behave as if nothing's the matter! For Heaven's sake, behave as if nothing's the matter!

(Enter LANCELOT*)*

PRESIDENT.   Ah, how do you do? We didn't expect you, but all the same, you're welcome. There aren't enough plates, but never mind. You can eat off a soup plate, and I'll eat off a dinner plate. I'd order them to bring some more, but those fool flunkeys have all run away... We've a wedding going on here, so to speak, he-he-he — an intimate, personal sort of affair. We're such a cosy little party... May I introduce you to my guests?... But where are they? Ah! they must have dropped something, they're looking for it under the table. This is my son, Henrik. It seems you've met before. He's very young, but he's a Mayor already. He's forged ahead since I... since we... in a word, since the day the Dragon was killed. Well, what are you waiting for? Come in, please.

HENRIK.   Why don't you speak?

PRESIDENT.   That's true. Why don't you? Have you had a good journey? What's the news? Would you like to rest after your travels? The guards will show you the way.

LANCELOT.   Good day, Elsa!

ELSA.   Lancelot! *(She runs up to him)* Sit down, please do sit down! Come right in! Can this really be you?

LANCELOT.   Yes, Elsa.

ELSA.   And your hands are warm! And your hair's grown longer since I saw you last! Or am I imagining this? But your cloak is still the same, Lancelot! *(She makes him sit down at the little table in the centre)* Have some wine. Or better not, don't take

271

anything from them. Rest awhile and then we'll go away. Daddy! He's come, Daddy! Just as he did that evening. Just at the very moment when once again we were thinking that the only thing left to us was to die quietly. Lancelot!

LANCELOT.   Does this mean that you still love me as before?

ELSA.   Daddy, do you hear? How many times have we dreamt that he'd come in and ask: 'Elsa, do you still love me as before?' And I'd answer: 'Yes, Lancelot!' And then I'd ask him: 'Where have you been such a long time?'

LANCELOT.   Far, far away, in the Black Mountains.

ELSA.   Were you very ill?

LANCELOT.   Yes, Elsa. To be mortally wounded is a very, very dangerous thing.

ELSA.   Who looked after you?

LANCELOT.   The wife of a wood-cutter. A nice, kind woman. Only she took exception to my calling her 'Elsa' all the time when I was delirious.

ELSA.   Does that mean that you were longing for me, too?

LANCELOT.   Yes, I was.

ELSA.   And I was killing myself with grief. They've been tormenting me here.

PRESIDENT.   Who? That's impossible! Why didn't you complain to us? We'd have taken measures against it.

LANCELOT.   I know everything, Elsa.

ELSA.   You know everything?

LANCELOT.   Yes.

ELSA.   How?

LANCELOT.   In the Black Mountains, not far from the wood-cutter's hut there's a huge cave. And in that cave there is a book, the Book of Complaints — it's almost full now. No one ever touches it, but page after page keeps being added to the others

272

which are already covered with writing. Something
is added every day. Who writes in that book? The
world! All the misdeeds of criminals, all the mis-
fortunes of those who suffer innocently — all is
written down.

(HENRIK *and the* PRESIDENT *steal on tiptoe
towards the door*)

ELSA.   And you read about us in it?

LANCELOT.   Yes, Elsa. Hey, you there! Murderers!
Stand still!

PRESIDENT.   Why. . . why be so abrupt about it?

LANCELOT.   Because I'm not the same man I was a
year ago. I liberated you, and what have you done?

PRESIDENT.   Ah, my goodness gracious! If I don't
give satisfaction, I'll simply go into retirement.

LANCELOT.   You won't go anywhere.

HENRIK.   You're absolutely right. The way he behaved
here without you was quite incredible. I can
give you a complete list of his crimes, ones that
haven't been entered into the Book of Complaints
yet, but were only projects for the future.

LANCELOT.   Be quiet!

HENRIK.   But allow me! If you examine the matter in
depth, you'll see I'm not personally guilty of
anything. I was taught to behave in that way.

LANCELOT.   Everyone was taught that way, but
why have you got to the top of the class, you
swine?

HENRIK.   Dad, let's go. He's swearing at us now!

LANCELOT.   No, you're not going! I've been back a
month already, Elsa.

ELSA.   And you didn't call to see me?

LANCELOT.   Yes, I did, but I was wearing my
invisible cap. It was early one morning. I kissed
you quietly so that you wouldn't wake up, and
then I went walking about the town and I saw
what a terrible life people were leading. It was
painful enough to read about it, but much worse
to see it with my own eyes. Hey you, Miller!

(The FIRST TOWNSMAN *gets out from under the table)*

I saw you wept with joy when you shouted to the Mayor: 'Glory be to you, Conqueror of the Dragon!'

FIRST TOWNSMAN.   That's quite true, I did weep, but I wasn't pretending, Mr Lancelot.

LANCELOT.   But you knew that it wasn't he who killed the Dragon?

FIRST TOWNSMAN.   Yes, I did know that. . . at home. . . But on parade. . . *(He makes a gesture of helplessness)*

LANCELOT.   You, Gardener!

(The GARDENER *emerges from under the table)*

LANCELOT.   Didn't you teach the snap-dragons to shout: 'Hurrah to the President'?

GARDENER.   Yes, I did.

LANCELOT.   And did they learn to do it?

GARDENER.   Yes, they did. Only after having shouted it, they put their tongues out at me. . . I thought I'd get money for new experiments, but. . .

LANCELOT.   Friedrichsen!

(The SECOND TOWNSMAN *emerges from under the table)*

LANCELOT.   Is it true that the President, when he was angry with you, put your only son in an underground dungeon?

SECOND TOWNSMAN.   Yes. The boy was coughing all the time and the dungeon's a damp place. . .

LANCELOT.   And after that, you presented the President with a pipe bearing the inscription 'For ever yours'?

SECOND TOWNSMAN.   But how could I soften his heart otherwise?

LANCELOT.   What am I to do with you all?

PRESIDENT. Just spit at them. This isn't a job
for you. Henrik and I will know just how to
manage them. That'll be a much more fitting
punishment for these miserable people. And
you just take Elsa by the arm and leave us to live
in our own way. It'll be more humane and democratic that way.

LANCELOT. I can't do that. Come in, friends!

(Enter the WEAVERS, the SMITH, the
HATTER and the MUSICAL INSTRUMENTS'
MAKER)

LANCELOT. You've disappointed me a lot, too. I
thought you'd manage to control them without me.
Why did you obey them and go to prison? There
are so many of you, after all!

THE WEAVERS. They were too quick for us.

LANCELOT. Take away these people — the Mayor
and the President.

THE WEAVERS. (Taking hold of the MAYOR and
the PRESIDENT) Come along!

THE SMITH. I've checked the bars myself. They're
nice and strong. Come on!

THE HATTER. Here, take these fools' caps! I used
to make beautiful hats once but the prison's
made me callous. Come along!

MUSICAL INSTRUMENTS' MAKER. In my cell I
made a violin out of black bread, using spider's
web for the strings. It plays quietly and sadly,
but you yourselves are to blame for that. You're
going to a place from which there's no return!
Our music will accompany you.

HENRIK. But this is nonsense, this is quite irregular!
This sort of thing simply doesn't happen! A
tramp, a beggar, such an impractical man —
and then all of a sudden. . .

THE WEAVERS. Come along!

PRESIDENT. I protest! This is inhuman. . .

THE WEAVERS. Come on!

(Faintly audible music, simple and grim. HENRIK *and the* PRESIDENT *are led away)*

LANCELOT. Elsa, you see, I'm not the same as I was, don't you?

ELSA. Yes, but I love you even more.

LANCELOT. We won't be able to go away.

ELSA. Never mind. It's quite possible to enjoy life even at home.

LANCELOT. We've got a very tricky and dreary task ahead of us. Even worse than doing embroidery. We shall have to kill the dragon in every single one of them.

BOY. And will it hurt us?

LANCELOT. Not you.

FIRST TOWNSMAN. What about us?

LANCELOT. I'll have to do a lot of work on you.

GARDENER. But please be patient, Mr Lancelot. I do implore you, be patient. You must do grafting. You must make bonfires — warmth helps growth, you know — and do remove the weeds carefully, take care not to damage the healthy roots. When you come to think of it deeply — and notwithstanding all sorts of reservations — men are basically worthy of cultivation after all.

FIRST GIRL-FRIEND. And let the wedding take place today, despite everything.

SECOND GIRL-FRIEND. Because people grow better looking just from joy.

LANCELOT. That's true! Hey, music!

(Music thunders)

Elsa, give me your hand. I love you all, my friends. Otherwise, why should I want to bother with you? And if I love you, everything's

sure to come out fine. And after many long
months of worry and torment, we shall all be
happy — very happy — in the end.

CURTAIN

1940